Madam Speaker

NANCY PELOSI'S LIFE, TIMES, AND RISE TO POWER

Marc Sandalow

MODERN TIMES

TO MARCIE,

the love of my life

★

© 2008 by Marc Sandalow

Modern Times is a trademark of Rodale Inc.
Rodale books may be purchased for business or promotional use or for special sales. For information, please write to:
Special Markets Department, Rodale Inc., 733 Third Avenue, New York, NY 10017

Printed in the United States of America
Rodale Inc. makes every effort to use acid-free ♾, recycled paper ♻.

BOOK DESIGN BY SUSAN EUGSTER

Library of Congress Cataloging-in-Publication Data

Sandalow, Marc.
    Madam speaker : Nancy Pelosi's life, times, and rise to power / Marc Sandalow.
        p.   cm.
    Includes bibliographical references.
    ISBN-13 978–1–59486–807–8   hardcover
    ISBN-10 1–59486–807–7   hardcover
    1. Pelosi, Nancy, date   2. United States. Congress. House—Speakers—Biography.   3. Women legislators—United States—Biography.   4. Legislators—United States—Biography.   5. United States. Congress. House—Biography.   6. Democratic Party (U.S.)—Biography.   7. Women in politics—United States—Case studies.   8. United States—Politics and government—date   9. California—Politics and government—date   I. Title.
E840.8.P37S26   2008
328.73092—dc22
[B]   2008002021

Distributed to the trade by Macmillan

2   4   6   8   10   9   7   5   3   1   hardcover

Contents

PREFACE ix

INTRODUCTION 1

PART I: BALTIMORE

CHAPTER ONE: A Girl in a Boys' House 11

CHAPTER TWO: The Mayor's Daughter 21

PART II: SAN FRANCISCO

CHAPTER THREE: Out of the Kitchen 43

CHAPTER FOUR: Up the Party Ladder 61

CHAPTER FIVE: Candidate Pelosi 83

PART III: WASHINGTON, DC

CHAPTER SIX: A Woman in a Man's House 115

CHAPTER SEVEN: Gay Pneumonia 125

CHAPTER EIGHT: The Presidio 133

CHAPTER NINE: The Butchers of Beijing 139

CHAPTER TEN: Life in the Minority 157

CHAPTER ELEVEN: The Path to Leadership 171

CHAPTER TWELVE: Woman with a Whip 203

CHAPTER THIRTEEN: Another Step up the Ladder 219

CHAPTER FOURTEEN: War 229

CHAPTER FIFTEEN: Madam Leader 247

CHAPTER SIXTEEN: Winning Back the House 265

CHAPTER SEVENTEEN: Madam Speaker 285

ENDNOTES 301

ACKNOWLEDGMENTS 307

INDEX 311

PREFACE

I FIRST MET NANCY PELOSI at a Democratic Party fund-raiser in the San Francisco Bay Area in June 1993.

Roughly 300 guests ate duck tamales wrapped in banana leaves and pledged nearly half a million dollars to the party at a lavish home in Portola Valley, a half-hour's drive south of San Francisco.

I had written about Pelosi sporadically for the *San Francisco Chronicle* since she first won election to Congress in June 1987. I had no inkling, as I introduced myself to the then 53-year-old congresswoman, of the role she would play in my professional life, let alone of her place in history.

I joined the paper's Washington Bureau later that summer, and over the next 14 years wrote hundreds of stories that chronicled Pelosi's evolution from a junior member of Congress to the most powerful member of the House.

My relationship with Pelosi has been ambiguous—sometimes warm and at other times cold.

She was always generous with her time when I served as a writer and then bureau chief for her hometown paper. She agreed to regular interviews and lunches and politely returned phone calls, once telling me she regarded me as "an ambassador for her constituents."

As Pelosi began to cultivate a national following, I traveled with her to each region of the country, traversing the Rocky and the Pocono mountains in vans, flying across the country in commercial planes (many rows behind her), and trying to keep up with her frenetic and seemingly tireless pace. She never wanted it said that she was "too good" for her hometown paper, and she never behaved as if she were. She has kindly shown me around her office, asked after my family, and inquired about what costumes my kids were wearing on Halloween.

She has also made plain her disdain for the press. Pelosi objected strenuously to some stories I wrote, particularly those that did not put Democrats in a positive light. She has complained to me about the news media trivializing her accomplishments and fixating on political division. My editor in San Francisco was awakened one morning by Pelosi's voice on a public radio program, answering the host's question by asserting, "Marc Sandalow is ill-informed" (she had objected to my assertion in a story that she would be spending "the bulk" of her time that month pushing trade sanctions against China, when in fact she said she'd be spending more time on AIDS and other matters).

This is not an authorized biography. Though I have written hundreds of news stories about Pelosi and conducted dozens and dozens of interviews with her over the past 14 years, Pelosi did not make eye contact with me after I informed her staff that I was writing this book. Repeated requests for interviews, information, or cooperation were denied and a direct appeal to Pelosi in writing went unanswered.

As this book was being completed, Pelosi announced plans to write a memoir. Several of her associates suggested that her refusal to cooperate was based on her desire to tell her own story. Others speculated her suspicions of the news media played a role. She offered no explanation.

Pelosi's story is well worth telling. Like the president and vice president, the Speaker of the House is a national figure charged with overseeing a national institution, in this case the entire House of Representatives. The Speaker is second in the line of succession—after the vice president—to the presidency. Yet unlike the president or vice president, the Speaker represents a single congressional district and rarely faces the same scrutiny as a senator or governor, let alone a national candidate. Beyond the 700,000 residents of her San Francisco district, Pelosi's decisions are critical to all Americans. It is my hope that exploring the forces that enabled her to win the speakership—forces rooted in her Baltimore childhood and unleashed in San Francisco and Washington—will provide wisdom and insight into how she will lead.

Nancy Pelosi is a pioneer. When she was sworn in as Speaker on January 4, 2007, no other woman had come close to securing that post. Of the roughly 12,000 Americans who had served in Congress, just 230 had been women, and of them, Pelosi was the first to rise higher than number four in her party's hierarchy. I further hope that telling Pelosi's story will make it more likely that girls will view politics as a noble and attainable profession, that more women will lead with Pelosi's confidence, and that all Americans will expand their notions of what a leader looks like.

The woman I met in Portola Valley 20 years ago is still making history. As these words are being written, Pelosi is embroiled in many of the issues that will define her success as Speaker. Much of that history has yet to unfold.

What follows was written without Pelosi's cooperation, approval, or blessing. The story I am telling is based on 21 years of following Pelosi, 14 years of focusing on her in Washington, and the better part of a year conducting intensive research to fill in portions of her life.

—*Marc Sandalow,*
OCTOBER 2007

INTRODUCTION

"The gene pool for politics and political operation begins with Nancy Pelosi. If you wanted to infect people with political skills, political operation, Nancy Pelosi would be the repository."

—FORMER SAN FRANCISCO MAYOR WILLIE BROWN

"If they allow a woman to be pope, she might do that. I mean, who the hell thought Speaker?"

—FORMER CONGRESSMAN JOHN BURTON

THE PHONE RANG AT 7:15 A.M.

Nancy Pelosi was sound asleep. Seven hours earlier she had been on national television declaring victory in a Democratic rout that would soon make her Speaker of the House.

Pelosi had returned to her apartment overlooking the Potomac River after 2:00 a.m., and the phone jarred her back to the thought that had consumed much of the past two weeks.

The baby.

Alexandra, her youngest daughter, was already eight days past her due date. For the past week Pelosi had campaigned within a two-hour drive of Alexandra's Manhattan apartment so she could be at her side at a moment's notice. Her staff had drawn up elaborate election night contingency plans to handle every scenario: Democrats win and baby comes; Democrats lose and baby doesn't come; Democrats lose and baby comes; Democrats win and baby doesn't come.

Pelosi reached across her king-size bed and spoke excitedly into the receiver without bothering to say hello: "Are we getting a baby this morning?"

It was not a baby. It was the White House. The confused operator on the other end of the phone announced that the president was on the line.

"Is this Madam Speaker-to-Be?" President Bush asked as the expecting grandmother collapsed back into bed.[1]

TALES OF POLITICAL TRIUMPH ABOUND in Washington. Yet this is a story that has never been told. In the 230-year history of the nation, never before had a woman, let alone a mother or grandmother, risen to a position of such power.

Other women have blazed trails and left their marks in the halls of Congress. Geraldine Ferraro was her party's nominee for vice president; Lynn Martin was named secretary of labor; Shirley Chisholm fashioned a national following as the first African American congresswoman; Mae Nolan was the first woman to chair a House committee as a representative from San Francisco in the 1920s; and Jeannette Rankin of Montana became the first woman to serve in Congress in 1917, three years before the 19th Amendment guaranteed women the right to vote.

But of the 230 women elected to serve in Congress by 2006, Pelosi was the first to lead her party, to preside over the entire House of Representatives, to be trusted with the responsibility of being just two heartbeats from the presidency.

THE MORNING OF NOVEMBER 7, 2006, was no time for Pelosi to savor history. She bounded out of her penthouse apartment, with its sweeping view of the Kennedy Center, and into the black SUV that delivered her to the US Capitol 3½ miles away, moving rapidly through a series of meetings with her senior staff, an encounter with visiting schoolchildren from Queens, a news conference in a room overflowing with reporters, dozens of congratulatory calls to and from members of Congress and luminaries around the country, and a round of television interviews with CBS, NBC, PBS, CNN, FOX News, and reporters from San Francisco.

Pelosi fielded questions about the war ("Nowhere was the call for a new direction more clear from the American people than in the war in Iraq"), impeachment ("Off the table"), and the integrity of the Congress ("We will make this the most honest, ethical, and open Congress in history").

The nation was in transition. Americans were turning against President George W. Bush and the war in Iraq. The post–September 11 jitters that had defined the nation's politics for five years no longer guaranteed Republicans victories. The "netroots"—a potent mix of grassroots activism and Internet activity—fired up the Democratic base as it tugged the party to the left.

Pelosi told reporters shortly after noon that the best way for Bush to signal a change of direction in Iraq would be to replace the civilian leadership at the Pentagon. Forty-five minutes later, Bush announced that Defense Secretary Donald Rumsfeld was leaving his post. The president was not heeding her advice so much as responding to the same forces that had propelled Pelosi and her party to power.

Democrats had reclaimed the majority in the House after 12 years of Republican rule. And while votes were still being counted in Virginia, it would soon be learned they'd taken over the Senate as well. Bush would have to deal with a Democratic Congress for the first time.

As reporters shouted their questions and scurried to file stories on the busy day's developments, what made this moment most different from any before it was the figure before them.

3

Of the 51 previous Speakers of the House, there had been eight Johns, four Josephs, three Jameses, and even a Newt. Never a Nancy.

Tip O'Neill, with his craggy face, oversize belly, and shock of white hair, had embodied the modern-day image of a Speaker. In many history books, the quintessential Speaker was Sam Rayburn, the fiery Texan who served longer than any Speaker in history and was said to be able to melt collars with his glare.

It certainly was not a slender, neatly coiffed, Italian American grandmother who in her youth had reminded some of Audrey Hepburn. A visitor could spend hours marveling at the portraits and statues lining the corridors of the Capitol before stumbling across the few women who are memorialized. Pelosi liked to say that she shattered a marble ceiling. She also shattered a centuries-old caricature.

Her story, on its face, was radically different from that of any of her predecessors. When O'Neill was 37 years old, he was Speaker of the Massachusetts House of Representatives. When Rayburn was 37, he'd been Speaker of the Texas House of Representatives and elected to the US House four times.

When Pelosi was 37, she had five children at home, ages 12, 10, 9, 8, and 6.

As the sound system at her afternoon news conference faltered, Pelosi displayed a quality that neither O'Neill nor Rayburn had possessed.

"I'm not in charge of the technical arrangements," Pelosi told the crowd of reporters, her voice suddenly booming. *"I could use my mother-of-five voice!"*

The question of how Pelosi became the first woman to rise to such heights confounded some who knew her only from her sound bites. As she rose through the ranks, the Pelosi many Americans saw when they turned on the evening news was a strident partisan who stuck it to President Bush and the Republican Party at every opportunity.

>> *"President Bush is an incompetent leader. In fact, he's not a leader. He's a person who has no judgment, no experience, and no knowledge of the subjects that he has to decide upon."*

» *"[The GOP-run House] is the most corrupt Congress in history."*

» *"The cronyism in Katrina was criminal. I will say that again. The cronyism in Katrina was criminal."*

Opponents mocked her staccato clichés and alliterations as the rants of a San Francisco liberal. Even some supporters conceded that in front of a camera, Pelosi was sometimes scattered, often shrill, and always partisan.

Yet the caricature of Pelosi as a strident San Francisco liberal misses what made her history's most powerful female lawmaker. Pelosi did not become Speaker because of what she did in public. Pelosi reigned because she was a master of the inside game, a charming and cunning party operative who unified Democrats, seized upon Republican disharmony, and led her party to reclaim the majority. Belying her public image as a liberal ideologue, Pelosi is a pragmatic tactician with a long record of success.

Had Nancy D'Alesandro never left her home in Baltimore, never married Paul Pelosi or moved to his childhood home of San Francisco, there might be less confusion over her political core. Had she been elected Representative Nancy D'Alesandro from Baltimore's Little Italy, where her father was elected five times to Congress and served three terms as mayor, people would more easily grasp the depth of Pelosi's instincts.

"The gene pool for politics and political operation begins with Nancy Pelosi," said Willie Brown, the former California Assembly Speaker and San Francisco mayor. "If you wanted to infect people with political skills, political operation, Nancy Pelosi would be the repository."

As Pelosi raced through the Capitol that day, the *click-click-click* of her heels a constant reminder of her intensity, at least three reasons were apparent for her historic rise.

The first was her pedigree. She was literally born into politics, sleeping with copies of the *Congressional Record* beneath her bed in a household where patriotism, Catholicism, and the Democratic Party were all revered, and not always in that order. It was no reach for Pelosi to serve as chair of the California Democratic Party, to be named host of the 1984 Democratic Convention, finance chair of the party's 1986 Senate campaign, or cochair of the 1992 platform committee or to rise through the ranks in Congress. It was instinct. In Washington, she is the ultimate inside player. She understands the needs and the egos of her 434 colleagues. She knows how to win.

The second was the timing. It took 131 years following ratification of the Constitution for women to be guaranteed the right to vote. It took another 73 years before the number of women serving in Congress exceeded 10 percent. When Pelosi was born in 1940, only eight women served in the House. The number had tripled by 1987, when Pelosi was first elected to Congress, and climbed to 74 by the time she became Speaker. That means that more than one-third of all the women who had *ever* served in the House were serving when Pelosi became Speaker.

And finally there was Pelosi's toughness. Packed in her trim Armani suits, behind the wide eyes and soft voice is an unflinching toughness—Pelosi prefers the word *strength*—that accompanies the 18-hour workdays and fuels the relentless drive. She relaxes by racing through crossword puzzles, devouring chocolate, reading on cross-country flights, and competing alongside contestants on *Jeopardy!* She is rarely off. She does not drink wine or alcohol. Her social time is often spent at party functions and fund-raisers, where she has raised almost as much political money as anyone in history. She distributes the money with cold-blooded calculation. She is unfailingly gracious and devoted to her allies. At the same time, she can be tough on her colleagues and even tougher on her staff. She does it without apology and without any sign of self-doubt.

"*Fear* is not a word that is in my vocabulary," she said a few days before the election that would make her Speaker. Twenty years earlier, with a house full of kids, she'd put it this way: "I'm not afraid of anything. I put all my problems in the following terms: If they can't take my children away, then I can handle it."[2]

Pelosi was mindful of her historic role that first morning. She spoke of having a responsibility to conduct herself in a way that will make other women "proud, make them want to be Speaker, and ensure another one will be soon."

But there was little time to celebrate. She had a long list of things she wanted to get done.

Pelosi hardly cracked a smile when she was asked whether she was offended by Bush's postelection offer to help her find an interior decorator to pick out drapes for her new office.

"I don't get bogged down by things like that. I'm offended by one in five children in America living in poverty, 5 million more people not having health insurance," she said.

Dennis Hastert, the man Pelosi replaced as Speaker, had needed to be convinced to take the job eight years before.

"The last thing in my mind going to work on that fateful day, December 19, 1998, was becoming Speaker of the House," Hastert wrote. When Republicans appealed to him, he disappeared into a room in the bowels of the Capitol, then looked up and said, "Why me, Lord?"[3]

Pelosi required no push. She knew exactly what she was after. She had succeeded at everything she had pursued, whether it was raising five children; winning a seat in Congress; or fighting for AIDS victims at home, human rights in China, or control of the House of Representatives. Becoming Speaker, in that context, seemed almost natural. Yet it is an accomplishment that was unthinkable just a generation before.

SPECIMEN BALLOT For Voting Mach
General Election, Tuesday, November 5, 1940

District

Polls O

HOW T

PART I

BALTIMORE

CHAPTER ONE

A GIRL IN A BOYS' HOUSE

"I don't know how many other Speakers of the House worked a precinct in an ethnic area when they were 13 years old, seeing human nature in the raw. You think Tip O'Neill or Newt Gingrich did that?"
—TOMMY D'ALESANDRO III

"Don't think she's from San Francisco. She's from Baltimore."
—REPRESENTATIVE JACK MURTHA (D-PA)

ON THE DAY NANCY PELOSI WAS BORN, her father was on the floor of the House of Representatives trolling for votes.

Representative Thomas D'Alesandro was a sharply dressed son of Baltimore's

Little Italy and a fierce devotee of President Franklin D. Roosevelt. The legislation before the House that day was an FDR-backed measure to provide job training to kids. It was precisely the kind of initiative that D'Alesandro had come to Congress to support.

Word reached D'Alesandro that his wife, Annunciata, known as Nancy, was in labor, and he quickly shifted gears. He sought another congressman with whom he could pair off; D'Alesandro would pledge not to vote in favor of the legislation in return for the partner's pledge not to vote against it. Then, satisfied that his absence wouldn't endanger the bill, he raced off to Baltimore's St. Joseph's Hospital to be with his wife.

They'd been through the drill before. This was Tommy and Nancy D'Alesandro's seventh child. If there were two things D'Alesandro understood, it was deal making and parenting. At age 36, D'Alesandro had been a father for 11 years and an elected official for 14.

On March 26, 1940, House Resolution 436, the National Youth Administration Bill, passed easily. Nancy Patricia D'Alesandro weighed in at 8½ pounds.

The birth of a baby girl thrilled Nancy and Tommy, who had produced six consecutive boys, and her gender was immediately the storyline for Baltimore newspapers, which first printed baby Nancy's picture when she was just a few hours old.

The *Baltimore News-Post* showed the future Speaker of the House as a tightly wrapped newborn being held by her mother, who was lying in bed in a hospital gown, surrounded by her father and brothers. "It's a Girl for the D'Alesandros," read the headline.

In the picture, as in the world where she would spend her professional life, Pelosi is surrounded by boys. There is her father, "Big Tommy," and her brothers "Young Tommy," Roosey, Nicky, Hector, and Joey. A sixth D'Alesandro boy had tragically died of pneumonia a few years before.

Word spread quickly that there was now a D'Alesandro girl.

"D'Alesandro Will Find New Boss in First Daughter," declared a headline in another publication.

"We predict that this little lady will soon be a 'Queen' in her own right," the newspaper wrote.[1]

Becoming queen would have seemed as likely as Speaker in 1940. Politics was the domain of men. A woman had never been elected to the Baltimore city council. There was not a single woman governor in America. One woman served in the Senate. Eight women served in the House. None held a position of prominence.

Decades later her oldest brother, Tommy, recalled affectionately how "the whole community was rooting for a girl."

The boys were not so certain at the time. The proud father said that when he announced to his sons that they finally had a sister, the boys agreed, "We don't want any girls around here."[2]

BALTIMORE IN 1940 WAS a congested industrial city with an architecturally rich skyline and nearly a million residents. Its deep harbors and position midway along the eastern seaboard had made it a trading destination since the 1700s. World War I had brought industry and thousands of new working-class jobs. Bethlehem Steel Corporation was the city's largest employer, and thousands of workers flocked in from the South.

Pelosi was raised at 245 Albemarle Street, in the heart of Baltimore's Little Italy. The neighborhood was a tightly knit enclave just off Baltimore's brackish waterfront. A short walk from downtown, Little Italy encompassed roughly 10 square blocks at the eastern edge of the city's run-down and at times putrid inner harbor.

Italians had been living in the area for roughly a century, drawn to its cheap housing and proximity to the port. The neighborhood flourished in the late 1840s—at almost exactly the time that California's gold rush led to a boom in Pelosi's adopted home of San Francisco—when a train station was erected there as a stopping point between Philadelphia and Washington, DC.[3]

By 1900, Italians occupied almost every home in the neighborhood. Families arriving from Genoa and Abruzzi crowded into the two-story brick row houses, many of which lacked running water. The small houses were often home to multiple generations. As families got larger and more relatives came from overseas, those who could afford it found new housing next door or down the street. Those who couldn't crowded into the rooms they had.

Pelosi's mother grew up across the street at 204 Albemarle Street, her father at 235 Albemarle. Her mother's grandparents lived at 206 Albemarle. Aunt Jessie lived at 314 Albemarle. Aunt Mary lived around the corner on Eastern Avenue. Cousins were everywhere. The same could be said of every family.

The enormous pumping station that opened in 1911 at the harbor's edge offered modern sewage treatment for Baltimore as well as jobs and bocce courts for the neighborhood men. Pelosi's grandfather worked there during the Depression, earning between $15 and $16 a month. Men who didn't work at the pumping station found jobs at rail yards and steel mills or worked as bricklayers or stonemasons. It was a working-class neighborhood, virtually devoid of doctors, lawyers, and other professionals.

Residents sat on the stoop to pass the time in the days before television and air-conditioning beckoned them inside. The municipal bathhouse on High Street, which in Pelosi's grandparents' day had offered scalding hot showers for three cents, had been replaced by household plumbing, but laundry was dried on lines that hung from windows. Neighborhood boys were known for the corner they hung out on. Kids bought candy at Mugavero's (Mugs) Confectionery, a block from Pelosi's home.

The center of the community was St. Leo's Church, built in 1880, which towered above the neighborhood's row houses. Its bells could be heard at Pelosi's home on Sunday mornings, when the entire neighborhood walked up its steep front steps for Mass, held in English and Italian. On church days, the scent of tomato sauce simmering in dozens of kitchens filled the narrow streets as women prepared the Sunday dinner. Anyone was welcome into anyone else's home for food. Everyone was family.

War took a heavy toll in Little Italy. Hundreds of young men enlisted to fight the Germans, the Japanese, and even the Italians. The red brick walls outside St. Leo's hold plaques bearing long lists of the names of those who gave their lives and served: four Delorenzos, seven Picarellis, eight Iannatuonos. Six neighborhood boys were killed in World War I, 15 in World War II—a terrible toll for such a tiny slice of Baltimore. The Italians of Baltimore aspired to be American. They were traditionalists, fierce patriots, and very proud of their assimilation.

A block away was St. Leo's School, where Pelosi attended grade school in her blue uniform and where her father and brothers were schooled. When her older brother entered, tuition was 25 cents a week. Elderly men—and even a few women—still throw bocce balls on the courts outside the school and sit on the red, white, and green benches painted the colors of the Italian flag.

The neighborhood oozed politics. Even before Pelosi's father established a dynasty at the corner of Albemarle and Fawn Streets, Congressman Vincent Palmisano lived just across the street. Senators and presidents came by. On the night when Spiro Agnew resigned as vice president half a century later, he dined at Sabatino's, a neighborhood institution he knew well from his days as Baltimore County executive.

Baltimore, like many eastern cities, was defined by its ethnic neighborhoods. There was little diversity or ethnic mixing inside Little Italy. People born in the neighborhood stayed in the neighborhood. The women mostly worked at home. The adventurous ones got jobs working in downtown department stores or textile factories.

Pelosi would be different. She left the neighborhood for high school each day. She left the city to go to college. And she left the East Coast to raise her family on the other side of the country.

PELOSI'S ROOTS IN THE NEIGHBORHOOD ran deep. Her mother was born in Italy but moved when she was an infant to Albemarle Street—just a block from where she would raise her own family. The family returned to Italy for a few years but then moved back to Baltimore. As a result, Annunciata spoke perfect Italian, in contrast to her future husband, who joked that he spoke "Chinese Italian," meaning that he could hold a conversation but really chopped it up.

Annunciata Lombardi was a distinguished graduate of the Institute of Notre Dame, a well-regarded Catholic high school a few miles outside Little Italy, where young Nancy would be schooled a generation later.

Annunciata—Nancy—was an accomplished woman with seemingly boundless potential. She was smart, quick, and confident. She got good grades and had a sharp mind and would develop a quick wit and a keen political sense that would become invaluable to her husband's career. "Big Nancy's" dark hair and big, dark eyes and her impeccable dress made her quite an attraction. Her eldest son, Tommy, described her as "a cross between Elizabeth Taylor and Ava Gardner."

Upon earning her diploma from the Institute of Notre Dame, Pelosi's mother got a job that suited her quick mind: auctioneer, a role practically unheard of for a woman. She was good enough to be asked by her employer to go to New York to earn national certification, a feat that would have been pioneering in the 1920s, let alone today.

Instead, at age 19, she married Tommy D'Alesandro, a 25-year-old dapper politician already serving in the Maryland statehouse. She had known Tommy from the neighborhood since she was a little girl.

The wedding of Annunciata Lombardi and Tommy D'Alesandro was an extravagant affair. On the morning of the wedding, Sunday, September 30, 1928, Tommy sent the 18-piece St. Gabriel's Society band, waving red, white, and green Italian flags, to Nancy's Albemarle Street home to serenade her as she got ready and to trumpet her departure to St. Leo's, where they were to be wed. Nancy made it known that if the band didn't depart, the wedding was off. The groom waved them away.

The festivities lasted more than 12 hours. With Tommy's extensive contacts in Little Italy, Baltimore, and Annapolis, the neighborhood streets were crowded with thousands of celebrants in one of the largest wedding ceremonies the city had ever seen. It was past 11:00 p.m. by the time the groom cut the cake. Years later Tommy confessed that the festivities had interfered with their honeymoon travel plans.

"I got sick," Tommy confessed. "I ate too much."[4]

THOMAS D'ALESANDRO JR. WAS the fourth of 13 kids, born August 1, 1903. He was the son of Thomas—Tomaso—D'Alesandro, who had come from the mountains of Abruzzi, Italy. His father opened a store at the edge of Little Italy but earned more money swinging a pick at a local quarry. His mother, Mary Annie Foppiano D'Alesandro, was born on Albemarle Street two decades after the Civil War.

D'Alesandro's formal schooling ended at age 13. Just weeks before graduating the eighth grade, D'Alesandro got in a fight with a classmate and, rather than bringing his parents in to face the principal, left school. His first job was selling newspapers on the streets of Baltimore. Like so many of the neighborhood boys who saw where the authority lay, he wanted to become a priest.

He soon got a job collecting insurance fees from neighbors. He earned $5 a week. The insurance industry took D'Alesandro out of the neighborhood. He ventured past Pratt Street and Eastern Avenue and beyond Little Italy's familiar boundaries. At first he collected dues, often as little as a few pennies a week. Eventually he sold policies. He took classes at Calvert Business College and began hanging around Democratic Party headquarters. He was a precinct runner before he was old enough to vote.

He was also an accomplished dancer, an award-winning ballroom-style dancer. He entered competitions and won. Decades later, when his eldest son was campaigning for city council, young Tommy would sometimes knock on a door to have a woman say admiringly, "I danced with your father."[5]

It was this young, well-spoken, dapper, insurance-selling ballroom dancer who was spotted by Baltimore sheriff Joseph Deegan, a fixture in the Democratic machine. Deegan immediately recognized his political potential and, perhaps, a chance to unseat his rivals.

Deegan took him to the political bosses who played pinochle at the grand Rennert Hotel and told the men, "This is Tommy D'Alesandro, a very popular person in our district. I'd like to make him a candidate for the House of Delegates on our ticket."

Legend has it that the men never looked up from their game.

"Tell him to go out and get 500 signatures" was the response.

That was not difficult for a young man who knew 500 people in Little Italy, not to mention thousands of others from selling insurance door-to-door. D'Alesandro returned with the 500 signatures.

The men at the card table acted unimpressed. "If you've got 500 signatures, you don't need us," they said.

The bosses were right. Between his relatives and friends in Little Italy, his contacts from going door-to-door selling insurance, and friends from his dancing days, D'Alesandro was well known. On election day, D'Alesandro went downtown to watch the numbers come in. He didn't have the money to buy a radio to hear the returns, but the *Baltimore Sun* displayed results on the side of its building. It was there he learned that he had been elected, at age 22, to represent Little Italy as the youngest member of the Maryland House of Delegates.

D'Alesandro arrived in Annapolis wearing an oxford gray suit, a polka-dot tie, leather slippers, and a derby. He was so green that he hopped off the train, proudly jumped into a taxi, and asked to be driven all the way to the Capitol. The driver started the car, drove him half a block, and stopped.

"I said, 'What's the matter? Do you have a flat tire?' He said, 'No. This is the Capitol.'"[6]

D'Alesandro was not impressed by the caliber of his peers.

"I went in and looked at [the Maryland statehouse]. I walked upstairs and I looked for Henry Clay, George Washington, and Abraham Lincoln. All I saw was a bunch of drunks," D'Alesandro recalled.[7]

He left the statehouse in 1936 for an appointment as a deputy collector for the Internal Revenue Service. Like most aspects of the D'Alesandro household, politics played a guiding role in his job path. D'Alesandro believed he was given the appointment by political opponents who wanted him out of the way so he wouldn't run for a vacant city council seat. Happy to earn a stable salary, D'Alesandro commuted regularly to New York for a couple of years. But he ran afoul of his Little Italy neighbor Vincent Palmisano, who was among the first Italian Americans to serve in Congress.

The two didn't like each other politically; Palmisano was against the New Deal, and D'Alesandro was a devout Roosevelt man. They didn't like each other personally, either. Palmisano had been fickle in his support for D'Alesandro in his assembly race. And D'Alesandro took it hard when Palmisano—who lived just across Albemarle Street—hadn't come to visit when his boy was dying of pneumonia.

Palmisano complained to federal officials that IRS employees were not supposed to engage in political activity. D'Alesandro wanted to keep his job, but he could not stomach the thought of remaining on the political sidelines.

At a going-away party as he left his job in New York, D'Alesandro vowed to challenge Palmisano for his seat in Congress. D'Alesandro returned to Baltimore to sell insurance and serve two terms on the city council. He then exacted his revenge.

"He always saw my father as an irritant. Didn't like his style," young Tommy said of Palmisano. "So instead of taking him in, my father built and built and built, and when the time came, my father ran against him."

The 1938 Democratic primary to represent Maryland's Third Congressional District, between D'Alesandro and Palmisano, split the community apart.

"Can you imagine? Neighbor against neighbor. Son against son. Daughter against daughter. Husband against wife. There were houses with both placards," recalled Tommy, who was 10 years old at the time.

D'Alesandro had the backing of William Curran, the city's biggest boss. D'Alesandro was pro-labor and pro–New Deal. In Democratic Baltimore, that was a good place to be. On election day, all the New Dealers won big—except D'Alesandro. It was a nail-biter. The first count had D'Alesandro winning by 48 votes. Another count showed Palmisano winning by 1. In the end, of 27,878 votes cast, it was D'Alesandro by 61 votes.

Winning the subsequent general election should have been easy, but it was marred by personal tragedy. D'Alesandro was eating lunch at the Horn & Horn restaurant with his Republican opponent, of all people, when a call came to rush home. His mother was sick. By the time he got home, she was dead. For 10 days he stopped campaigning. But the Third Congressional District was safely in the Democrats' hands, and he won by 6,200 votes.

And so D'Alesandro went to Washington. Life as a member of the 76th Congress was dramatically different than it was when D'Alesandro's daughter would become its Speaker. It was a homogeneous crowd that drank together by night and often spent months at a time in Washington when Congress was in session.

In 1938 there were four women in the House and none in the Senate. House members earned $10,000 a year. The Speaker was William Bankhead of Alabama, and President Roosevelt was at the halfway point of his 12-year presidency. Adolf Hitler was in power in Germany, and the world was on the brink of war.

This was the world into which Nancy D'Alesandro was born.

CHAPTER TWO

THE MAYOR'S DAUGHTER

"I'm a Democrat, and I'll live a Democrat and die a Democrat."
—TOMMY D'ALESANDRO JR., 1958

"My parents did not raise me to be Speaker of the House.
My parents raised me to be holy."
—NANCY PELOSI, 2007

THOMAS D'ALESANDRO WAS A big-time politician who took his family along for the ride.

Among Pelosi's first memories is arriving at the Capitol in a white dress as a four-year-old to visit her dad. As the family approached the north side of the gleaming dome, her mother instructed one of her older brothers to "show Nancy the Capitol," confusing the little girl who had just mastered the alphabet.

"I'd say, 'Capital what? Capital A, capital B, capital C?'"[1]

It was a political life. D'Alesandro was in the second year of his first term in Congress when his daughter was born. He kept copies of the *Congressional Record* under her bed. Constituents were in and out of the house at all hours.

Life as a member of Congress from Baltimore was good. It meant an easy commute by congressional standards. Most members had apartments in Washington, but the D'Alesandros were able to stay in Baltimore. D'Alesandro tried to make it home by 7:00 each night, but he told his wife and the family not to wait to have their dinner.

In Washington, D'Alesandro got to live out his New Deal ambitions. He pushed spending for jobs, public works, and youth programs. He delivered his first address on the House floor on February 7, 1939, a five-minute speech calling for a veterans' hospital in his district. That November he first met President Roosevelt, who offered him a cigarette and called him "Tommy."[2] D'Alesandro hung a picture of FDR in his living room.

He rode the eight o'clock train into Washington, often pushing his way past job seekers as he left his house. A decade after the Great Depression, being in public office was about getting people jobs. Constituents stopped by his office and home. They called at all hours. D'Alesandro always carried a sheet of paper with him. On one side was a list of people he'd found jobs. On the other side was a longer list of those who still needed them.

"They all want jobs. Something must be done about this unemployment," he complained. "People down here have large families. It works a hardship when somebody in the family loses a job. Your heart goes out to them, and you try to help them. . . . Since I was elected, nine out of every ten people who have come to see me have been out of work, and hunting it or just wanting jobs."[3]

It was impossible to find jobs for everybody. He told people that a congressman needed to make new friends every day to make up for the people he couldn't satisfy.

Sharply dressed, with a kerchief in his pocket and a neatly trimmed mustache, D'Alesandro fit the image of a congressman. He was soon the best known of the state's six representatives, and he seemed quite comfortable in the House.

But his home was Little Italy, not Capitol Hill. On the train each day, D'Alesandro would hear from people who talked politics and asked for favors.

D'Alesandro realized that most of what they were interested in could be better delivered from Baltimore than Washington. His notion of public service was person-to-person. He was a *paisan*, a man of his neighborhood.

He won a seat on the influential Appropriations Committee, which doles out money, and became chair of the District of Columbia Committee, which essentially governed the city until the district got its own government in the 1970s. The chairman of the committee was unofficially known as the "mayor of DC."

One day Vice President Truman was in Baltimore to deliver a speech, and D'Alesandro took him to the home of a judge to share some whiskey.

"Harry, how would you feel about D'Alesandro for mayor of Baltimore?" the congressman asked the vice president.

"I'd be for you," Truman responded. "If you're good enough to be mayor of Washington, you're good enough to be mayor of your own hometown."[4]

It became the theme of his campaign for mayor, a job D'Alesandro had long desired.

It was a tough campaign, partly because of his name. D'Alesandro was a familiar name inside Little Italy, but for many outside the neighborhood, it was difficult to pronounce and oozed ethnicity.

So he ran radio ads that literally sang his name: "D'Alesandro. D'Alesandro stands for good government," went the jingle. "Vote for Tommy D'Alesandro. Paved streets, more schools . . ."[5]

It worked. As he walked the streets, people would sing "D'Alesandro" at him.

His opponent, the city's comptroller, had a less fortunate name for politics: Howard E. Crook.

Pelosi's father took elections very seriously. He was a tireless campaigner who won 26 elections in a span of 30 years. No detail was too small for his attention. He made sure the sons and daughters of supporters were registered as soon as they turned 21, and he pored over precinct lists, walked door-to-door, and campaigned neighborhood-to-neighborhood.

He once said he best liked running against bankers or businessmen because they were easily intimidated. You could "hit them in the solar plexus," he said, and their wives or mothers would say, "'Stay away from the Italian boy. He's too rough. You stay away from him.'"[6]

No matter whom he faced, he threw everything he had against him. Asked once whom he was running against, D'Alesandro responded, "I don't know, but it's some no-good son of a bitch. That's all I can tell you."[7]

A yellow legal pad sat inside the front door of the D'Alesandros' Albemarle Street home, and everyone in the family knew the drill. Constituents came by at all hours looking for favors. They needed jobs. They needed help with permits. They needed their sidewalks fixed, their streetlights replaced, to get a loved one into a hospital or out of jail. Names and numbers were carefully taken down. D'Alesandro would do what he could. The information would be transferred by manual typewriter onto index cards, which were then organized in a file.

Other households had a recipe file. The D'Alesandros had a favor file. Come election time, there would be a long list of the names and numbers of those who could be called upon to return the favor. Some would walk precincts. Some would drive voters to polls.

Before the sun rose on election day, May 6, 1947, D'Alesandro climbed to the roof of the family home with his eldest son. It was still dark, and they gazed at the car headlights driving toward them from the east. Some carried poll workers, some carried placards, some carried the volunteers who would go door-to-door.

"All these favors showed up," young Tommy recalled. "My father said, 'I don't know if we're going to win tonight. But it's going to be a hell of a fight.'"

D'Alesandro won by 24,272 votes. He was 43 years old. Little Italy celebrated the coronation of one of its own. Car horns honked and confetti flew. When D'Alesandro spoke to the crowd that night, the *Baltimore Sun* noted, it seemed "he knew them all."

The front page of the next morning's paper featured a photo of a smiling D'Alesandro holding seven-year-old Nancy in his arms.

PELOSI'S CHILDHOOD WOULD BE defined by that victory. Over the next 12 years D'Alesandro became a Baltimore institution. From the time little Nancy was in first grade through her years in college, her father was the biggest man in the neighborhood and possibly the best-known man in town. They could have moved out of Little Italy into a more spacious home in a more desirable neighborhood. But Tommy was a *paisan*. He was one of them.

Little Nancy was special. She was the youngest. She was a girl. Babysitters had to be relatives, and there wasn't any shortage. The mayor's driver picked little Nancy up each morning to drive her to school, a source of embarrassment for the mayor's daughter when she was older. She sometimes had the driver stop short so she could walk the final few blocks.

Politics were a daily part of Pelosi's childhood: ground-breaking ceremonies, picnics, community events, carnivals, church gatherings, weddings, spaghetti dinners, crab feeds, dances, even funerals. Sometimes the mayor would go alone. Sometimes it was the entire family.

D'Alesandro possessed remarkable energy. And he liked to be among people. Every New Year's he would shake as many hands as possible. On December 30, 1956, he shook 5,197 hands, and the paper ran a picture of his swollen hand wrapped in bandages. The following year it was 6,234 handshakes and another picture of his bandaged right paw. His 17-year-old daughter joined him in the greeting line and displayed no such swelling. She was wearing gloves.[8]

When things happened to Pelosi and her family, news of it appeared in the paper. Young Tommy fell down some stairs on Albemarle Street one day and needed go to the hospital for cuts and bruises. "D'Alesandro's Son Hurt: Thomas 3rd Falls into Cellar Stairway Near Home," the story read the next day.

Pelosi was in the newspaper regularly. Her dark hair and piercing eyes were often visible beside her father, who would be presenting a dignitary with the keys to the city or attending a social function.

Pelosi was quiet and reserved. She was surrounded by brothers who did plenty of talking. Nancy took it all in. She observed.

She absorbed the family's reverence for public service and its faith in government to deliver to the needy. She became politically astute at a young age. Pelosi recalled her parents taking her to a polling place as a little girl. A Republican poll worker handed her a little toy elephant as a souvenir. Pelosi recoiled, quickly handing it back.

"He thinks I don't know what this is," Pelosi recalled thinking many years later with a laugh. "I was offended."[9]

She also picked up the family business very quickly.

The D'Alesandro house was always busy. It was not uncommon for Pelosi to come downstairs in the morning to find men inquiring about work or women inquiring on behalf of their sons. Her mother often prepared a large pot of stew, and anyone who wanted it would be served throughout the day or even invited to stay for supper.

The home phone line—Calvert 4890—was so busy the mayor had eight more lines installed in the house. Three were on the third floor, where the mayor slept with Tommy, Roosey, Nicky, and Hector. His wife slept on the second floor with Nancy and Joey, the two youngest children.

The formal living room on the first floor was decorated with an Oriental rug and contemporary parlor furniture. There was the portrait of FDR, whom D'Alesandro sometimes referred to as "my idol." There was also a small statue of Frances Xavier Cabrini, known as Mother Cabrini, a newly canonized saint who, like D'Alesandro, was Italian and one of 13 children and who had come to the New World and helped build schools, hospitals, and orphanages.

When the family gathered for dinner, the conversation was sometimes about school, church, or sports. Quite often it was about politics—not necessarily the great issues of the day, but matters like what was new in the Third Precinct and whose children were reaching voting age.

As a 10-year-old, Pelosi could handle the constituents by herself. She would take turns with her siblings manning the office that doubled as their living room. She was well versed in the workings of the box of index cards known as the favor file.

"I knew how to answer the phone and tell people where to go if they needed a bed in a city hospital, or where to call to get into a housing project," Pelosi said 30 years later.[10]

St. Leo's was always a fixture. The D'Alesandros never missed Mass on Sunday. Communion and daily prayer were an unshakable part of the family's upbringing. Just like her father, Pelosi saw where the power was centered, and one day she announced to her mother that she wanted to be a priest. At first no one had the heart to tell her that only men could be priests. Little Nancy kept telling people that when she grew up, she would be a priest. Finally she was told that if she wanted to pursue such work, she could become a nun. That didn't hold the same allure.

After Pelosi graduated from elementary school, her mother insisted that she attend the Institute of Notre Dame. While her brothers attended St. Leo's school with the neighborhood's Italian kids a few blocks from home, Pelosi met Irish, German, and Polish kids from all over the city at the prestigious all-girls school that her mother had also attended.

"My father was a committed parochial guy. My mother was for opening the windows," her older brother Tommy said.

Pelosi blossomed in her new environment. She was popular in class and spoke up more frequently. Though she still regarded herself as shy, she was a member of the debate team and was known for her sharp rebuttals. She had parties at her house—usually just for girls—and went to the prom with a boy who would go on to become the Baltimore County executive.

Her mother kept close tabs on her progress at school. A classmate remembers a nun telling Pelosi her mother was at school one day. It was a somber occasion.

Report cards had arrived in the mail that day, and little Nancy's Latin mark had fallen a grade. Her mother wanted an explanation. She had high expectations for her daughter's success.

Her classmates assumed Pelosi would go on to work in law or government—not politics. Elected office, even for the mayor's daughter, was not regarded as an option at an all-girls school (though Barbara Mikulski, who would go on to represent Maryland in the House and Senate, had graduated from the same school just a few years ahead of Pelosi). For those interested in working outside the home, nursing and teaching were the most likely careers. Politics was the domain of men.

Pelosi met scores of national figures. In part because D'Alesandro was an influential Democrat and in part because Baltimore was the biggest city close to Washington, future presidents, vice presidents, and others running for high office often stopped by the house at the corner of Albemarle and Fawn.

Bill Clinton's 1962 high school encounter with President John F. Kennedy in the Rose Garden produced a well-known photograph that foreshadowed the young southerner's ambitious rise. Pelosi's encounter with Kennedy had come several years earlier, when her father took her to a formal function at Baltimore's Emerson Hotel, where the then senator was being honored for his book, *Profiles in Courage*. Pelosi, dressed in a formal gown with white gloves, turned down an invitation to sit at a table with her Institute of Notre Dame classmates so she could sit with her father next to the man who would soon be president. A framed picture of Kennedy smiling at the teenage Pelosi hung in her office for many years.

When he introduced Speaker Sam Rayburn at the same hotel in January 1956 as a man "among American immortals," D'Alesandro could hardly have imagined that a half century later his own daughter—at the time 15 years old—would step into that very role.

PELOSI LEARNED POLITICS FROM a man who looked the part of a politician. His hair was cut weekly. He sometimes wore bow ties and usually had a silk handkerchief in his breast pocket. He wore a three-diamond ring on the little finger of his right hand and a diamond-and-gold monogrammed ring on his left.[11]

When Hollywood shoots scenes of smoke-filled rooms, it is characters like D'Alesandro who are puffing on the cigars (something he did only rarely). He was a natural operator. He was a delegate at seven consecutive Democratic conventions, served for many years on the Democratic National Committee, and cut deals to win support for Adlai Stevenson's presidential runs.

Pelosi recalls her father "was totally consumed with politics. He didn't play golf or anything else. He said the Catholic Church and the Democratic Party— and his family, of course—were his loyalties."[12]

Pelosi's own passion for Democratic politics can easily be traced to her father.

"Republicans always play the same game. They are for big business and money interests," the mayor said, using words remarkably similar to those that would later be used by his daughter.[13] D'Alesandro was an unwavering partisan who implored his fellow Democrats to patch up their differences in order to advance the party, much as his daughter would do in Congress 50 years later.

"We know from long experience that the people are better served by Democratic public officials, and we are letting the people down when we permit factional fighting to put Republicans in office," he said.[14]

D'Alesandro was very clear in his own mind on the difference between his brand of New Deal liberalism and the socialism that was fashionable among some leftists. He took umbrage when an opponent during the 1950s accused him of "socialistic" thinking, which implied the authoritative hand of Big Brother—as demonstrated in the Soviet Union—and not the social safety net that New Dealers like D'Alesandro embraced.

Like most politicians of his day, he was a fierce anti-Communist. Communism was particularly reviled by the Catholic Church, and D'Alesandro railed against what he sometimes called the "evil doctrine of Communism" and other times simply "ungodly Communism."

Growing up in a self-contained neighbored, Pelosi knew little discrimination.

Yet as an Italian, D'Alesandro understood that he faced prejudice because his name "ends in a vowel."

"Every time I run for anything, someone wants me to take an oath of allegiance or be repatriated. My grandfather fought in the Civil War and my brother was killed in the Battle of the Bulge. The bullet didn't ask his name, race or religion. I am a better American than my critics think they are."[15]

D'Alesandro believed that his success paved the way for the next generation of Italian Americans, allowing voters to elect future politicians like his son—and his daughter—without hesitating over their ethnic background.

The news media was a constant presence and not always a friend. Early news coverage of his mayoralty was by and large favorable, and D'Alesandro seemed to be around a camera or a reporter virtually nonstop. But he did not always cooperate. One young reporter repeatedly asked D'Alesandro for his views on a matter and kept getting no response. Out of frustration, the reporter finally blurted out, "My desk wants to know your position."

D'Alesandro is said to have put his ear to his desk and bellowed back, "My desk tells your desk to go fuck itself!"

Relations with the media appeared to sour midway through his mayoral tenure following an incident involving his family. D'Alesandro and several of his children, including Nancy, boated off to Europe in the summer of 1953, where he was representing the US Conference of Mayors.

Upon returning home, they learned that their second-oldest son, Roosey, then 21, along with 15 other kids from the neighborhood, had been arrested for renting an apartment to board two underage girls. He was indicted on charges of statutory rape and perjury. The charges were ultimately dismissed, but the story got far more ink than it might have because it involved the son of the mayor.

He was also displeased over the media's coverage of a scandal involving a local contractor—whose daughter was married to young Tommy—who had lent money to D'Alesandro's wife. There was no evidence of illegal activity, but the attention was among the reasons he decided against running for governor when Pelosi was 14.

His years in public office left him with disdain for the Fourth Estate.

"No decent man will run for office on account of the Sun papers," he told an interviewer many years after he left office, referring to the *Baltimore Sun* and its afternoon edition, the *Evening Sun*. "They got nothing but tripe working for them. . . . They got nothing but garbage working for them. They pay them such lousy salaries, they can't get anybody to work for them, you know. They're no good."[16]

The mayor held as little regard for the Hearst-owned *Baltimore News American*.

"It's a yellow sheet," D'Alesandro said. "If it's a one-alarm fire down here, they got 50 pages that the whole town is burning up. . . . Anything good, they don't put in the paper."

Pelosi would never use such language when she served in public office, though many reporters suspected she shared the sentiment.

Pelosi watched as her father helped guide Baltimore into the modern age. It was during D'Alesandro's tenure that the city made the conversion from gas lamps to electric lights, built a freeway tunnel below its harbor, paved its cobblestone roads, became one of the first major cities in the world to introduce fluoride into the water supply, and opened its airport.

D'Alesandro accompanied President Harry S. Truman on a flight from Washington, DC, to Baltimore to inaugurate the airport, no small accomplishment for a man who was so terrified of flying that he did not ride in an airplane for the first 46 years of his life.

The night before the flight, D'Alesandro recalled, "I said 300 Hail Marys, 50 Our Fathers and the best doggone Act of Contrition of my life."[17]

It was during D'Alesandro's tenure that the Baltimore Colts and Orioles came to a town that had been without professional sports teams for half a century. As a teenager, Pelosi joined her father at football games, where she watched Johnny Unitas lead the Colts to back-to-back championships. The day the Orioles played their first game at Memorial Stadium (one sportswriter suggested it be named "D'Alesandro Stadium"), April 15, 1954, was a big day in Baltimore. Schools closed and parades featured 32 floats and 20 bands. Vice President Richard Nixon threw out the first ball.

D'Alesandro missed it. He was in Bon Secours Hospital suffering from what was alternately described as fatigue and nervous collapse. The mayor had lost 40 pounds and according to *Time Magazine* was a "shadow of his once proud, pudgy self."[18]

It was almost exactly one month after the Orioles' opener that the Supreme Court handed down its *Brown v. Board of Education* decision and ordered school districts around the country to desegregate.

The decision had a profound impact in Baltimore, which still operated much like a Southern city, having desegregated its golf course and hired black transit workers only a few years earlier. New Deal liberalism clashed with blue-collar prejudice, and City Hall expressed alarm at whites' possible reaction to integration.

School board president Walter Sondheim Jr. went to see D'Alesandro in the hospital to inform him that the school board had voted to integrate the schools in time for the new school year.

"I'll never forget what he did," Sondheim recalled. "He kind of shook his hand at me and said, "I don't know whether what you did was right, but the priests tell me you were right."

And that, Sondheim recalled, ended any doubts that City Hall might not back integration.[19]

Of course, it didn't solve Baltimore's racial problems. The riots after Martin Luther King Jr. was killed in 1968 were among the reasons that young Tommy, who would succeed his father as mayor, served only one term.

Being part of the mayor's family was not all glamour. Pelosi never forgot the odor of the rotting garbage that was strewn over the sidewalk in front of their home during a contentious street cleaners' strike when she was a teenager.

"What a mean thing to do to my mother," she said many years later.[20]

Pelosi learned politics from her father, but it was her mother she credits with having made her a success. "Big Nancy" was a dynamo who simultaneously ran a household with six children and the mayor's constituent service operation at the corner of Albemarle and Fawn streets.

She decided to resume her education when Little Nancy was an infant, enrolling at the University of Baltimore to earn a law degree while caring for six children ages six months to 11 years.

"When my children grow up, I'll need another interest to keep me busy," she explained to a reporter when Nancy was a toddler. "Even now the house seems empty because three of the children are in school. Tommy is in the seventh grade, Roosey is in the second, Nicky started in the first grade this week. That leaves me only Hector and Jo-Jo and Nancy during the daytime."

She figured she could learn the law at night because her kids were in bed by 7:00.

"I will go to school from 7:30 until 10:30. My studying will be done in the daytime.

"I feel that I should do something constructive to learn more," D'Alesandro said. "I was married a year after I finished school, and this has been my first chance to study. If God is willing, I want all the children to go through high school and college. I must keep up with them, or even a little ahead of them, mustn't I? That is why I go to school this winter."[21]

The law degree never came, but the energy never let up.

She organized a mothers' club at St. Leo's and a women's political club that would meet in the D'Alesandros' basement. Young Tommy remembers few things as intimidating as the charged-up army of women marching up from his basement each week.

In the newspaper, Annunciata D'Alesandro was always pictured wearing formal clothes, frilly satin blouses, and elegant necklaces. Two maids helped with housework, but she did all the cooking, including a spaghetti dinner at least twice a week. She said she only needed six hours of sleep, going to bed after midnight and getting up before 6:30.

"If she lived today or 20 years hence, the sky would be the limit for her," young Tommy said. "We'll never know what she could have accomplished, but she lived in a time when her options were very limited. She had seven children; she was in an Italian American family and all that that implies in terms of her ability to spread her own wings to fly."

Yet she saw a chance for her daughter to pursue the opportunities that were not available to her. It was Pelosi's mother who insisted she leave the neighborhood to attend the Institute of Notre Dame and who stood by her when her father objected to her leaving town to go to college.

"Over my dead body!" D'Alesandro was said to have thundered when he heard of his daughter's plans to leave Baltimore for Trinity College.

"That could be arranged," his wife responded.

Pelosi's mother was also known for her long, and at times unforgiving, memory. She never forgot who was on her husband's side and who had been against him. Her husband would tell the story of introducing his wife to President Lyndon B. Johnson in the heat of the 1964 campaign. The president had known D'Alesandro from his days in Congress and referred to him—and most other Italians—as "Tony." D'Alesandro took less offense than his wife. Upon her husband's introducing her to Johnson, she gave him a sharp look and told him, "My husband's name is Thomas John D'Alesandro. It is not Tony," drawing a stunned look from the rebuked president.[22]

Tommy D'Alesandro had won 23 consecutive elections when he announced a bid for a seat in the US Senate in 1958.

"If you go to Pimlico and find a horse that ran and won 23 times," D'Alesandro liked to tell audiences, referring to the Baltimore area's famed track, "that's the one you're going to drop your deuce on."

But the string came to an end. The party bosses had convinced D'Alesandro that he'd be anchored by a strong Democratic ticket. But they were unwilling to help him outside of ethnic Baltimore. D'Alesandro won in his own city by more than 31,000 votes, but it wasn't enough.

Young Tommy recalls that his mother had seen it coming.

"My father came back from making that deal, and when he came home . . . my mother said, 'You're beat.' She said, 'They boxed you in. You made a bad deal. You should have talked to me before you made a deal. You're the only one running against an incumbent. They got all open fields. This guy is going to lay and wait for you. They're not going to be burdened by you,'" he recounted. "Everything she said came to fruition."[23]

The following year D'Alesandro ran for a fourth term, but voters wanted someone new. He lost the primary by 33,000 votes. It was his last election.

Asked shortly after the defeat if he would support the Democrat who had just beaten him, D'Alesandro displayed the partisan fervor that could be seen in his daughter a generation later.

"Hell, yes," D'Alesandro said. "I'm a Democrat, and I'll live a Democrat and die a Democrat."[24]

And he did. After leaving the mayor's post, D'Alesandro was rewarded by President Kennedy, whom he had helped regularly, with a job on the Renegotiation Board, an agency that reviewed federal contracts. Pelosi, by then a student at Trinity College, accompanied him to the White House swearing-in ceremony.

There was talk about D'Alesandro, who remained the best-known figure in Little Italy, entering the 1963 mayor's race. But he deferred to his eldest son, who was now serving as president of the city council.

"I love him, and he deserves his chance," the elder D'Alesandro said.

D'Alesandro had no objection to his daughter attending college. But Trinity was an hour's drive—nearly 50 miles—from Little Italy. His sons hadn't traveled outside Baltimore for school. Most of Pelosi's classmates at the Institute of Notre Dame remained in town. People from Little Italy stayed close to home.

But Pelosi's mother was adamant. She was going to open windows that had been closed to her in the 1920s. Trinity offered young women a liberal arts education in a Catholic setting, and she insisted that Pelosi attend.

Pelosi set off for college on a Sunday afternoon in September 1958, when her father was in the final months of his Senate campaign. It was an adventure that would expand her horizons farther than anyone could have imagined.

Pelosi, her mother, and her brother Nicky all piled into a Mercury belonging to local law student Peter Angelos, a friend of Nicky's, for the drive to Washington. Looking back on that day nearly 50 years later, Angelos said that Pelosi seemed to understand that great adventures lay ahead but characteristically handled it like "she had everything under control."[25]

Angelos would go on to serve four years on the city council, become one of Baltimore's most successful attorneys, buy the Baltimore Orioles, and contribute hundreds of thousands of dollars to Democratic candidates.

As a student Pelosi was swept up by the idealism and promise of President Kennedy—a fellow Catholic—who inspired an entire generation of leaders. Pelosi trudged through newly fallen snow to the east side of the Capitol on January 20, 1961, to hear Kennedy speak the immortal words: "And so, my fellow Americans: Ask not what your country can do for you—ask what you can do for your country."

Hundreds of times in the course of her own political career, Pelosi would remind audiences of the less-well-known lines that followed: "My fellow citizens of the world: Ask not what America will do for you, but what together we can do for the freedom of man."

Trinity was an all-women's school, and Pelosi by all accounts was intense and studious. Her yearbook photo shows her with short hair coiffed below her ears, wearing a strapless gown. She volunteered for the Kennedy for President campaign in 1960 and was a member of the college's Democratic club.

For many students, Washington's highly charged political atmosphere is an eye-opening experience. For Pelosi it was a respite from the electoral intensity of Little Italy.

"For me it was a break from politics. My family was steeped in politics and so it was a nice break," Pelosi said of her college years.[26]

Pelosi's Catholicism showed no signs of wavering. Pelosi was surrounded by Catholics at Trinity, as she had been in Little Italy, and as she would be for much of her adult life. Going to mass was an unshakeable ritual, and it remained so even decades later when politics took her on the road and led her to worship in churches in all corners of the country.

Among the courses Pelosi took while at Trinity was one in African history, offered a few miles away at Georgetown University's School of Foreign Service and taught by the legendary professor Carroll Quigley. President Bill Clinton, who took a class from Quigley several years later, would comment, "Half the people at Georgetown thought he was a bit crazy, and the other half thought he was a genius and both were right."[27]

It was while taking the History of Africa, South of the Sahara, at Georgetown in the summer of 1961 that Nancy met a tall, strapping San Franciscan named Paul Pelosi. He had been raised in the city's Marina District and attended Malvern Preparatory School, a Catholic boarding school in Pennsylvania.

His father owned a pharmacy at 115 Mission Street but had earned considerably more money when he was awarded a contract to operate concessions in Lake Tahoe's Squaw Valley, where the 1960 Olympics were held.

Paul would graduate from Georgetown and study economics at New York University.

"She was just special," Paul said of his wife two decades after they were married. "She was just special. She was very bright, had a terrific personality. She had a very uncanny way about her. She was also pretty. So it was easy, very easy."[28]

The pair was inseparable. Pelosi had been considering a career in law, but her plans were interrupted when Paul proposed to her at St. Joseph's Church, two blocks from the US Capitol. Pelosi confided to a friend many years later that she knew the moment they were engaged that Paul would be a fantastic father. She wasn't as certain what kind of husband he would be.

As she prepared for the wedding, Pelosi worked her first job on Capitol Hill as a receptionist for Maryland senator Daniel Brewster. Brewster was, among other things, a civil rights advocate, and he would later place his name on the ballot for Maryland's 1964 Democratic presidential primary to deprive segregationist George Wallace of delegates. His civil rights stand did not make him a beloved figure throughout all of Maryland.

Just out of college, sharp, attractive, gracious, and with a name that all Maryland constituents knew, the youngest D'Alesandro was a highly valued addition to the office. Forty years later, Brewster recalled that when Pelosi applied for the job, "I grabbed her with both my hands."[29]

The senator recalled putting Pelosi at the front desk with a huge nameplate in front of her so everyone walking into his Dirksen Building office would see the family name.

"Having the D'Alesandro family supporting me was very helpful," he said.

It was at Brewster's office that Pelosi befriended the senator's young legislative aide, another Marylander named Steny Hoyer, who 45 years later would be the House majority leader.

Hoyer recalled that the two knew each other but never saw each other socially. He was newly married, she was soon to be married, and both were incredibly busy. But he certainly knew who she was. Everyone knew the D'Alesandros.

In an interview conducted a few months before he died, Brewster marveled at the good fortune that had brought the future Speaker and the majority leader together on the same staff. He also reflected on the drinking problem that had plagued him during his political years and said he hoped Pelosi and Hoyer had "learned some of the things you shouldn't do in political life" from working for him.

Nancy wouldn't be a D'Alesandro much longer. She left Brewster's office at the end of the summer to wed Paul and would forever be a Pelosi. It was preparations for the wedding that prompted her early departure from a civil rights rally at the Lincoln Memorial at the end of August. Pelosi had been among the

250,000 demonstrators on the Capitol Mall, but she left shortly before Dr. Martin Luther King Jr. delivered his "I have a dream" speech.

Nancy and Paul were married on September 7, 1963, at Mary Our Queen Cathedral in Baltimore, about a 20-minute drive from Little Italy. Pelosi wore a white silk satin gown with a floor-length lace mantilla, according to newspaper accounts.

The Pelosis moved to midtown Manhattan, where Paul worked in banking and Nancy had babies. Over the next seven years, Pelosi would be pregnant for more than 1,300 days. In a span of six years and one week, Pelosi gave birth to four girls and a boy: Nancy Corinne, Christine, Jacqueline, Paul Jr., and Alexandra. Her New York days were a blur of diapers, playgrounds, and toys. Pelosi had broken the mold by leaving Little Italy, but she was leading a very traditional life.

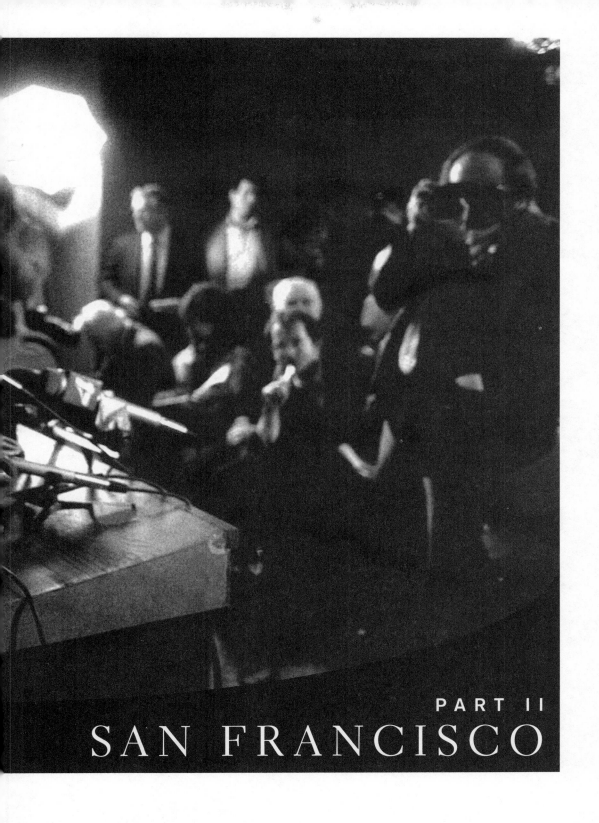

PART II
SAN FRANCISCO

CHAPTER THREE

OUT OF THE KITCHEN

"My parents would say, 'Never mind politics. Enjoy your family.'
And then, I don't know, you just discover it's in your DNA, in your blood."
—NANCY PELOSI, 2002

"I used to think as I was sitting in the park for eight hours a day watching
[my kids] play, that when they're in school, and I have enough time,
I could do something—like feed all the hungry people in the world."
—NANCY PELOSI, 1984

PELOSI MOVED TO HER HUSBAND'S HOMETOWN IN 1969, two years after the Summer of Love. San Francisco was a vibrant city that offered an abundance of beauty and happenings to a couple in their twenties. The Grateful Dead and Jefferson Airplane performed free concerts at Golden Gate Park. Janis Joplin played at Winterland, and the Doors appeared at the Cow Palace. The free speech movement had electrified the Berkeley campus across the Bay. Willie Mays, Willie McCovey, and Bobby Bonds all played for the Giants at windy Candlestick Park.

Nancy and Paul arrived from New York with children in tow. Nancy Corinne was four, Christine was two, Jacqueline was one, and Paul, just a few months old. Pelosi would be pregnant with Alexandra, her youngest daughter, before the year was out.

If leaving Little Italy for Trinity College was a big step, moving west was a life-changing ordeal. Baltimore is a flat city of redbrick row houses, narrow streets, and dark smokestacks. Working boats crowd the inner harbor's brackish waters. Heavy clouds bring urgent thunderstorms in the summer and ice in the winter. San Francisco is a place of preposterously steep hills, Spanish architecture, and sweeping vistas. The Pacific Ocean is deep blue as is the sky when it is not obscured by the thick summer fog. On clear days the hills offer views to the lush Marin headlands and the East Bay hills with remarkable clarity.

San Francisco is also 2,500 miles and three time zones from the East, and the elder D'Alesandros took it hard. When Nancy and Paul had lived in New York, they traveled down to Little Italy most weekends for a Sunday night dinner of ravioli and pasta. San Francisco was the city of Paul's youth, and his mother and father and brother still lived there. For Nancy, especially considering her father's fear of airplanes, California was a long way from home.

She and Paul looked for a place to rent until they found a neighborhood to settle in. But finding a comfortable house and a landlord willing to rent to a family with four young children proved challenging. When they finally found a home they liked, Pelosi asked the couple that was moving why they were leaving.

"'Oh,' the woman said proudly. 'My husband is going to Washington to work in the new administration,'" Pelosi recalled.

For Pelosi, who had pushed her children in baby carriages while serving as a Hubert Humphrey volunteer the year before and spent days crying when Richard Nixon won, it was too much to handle.

"I can't live here," she sputtered. "I can't live anywhere that's vacated because of the Nixon administration."[1]

Pelosi laughed as she recounted the story for an interview published in *California Living Magazine* 15 years later, insisting that she had since matured.

Instead of renting, Nancy and Paul purchased a large home on Presidio Terrace for $96,000, roughly two miles north of the corner of Haight and Ashbury.

Presidio Terrace was a particularly fancy cul-de-sac with huge, elegant homes built shortly after the 1906 earthquake. Studded with palm trees and tucked between the Presidio and the bustling Asian restaurants of the Inner Richmond neighborhood, it is a place few visitors to San Francisco see. The cul-de-sac's sole entry point secludes its 40 Tudor and Beaux-Arts homes, making it a wonderful place for kids to play.

It was not only the home of great wealth, it was also the home of great power. San Francisco mayor Joseph Alioto lived three doors away. Future mayor and senator Dianne Feinstein grew up on the block, and a decade later she would return to a home across the street.

It was not a gated community when the Pelosis moved in, though a guard stood at the entryway and walked the street for security. For city dwellers, it was very much like living in the suburbs.

The terrace's exclusivity was among its selling points when it was first established. A Baldwin & Howell advertisement from 1915 boasted: "There is only one spot in San Francisco where only Caucasians are permitted to buy or lease real estate or where they may reside. That place is Presidio Terrace."[2] The Supreme Court had ruled that racial covenants were illegal two decades before the Pelosis arrived.

Nineteen sixty-nine was a turbulent time in the Bay Area. In Berkeley, the free speech movement had evolved into a perpetual clash between a growing subculture and the police. In the middle of San Francisco Bay, nearly 100 American Indians occupied Alcatraz, home to an abandoned federal prison, to demand that the island be returned to the native people.

And it was in 1969 that the killer who called himself the Zodiac sent cryptic codes to the *San Francisco Chronicle,* demanding their publication and threatening more gruesome slayings. The last of his five known victims was a cab driver, shot point-blank in the head barely two blocks from the Pelosis' new home. The incident sent chills down the spines of residents, who began locking doors and looking over their shoulders for a killer who was never identified.

While the turbulence raged all around, Pelosi was raising a family. Paul was leasing equipment to businesses—including computers to firms in Silicon Valley—and dabbling in the real estate market. Business was booming and they had the money to pay nannies, but they had trouble finding someone both willing and competent to care for five young kids. A maid helped maintain the house, but the cooking and child care were handled by Pelosi, who seemed to be in her element.

"There is nothing I enjoyed more than taking care of babies," Pelosi said.[3]

When her kids were grown, she would wistfully note, "Sometimes I wish I could take them outside in the rain and shrink them back."

Pelosi was a master of efficiency as a young mother. She had no choice. She was in constant demand, balancing the competing needs of young schoolchildren, toddlers, and infants. For a number of years, she had three kids in diapers.

"Let's have some cooperation," Pelosi would tell her kids repeatedly.

When they asked what she wanted for Mother's Day or her birthday, the reply was often "good behavior."

Juggling multiple tasks became a Pelosi trademark, a skill she would rely upon later in Washington. Pelosi had grown up as the youngest of six, so to her, five seemed manageable. Being overwhelmed was not an option. Pelosi never seemed fazed by the frenetic pace. She was among the rarest of parents who seemed to gain energy from it.

"I used to think as I was sitting in the park for eight hours a day watching them play, that when they're in school, and I have enough time, I could do something—like feed all the hungry people in the world," Pelosi laughed to an interviewer when her youngest was in junior high school.[4]

Pelosi sounded remarkably like her own mother, who had enrolled in law school before young Nancy entered kindergarten.

"Babies have their own schedule. I was always moving. By the time they went to school, I was so super-charged that I was ready to do more. I don't think I had as much energy before I had babies."[5]

THE PELOSI NAME WAS known in San Francisco because of Paul's older brother, Ron, who had been best man at their wedding. Ron had served as president of the city's planning commission and was twice elected to the Board of Supervisors, in 1967 and 1971. But he was best known for a horrific incident that occurred shortly after Nancy and Paul moved to San Francisco.

Ron Pelosi and his wife had attended a gala black-tie fund-raiser for Mt. Zion Hospital aboard the S.S. *President Wilson*, leaving their four young children in the care of their housekeeper. They returned shortly after 12:30 a.m. to find their three-story home engulfed in flames.

Neighbors frantically kicked down the front door but were unable to enter because of the intense heat. Someone screamed that the kids were inside. Still dressed in his tuxedo, Pelosi threw a ladder against the side of the house and raced up to find his children. As he neared a second-story window, the ladder crashed to the ground, shattering Pelosi's hip. He did not learn the fate of his children until he awoke in the hospital many hours later.

His two sons, Brennan, nine, and Matthew, six, had found their way onto a second-story roof and, at the urging of the gathering crowd, leapt to safety.

Tragically, his daughters, 12-year-old Cynthia and one-year-old Caroline, and the 35-year old housekeeper could not escape and were burned almost beyond recognition.

Smoke from the spectacular blaze could be seen from Nancy and Paul's Presidio Terrace home several blocks away. The young boys and their distraught mother stayed with the Pelosis; Ron spent the next several months recovering in the hospital.

Ron Pelosi returned to work at city hall 5½ months later, vowing to remain in public office. He was the top vote getter in the following year's municipal election and became president of the Board of Supervisors.

Ron was a well-known and well-liked Democrat, though he was wealthier and more conservative than many San Franciscans. His prominence produced headlines in San Francisco papers that, years later, could prompt double takes after the Pelosi name became associated with his sister-in-law.

"Pelosi Bows to Women Libbers," read a 1972 headline in the *San Francisco Chronicle* after the supervisor publicly apologized for missing a meeting with a women's group.

Careful television viewers have reported seeing "Elect Pelosi" placards— referring to Ron, not Nancy—in old *Streets of San Francisco* episodes. It would be another three years before the newspaper would first mention Ron's sister-in-law.

SAN FRANCISCO WAS A solidly Democratic city when Pelosi arrived in 1969, though it hardly resembled a far-left outpost, let alone the "capital of the progressive movement in this country," as she would describe it a quarter of a century later.

The city had been a destination for adventurers, freethinkers, and renegades since the Barbary Coast days of the 19th century, a tradition carried on by Beats in the 1950s and hippies in the 1960s.

However, the San Francisco that Republicans tried to use against Pelosi

decades later had yet to emerge. The groups that form San Francisco's modern liberal base—renters, gays, Latinos, blacks—were only beginning to assert their influence when Pelosi arrived. In the mid-1960s, San Francisco was 95 percent white, mostly of German, Irish, and Italian descent. The Castro, then known as Eureka Valley, was home primarily to German Americans.

Before the 1960s, Republicans had not only won elections, they had thrived in the city. San Francisco had a string of progressive Republican mayors that stretched for 52 years, with the exception of two terms immediately following World War II. The streak lasted until Democratic congressman Jack Shelley traded his seat in Washington for one in city hall in 1964.

The city voted twice for Republican Dwight D. Eisenhower. Richard Nixon received 42 percent of San Francisco's vote in 1972, and Ronald Reagan received 38 percent in 1980. (In contrast, George W. Bush received 15.5 percent of the city's vote in 2000 and 2004.) The 1964 Republican National Convention came to San Francisco and nominated Barry Goldwater at the Cow Palace.

Pelosi arrived just as a great transformation was taking place. Thousands of Southeast Asians and Latin Americans moved to Northern California after passage of the 1965 Immigration Act. A boom in downtown office building reshaped San Francisco's skyline and transformed the labor force from working class to professional. Scott McKenzie sang San Francisco's appeal to young listeners around the world ("If you come to San Francisco, summertime will be a love-in there"[6]).

The most dominant figure in San Francisco politics at the time was Representative Phil Burton, who would play a critical role in Pelosi's ascent. Elected in 1964 to represent California's Fifth Congressional District, Burton was a chain-smoking, vodka-drinking, tough-talking legislative powerhouse who described himself as a "fighting liberal."

"His breath in the morning could sometimes melt steel," recalled the *Chronicle*'s Washington Bureau chief John Fogarty. "When he was hung over, he really became a bully."

Burton was as beloved as he was belligerent. A statue erected in his honor in San Francisco's Presidio shows, stuffed in his suit pocket, a partially visible note that reads: "The only way to deal with exploiters is . . ." Those who knew Burton know how the sentence ends: "to terrorize the bastards."

Burton was a master of Capitol Hill's inside game. In 1976 he came within a single vote of becoming Democratic majority leader, losing to Jim Wright, who went on to become Speaker two years later. He was a champion of unions and the environment and an early opponent of the Vietnam War. His legislative triumphs included instituting protections for coal workers and creating Northern California's Redwood National Park and the Golden Gate National Recreational Area.

When Pelosi arrived in 1969, Burton was in his early forties and still amassing power in Washington. It was Burton's seat that Pelosi eventually filled four years after his death. The one thing political observers in the Bay Area agreed upon at the time was that no matter who won the crowded race, no one would ever be able to fill Burton's shoes as a force in Washington.

Back home, Burton built a coalition of union members, blacks, environmentalists, gays, and working-class voters that would define the city's politics for decades after his death.

"Now you're not supposed to get the support of the environmentalists and labor. But how is it I've got the support of the cops and the gays as well? Ain't that a bitch?" he boasted in his prime.[7]

Among Burton's protégés was Willie Brown, a political mastermind who had come to San Francisco from Minneola, Texas, to attend law school and with Burton's help won a seat in the state legislature the year Burton went to Congress. Another was state senator George Moscone, a close Burton comrade who served as president of the California Senate until he was elected mayor in 1975. Burton's brother John served in the California Assembly until a neighboring district elected him to join his brother in Washington in 1974.

The Burton "machine" would be challenged and ultimately bolstered in the

1970s by politically active gays who were settling in the Castro. Harvey Milk moved to San Francisco a year after Pelosi and, from his camera shop on Castro Street, inspired an entire generation of gay activists. Milk ran for a seat on the Board of Supervisors the year after he arrived, a post he won four years later.

The governor was Ronald Reagan. Dianne Feinstein, then a 36-year-old appointee to the state's Women's Parole Board and a candidate for the Board of Supervisors, was at the beginning of a political path that would take her from supervisor and mayor to senator.

Pelosi had other priorities; she had a house full of young children. Upon Alexandra's birth in 1970, she had delivered five kids in six years and one week. Days and nights were consumed by diapers, naps, feedings, playgrounds, pre-school, and playtime.

Yet political inactivity was not an option. Her parents advised her to enjoy her family, and she did. But they had also imbued her with boundless energy and a longing to serve.

As she sat at neighborhood playgrounds, she often kept one eye on her children as she read through a stack of newspapers. She advised the National Conference of Mayors; was a trustee of the Leakey Foundation, a San Francisco–based group that funds research into human origins; and later served on a committee organizing the nation's bicentennial celebration. The annual San Francisco Film Festival hired the young mother as an event planner, and Pelosi cochaired the festival's opening night black-tie affair.

She had a big house, traveled in well-to-do circles, and possessed a deeply rooted desire to help the Democratic Party. It was only a matter of time before she offered to host gatherings to help the party raise money, endearing herself to the party's political establishment.

It was at a fund-raiser that she met Leo McCarthy, San Francisco's representative in the California Assembly. McCarthy was a soft-spoken man with a priestly presence that masked his big political ambition. McCarthy was born in New Zealand but had moved to San Francisco as a four-year-old. A devoted

Democrat, he served on the city's Board of Supervisors before winning election to the Assembly in 1968. McCarthy was 10 years older than Pelosi, was a fellow Catholic, and had four children.

The two struck up a friendship that would last until he died 35 years later, a month and a day into Pelosi's speakership.

When Pelosi arrived in San Francisco, McCarthy and Burton headed rival political factions that battled for power among San Francisco's Democrats.

Most voters understand ideological disputes. But every city also has political divisions based on personalities, alliances, grudges, egos, and opportunity. The battle lines, well understood by the participants, often appear petty, if not incomprehensible, to the outside world. Pelosi was accustomed to Baltimore's divisions involving the D'Alesandros, the Currans, the O'Malleys, and the Palmisanos. Now she had a new battlefield to navigate: McCarthy and John Foran, who were disciples of state senator Eugene McAteer, versus Burton and Brown.

Stylistically, McCarthy and Burton couldn't have been more different. McCarthy was respectful, reserved, and gracious. Burton was loud, confrontational, and crude. Both possessed sharp political minds and were dedicated Democrats. On matters of policy there was little substantive difference between them, though McCarthy was slightly more conservative, appealing to the Irish Catholics on San Francisco's west side, while Burton was more working class, appealing to minorities and union members. Most outsiders would have been hard-pressed to identify their political differences.

Pelosi was in the McCarthy camp. But luckily for Pelosi—who would count on both sides during her own political rise—the great divide was nearing an end.

By the mid-1970s, circumstance, need, and the city's incestuous politics brought the two camps together in a chain of interconnected elections: George Moscone, a Burton ally, left his seat in the California Senate to become mayor; Assemblyman John Foran, McCarthy's former law partner, ran for Moscone's seat; and Art Agnos, McCarthy's chief of staff, ran for Foran's Assembly seat. The paths became even more intertwined, tragically, when both Moscone and

Harvey Milk, the man whom Agnos defeated to win his Assembly seat, were assassinated by the same killer.

The complicated machinations made perfect sense to Pelosi, who had observed her father's alliances and knew the story of Tommy D'Alesandro seeking the blessings of Baltimore's bosses in the 1920s. The 1970s San Francisco version involved Agnos being told to secure Burton's blessings for the Assembly seat he sought, which was in the heart of Burton country—North Beach, Chinatown, South of Market, Potrero Hill, Hunters Point, and the Castro.

Agnos, a former social worker from Massachusetts, recalled McCarthy prepping him for every question Burton might ask. Agnos had never met the older Burton and was tentative when he walked into the representative's San Francisco office.

"Johnny says you're a good guy, so you're okay with me," said Burton, who was wearing a sleeveless T-shirt.

And then, to Agnos's great surprise, Burton said, "If anything ever happens to me, would you take care of my wife?"

That was a question that Agnos hadn't prepared for, though he figured it was a good sign; any politician asking such a question was unlikely to deny him an endorsement.

"What do you want me to do?" Agnos asked.

"I don't know," Burton responded.

"Well then, I'd go to John [Burton's brother], and he'll know."[8]

It was the perfect answer. Burton endorsed Agnos, who would later go on to be mayor. The 1976 election ended the Burton–McCarthy divide that had defined San Francisco politics for nearly two decades.

PELOSI GOT ALONG WITH THEM ALL. In one sense it is hard to imagine why Phil Burton took such a liking to Pelosi. He had struggled against McCarthy and other Catholic Democrats for a generation. His base was the unions and the working poor, and he used the wealthy as a foil. Pelosi was friends with McCarthy, Burton's longtime nemesis, and Mayor Alioto, with whom he had never gotten along.

But Pelosi possessed other traits that Burton cherished. She was "operational," which meant that she understood politics and how to win. And she was "on the level," which meant that she could be trusted. And that was good enough for Burton.

Pelosi told friends she had a confrontation early on with Burton in which he began raising his voice. She stood her ground. She told Burton why he was wrong. Burton grabbed her by the chin and shook it. He smiled. They were friends from then on.

Asked two decades later how big an influence on her Burton had been, Pelosi paused for a good five seconds.

"I thought I was an influence on him, too." she said.[9]

Among the items Pelosi brought into the Speaker's office was a foot-tall statue of Burton striking an assertive pose.

IN THE MID-1970S, WHEN her youngest was out of diapers, Pelosi became president of the Presidio Terrace Association and was named to the San Francisco Library Commission by her neighbor Mayor Alioto.

The first mention of Pelosi in the *San Francisco Chronicle* is in the June 6, 1975, edition, when the paper announced that "Nancy Pelosi, neighborhood leader and sister-in-law of supervisor Ronald Pelosi, was appointed yesterday to San Francisco's Library Commission. . . . Alioto originally appointed Mrs. Seymour Farber, but she quietly withdrew because she couldn't meet the residency requirements."[10]

Pelosi's youngest daughter was off to kindergarten, and Pelosi felt she had time on her hands. She was hosting more and more fund-raising parties, bringing contributors into her large home on behalf of local candidates, which made her very popular among the elected officials. McCarthy was making a push for the Assembly speakership, and Pelosi was there to help.

"When the children were small, I didn't do much. I walked the precinct. Had parties for candidates. Was a resource. When they were in school, then I could take real responsibility for things," Pelosi said.[11]

"There was no *decision* to go into politics," she explained. "It's what I always did."

FOR A FUND-RAISING DINNER Pelosi cohosted in early 1976, the speaker was California governor Jerry Brown. Brown was close to McCarthy. He was Catholic, a native San Franciscan, and familiar with many of the people Pelosi knew. Brown had sat behind Paul's older brother David at St. Ignatius School in San Francisco's Sunset district. Pelosi was impressed.

"After the dinner, I said to myself, 'He's the one person who really seems to be able to strike a chord with all in the party,'" she recalled.[12]

At the age of 38, Brown became a candidate for president as a late challenger to Jimmy Carter, the Georgia governor who some thought was unelectable. Brown's hope was to score a big victory in California's June primary and head into the convention with momentum.

Maryland's primary was a month before California's, but Brown had paid the contest little attention; the state had few delegates, and it seemed unlikely the young governor of California would have a serious shot at winning.

Pelosi thought otherwise. She went to Leo McCarthy and told him Brown needed to compete in her home state.

"I told him he should talk to Jerry about staying on the ballot, about going there, winning early, which will strengthen his hand when he comes to California," she said. "Otherwise, by the time he gets to California, he'll be an afterthought."[13]

Pelosi wrote a campaign memo for Brown, outlining how he could win the primary. The first thing he should do, it said, was contact Tommy, her brother, and Ted Venetoulis, the young man who had taken her to the prom 18 years before and was now Baltimore's county executive. She asked McCarthy to get the memo to the governor, and he did. Brown was intrigued. Pelosi understood politics, and she knew Maryland.

Tommy and Venetoulis were skeptical.

Venetoulis recalls telling Brown, "My professional judgment is that it is impossible for a 38-year-old bachelor from California to come into this state and run for president. It's ridiculous. But my gut feeling, what I feel instinctively, is that it might work."[14]

Brown flew to Baltimore and stayed at the D'Alesandro home on Albemarle Street. He had two weeks. D'Alesandro and Venetoulis escorted him everywhere. They knew the neighborhoods. They knew the labor leaders. They knew the media. Pelosi and Brown's girlfriend, Linda Ronstadt, joined them for the homestretch.

Brown won the Maryland primary, and suddenly his campaign had a national following. He went on to win the primaries in Nevada and California. Though he was unable to stop Carter from receiving the nomination, it was arguably the high point of his national profile.

"The secret weapon was Nancy," recalled Bill Press, a Brown staffer who would go on to become chair of the California Democratic Party.

Pelosi suddenly had enormous credibility among a widening circle of Democrats. Her efforts on Brown's behalf earned her a seat on the Democratic National Committee. Several local Democrats, including McCarthy, urged her to take the post of Northern California chair of the Democratic Party.

She was traveling in elite circles, with the players who had dominated the state's politics for a generation—Jerry and Edmund Brown, Phil Burton, Joseph Alioto—and those who would be the big players for the next—Willie Brown, Leo McCarthy, Art Agnos.

Each New Year's she'd cohost a gathering with Willie Brown, clothier Wilkes

Bashford, and *San Francisco Chronicle* columnist Herb Caen. Each host would invite 10 guests, and the crowd would take over a North Beach restaurant.

She had befriended Governor Brown, who would sometimes relax on a sofa in the Pelosi kitchen while she made dinner for the kids.

Pelosi's life had always been political, but she had not planned a life in politics. Her parents had always told her to "never mind politics. Enjoy your family."[15]

But her kids were now in school. She had time. "And you just discover it's in your DNA, in your blood. And you look around and see children in trouble and health issues and schools that aren't working and the economic troubles of families. And you find yourself in politics."

Pelosi said it was the Brown campaign that took her "out of the kitchen." In Little Italy, everyone knew that the D'Alesandros understood politics. Twenty-five hundred miles away in San Francisco, they were beginning to learn that about Pelosi.

Pelosi was 37 years old, the age her father had been when she was born, the age Tip O'Neill was the year he became Speaker of the Massachusetts House. Each of them also had households with children. But they also had something Pelosi did not have: a wife. Paul Pelosi was a devoted father who was very involved in raising the family. He was also working full-time.

Paul did not share his wife's passion for politics. He had the natural backslapping warmth and even the look of a candidate but never considered a career in government. He was perfectly content to golf and spend time with his family and would probably have been delighted, Pelosi said many years later, if she decided to walk away from public service. At the same time, he never suggested she do so. He dutifully stood by his wife as she followed the path that had been her family's calling.

Pelosi would spend the next decade working vigorously for the Democratic Party as she raised a family of five.

Each day was a logistical labyrinth. Car pools. Fund-raising letters. School plays. Donor meetings. Birthday parties. Printing deadlines. Teacher meetings.

Slate cards. Soccer practice. School supplies. Voter files. Press calls. Homework. Thank-you notes. Fund-raising dinners. Field trips.

When Agar Jaicks, chair of the county Democrats, caught a ride in Pelosi's red Jeep Wagoneer one afternoon, she had to clear a pile of handwritten envelopes from the passenger's seat to make room for him. It was apparent that she had been stuffing envelopes when stopped at red lights.

Efficiency was essential, as was energy. And so was the involvement of the entire family.

"Let's have some cooperation," Pelosi told her kids over and over again.

The girls attended the Catholic Convent of the Sacred Heart Elementary School, and their school uniforms were laid out the night before. On nonschool days, Pelosi often dressed her children in identical colors so they'd be easier to identify in crowds. Lunches were put together in assembly-line fashion—10 slices of wheat bread, meat, apples, and pretzels. Individual orders were not accepted.

"I'm not taking any complaints," she'd tell them. There wasn't time.

Dishes were cleared after dinner, and the table was set for the next morning. Like her mother, she was good at pasta, but she didn't spend time cooking. Food was ready-made, takeout, or something simple. Premade ravioli from Lucca's Delicatessen and sweets from Just Desserts, not to mention Swenson's ice cream, were staples. It was more efficient to have others spend time cooking.

There were fixed times for completing homework and other responsibilities. The household was very disciplined.

"Proper prevention prevents poor performance," she'd tell her kids, showing early signs of the alliteration that became a staple of her sound bites on Capitol Hill two decades later.

When the kids scuffled with other children, Pelosi cited her own father's admonition, one she would repeat many times in politics: "Throw a punch, take a punch."

The children were incorporated into everything. At party headquarters, Pelosi would race off to pick up a child, leaving Paul Jr. and Alexandra with co-workers to play with crayons or the photocopier. Her children recall their mother with a phone seemingly glued to her ear.

As they grew older, the kids would help sort and stuff envelopes and take them to the printer. It was less expensive for the party to send letters sorted by zip code, and the children would set up an assembly line of their own to get the job done. Alexandra complained that as the youngest, she always got stuck licking the envelopes.

While other children would sing: "He's got the whole world in his hands," the Pelosi kids sang, "He's got the stuffers and the mailers in his hands."

Pelosi accompanied her children on field trips to the Old Mint and other Bay Area attractions. She was a regular at school events. Each year she would enroll as a "class mom" for one of her kids.

Halloween was a big holiday in the Pelosi house. Pelosi would often make the costumes herself, including an angel costume with a pink dress that Alexandra has never thrown away.

The family skied regularly at Lake Tahoe and in the summertime visited Maryland's Eastern Shore, where Pelosi would visit family and sometimes stop by Little Italy for dinner at Chiapparelli's or her parents'.

Pelosi discouraged her kids from sleeping over at other kids' houses. The Pelosi home—stocked with plenty of yummy chocolate—became a favorite place for other kids to hang out.

Evenings were often busy with events. She and Paul were out roughly three or four nights a week. Their big house continued to be a common gathering place for politics and raising money. Governor Brown, Senator Alan Cranston, state senators, assemblymen, and members of San Francisco's Board of Supervisors took advantage of Pelosi's hospitality, as did national politicians eager to solicit donations from Northern California's well-to-do-Democrats.

New York governor Mario Cuomo and Senators Ted Kennedy (D-MA) and Gary Hart (D-CO) were among the guests of honor. Neighborhood children were invited over for a chance to meet celebrities and enlisted to hang coats.

Sometimes there was catering help at parties and, occasionally, cleaning ladies at the house. But there was no full-time staff. When guests arrived for functions at the Aliotos' house, three doors down, they were greeted by a butler. When they arrived at the Pelosis' home, they were more likely to be greeted by a kid with a tray of bagels and sliced lox.

The kids always participated. They learned to take jackets, distribute name tags, and pass hors d'oeuvres.

When Agnos, then an assemblyman, would come over for dinner, Pelosi would tell him not to bother with a babysitter. He'd bring his two young boys with him, and the Pelosi girls would look after them.

It was a life that Pelosi had lived on Albemarle Street. And like the young D'Alesandros, the Pelosi kids were very politically adept.

During the 1980 campaign for president, Pelosi backed Jerry Brown, while her daughters, then ages 9 through 15, backed Ted Kennedy and sat in his box at the Democratic convention at New York's Madison Square Garden. Her 11-year-old son was for President Carter. Paul wisely refused to divulge his preference.[16]

Periodically a local reporter would ask Pelosi for her thoughts on political affairs. But she neither sought nor received much public attention. When President Carter refused to participate in a 1980 debate against Ronald Reagan and Independent John Anderson, Pelosi expressed her disapproval in the *San Francisco Chronicle*, asserting that Carter "has been a good president, he's an articulate man and would be able to defend any action he has taken."[17]

Pelosi was outraged six weeks later when Carter conceded to Reagan two hours before the polls closed in California, fearing the news had discouraged thousands of potential Democratic voters.

Displaying a zeal that foreshadowed her efforts to come, Pelosi spoke of the need to shake up the Democratic Party and made it clear that she did not believe that enough party officials possessed her energy or drive to succeed.

"We have been delinquent, or lazy, or not hungry enough. Not just last month or the last three months, but for some time," Pelosi said.[18]

CHAPTER FOUR

Up the Party Ladder

"She's a good-looking woman. Her voice is soft and feminine and kind of retiring. There's a certain shyness to her. You don't get the sense that she's a dynamo. But I learned very early on . . . don't mess with Nancy."
—SAN FRANCISCO DEMOCRATIC PARTY CHAIR AGAR JAICKS, 2007

"I had a few persons say to me, 'Oh, do you work for the committee?' It was pretty exciting to say, 'I am the chair.'"
—NANCY PELOSI, 1981

THE SAN FRANCISCO BAY AREA was a turbulent place in the 1960s and 1970s. In addition to the Haight-Ashbury scene, the Alcatraz takeover, and the Berkeley riots, there were regular demonstrations against the Vietnam War. When four students were killed at Kent State University in Ohio, antiwar protesters stormed San Francisco's City Hall to voice their distress, and violence flared across the Bay. Patty Hearst was kidnapped from her Berkeley apartment and photographed robbing a San Francisco bank. Sara Jane Moore took a shot at President Gerald Ford outside the St. Francis Hotel.

But none of these events compared to the horror of November 1978. Over the span of 10 days, two events would rock the city to its core and shatter the political order in ways it would never fully recover from.

On the morning of November 18, 1978, San Francisco representative Leo Ryan and a delegation of Northern California political aides, physicians, and journalists were in South America visiting an American cult that had set up camp in Guyana, near the Venezuelan border. The group of nearly 1,000 people, the majority of whom were African Americans from Northern California, were devotees of the Reverend Jim Jones, a well-connected preacher who was on the periphery of San Francisco Democratic Party circles and had been appointed by then mayor George Moscone to the city's Housing Authority.

A 1977 report written by Marshall Kilduff and Phil Tracy and published in *New West Magazine* exposed the church's bizarre, cultlike practices, including beatings and mental abuse.[1]

Family members complained that relatives who had gone to live at the compound, known as Jonestown, had stopped responding to their letters. Ryan led a delegation of journalists and doctors to get a firsthand look at the home of the Peoples Temple. He would never return.

After spending roughly 24 hours at Jonestown, Ryan left with 15 inhabitants who had passed him notes expressing their desire to go home. The group's departure from a rural airstrip in Port Kaituma, 10 miles outside Jonestown, was delayed a few hours while a second plane was dispatched to carry the departing cult members.

As the first plane finally taxied for takeoff, gunmen opened fire on Ryan and his party. Those who could do so fled into the jungle. Ryan, three journalists, and one defector were killed.

Forty-five minutes later, Jones called together his congregation. He had already prepared them for the possibility of suicide. The time had come. Cyanide was mixed with Flav-R-Aid, a British powdered drink mix, in huge metal tins and administered to the entire village. Those who refused to drink it were shot. Dozens fled into the jungle. Hundreds died of poisoning. Jones shot himself.

On the 32nd floor of San Francisco's Embarcadero Center, Barbara Taylor was anchoring KCBS radio's Saturday evening news when reports of the murders began to come across the newswire. The station got a Guyanese official on the line and patched her through to Taylor on live radio.

Taylor asked the woman for the number of casualties, and through a thick accent she replied, "We found 500 bodies."

Taylor, assuming she had misunderstood, asked again.

"We found 500 bodies," the woman said again.

It took several rounds of questions before it dawned on Taylor that she had not misheard. The magnitude of the horror was beyond anyone's comprehension. It turned out that 500 was wrong. The death toll at Jonestown was 912.

The news shocked the world. It hit San Francisco particularly hard. Many knew victims. Jones had been known to San Francisco politicos. Prominent pediatrician Cyril Ramer, who lived just across the street from Pelosi, was among those who had been asked to go along on the trip. Ramer stayed home because she wanted her college-age stepson to join her; she had asked if she could go on the next trip to avoid interfering with his semester.

THE CITY WAS IN MOURNING when the next blow came. It was murder once again, and this time it happened much closer to home.

Mayor Moscone, who was part of the Burton team, had been elected in 1975. Harvey Milk was elected to the city's Board of Supervisors two years later, the first openly gay man elected to the board. Retired police officer Dan White was also elected. Ron Pelosi lost his seat on the board the same year.

Milk, representing the Castro, was a pioneer in a burgeoning political movement and loved the spotlight. White was from the city's more conservative western neighborhoods and was uncomfortable on the board. The job of supervisor paid just $12,300, and White felt the financial crunch. White resigned his seat, leaving a vacancy on the board for Moscone to fill.

As speculation mounted over whom Moscone would name, White changed his mind. He wanted the mayor to give him back the post. Moscone felt for White. At the same time, Milk reminded him that White's absence gave the board an even 5-5 split between the liberals and the conservatives, and if Moscone appointed another liberal, they'd have a majority.

KCBS's Taylor, working a Sunday night shift, phoned Mel Wax, the mayor's press secretary, to see if the mayor had made a decision. He had. Wax told Taylor that the mayor had decided against renaming White to the board.

Taylor called White at home to get his reaction. White sounded confused and kept asking Taylor, "What are you talking about?" He hadn't yet heard the news.

The following morning, as Moscone talked to the relatives of a Jonestown victim in his office, White crawled through a City Hall basement window to avoid the building's metal detectors. He was carrying a .38-caliber pistol. He walked up the two flights of stairs to the mayor's office and demanded to see Moscone. The mayor invited White in, taking him to an intimate back office where the two could have a private chat. He lit a cigarette and offered White a drink. It was then that he informed White that he had decided not to rename him to the board.

White pulled out his gun and fired a shot at Moscone. He then walked over and shot another bullet directly into his head. White left by a door that led straight to a public corridor and walked across the second floor to Harvey Milk's office.

Supervisor Dianne Feinstein saw White walking by and asked if she could have a word with him.

"I've got to see Harvey first," he told her.[2]

Moments later a shot rang through the office. Feinstein thought White had killed himself. Then another shot. Feinstein went into Milk's office to find him bleeding on the floor. The former wife of a doctor, she instinctively reached down to feel his pulse. Her finger entered a bullet hole in Milk's wrist.

Feinstein, as president of the Board of Supervisors, a position that Ron Pelosi had held six years before, faced a cluster of city hall reporters only minutes later.

"Mayor George Moscone and Supervisor Harvey Milk have been shot . . . and killed. The suspect is Supervisor Dan White," Feinstein said.

San Francisco was in turmoil. Its politics, always regarded as combative, had now turned to blood. Local politics would never be the same. Feinstein, who had told reporters just an hour before the shooting that she would not run for office again, took over as mayor and would remain among California's most popular politicians for the next three decades.

Portions of San Francisco's gay community became radicalized, particularly after White was found guilty of second-degree murder and sentenced to just seven years in prison for the double killing. Those involved in government and politics were traumatized. As in the aftermath of the 1906 earthquake, the trauma shattered assumptions about regular life, and no one could say when the horror would end.

"There was this sense of fear and uncertainty. The world was turned upside down. Everything became life *after* this happened, and life *before* this happened," KCBS's Taylor recalled.

IT WAS AMID THIS TURBULENCE that Pelosi immersed herself in the operations of the California Democratic Party. A succession of jobs would allow her to display to an ever-widening circle the political smarts that had been bred on Albemarle Street and transplanted across the country to Presidio Terrace.

Pelosi has an uncanny ability to befriend the rich, powerful, or famous—or, more often, those who will become rich, powerful, or famous. In part this is the natural result of traveling in certain circles, and in part it is cultivated. Other times, it has been luck. The young law student who drove her to college was Peter Angelos, who 35 years later would buy the Baltimore Orioles and become one of the Democratic Party's most reliable donors. The kid brother of one her best friends at Trinity was Chris Dodd, who went on to represent Connecticut in the US Senate. Her husband's roommate at Georgetown was Paul Tagliabue, who would become commissioner of the National Football League. In New York, while watching her children at the playground, she met a young writer named Truman Capote, who was working on his first book, *In Cold Blood*.

In 1980, after an earthquake in southern Italy killed more than 3,000 people, Pelosi was named by President Carter to an eight-member delegation that was to determine how best to spend $50 million in pledged relief aid. The delegation was comprised of Italian American political figures who were mostly unknown nationally. In addition to Pelosi, the delegation included freshman congresswoman Geraldine Ferraro from Queens and New York's lieutenant governor, Mario Cuomo.

By now Pelosi was fully engaged in the inner workings of California's Democratic Party, and it was natural after two terms as Northern California party chair that she was selected to be chair for the entire state organization. It was a post that had traditionally alternated between Northern and Southern California, and Pelosi was the consensus choice.

The role of a party chair is simple: Win elections.

Americans have the curious tendency to demand that their politicians not engage in overtly political behavior, and candidates routinely strive to appear above the fray. Not so party chairs. A good chair improves his or her party's chances of winning. Whether it is expanding voter registration rolls, manipulating ballots to favor their candidates, raising money, or issuing partisan diatribes, their role is to do what it takes to enhance the party's election record.

Pelosi was a natural.

On a typical day, she would drop her children off at school and then do the party's bidding from the Phelan Building, a classic 11-story flatiron building on Market Street built just after the 1906 earthquake.

Pelosi professionalized the operation, opening the party's first permanent headquarters in Sacramento, computerizing voter registration data, and commissioning its first statewide polls.

In her San Francisco office, she quickly made room for other party entities that had been spread out in less desirable locations, one of whom was Agar Jaicks, then chair of the San Francisco Democrats' central committee.

Pelosi brought Jaicks downtown and gave him an office next to hers, close enough that he recalls overhearing conversations with party officials punctuated with stern admonitions: "Stop hitting!" or "Homework!"

"She was a good mother, you could tell that," Jaicks recalled. "The way she handled her kids was warm and firm. They loved her."

As personal computers were just beginning to turn nearby Silicon Valley into the nation's most prosperous region, Pelosi inherited a magnetic tape with some names but nothing resembling a functional database. With the help of Rose King, a strategist whom she hired as the party's executive director, they created a database that at first included only information on 3,000 state central committee members and grew to include tens of thousands of activists from all 58 counties.

The party began for the first time to raise money on the phone, and Pelosi set the goal of registering 1 million new Democrats. They fell short of that goal but registered a record-setting 700,000 new Democrats.

"Nancy was willing to be bold," King remembered.

Pelosi became chair exactly three days before fellow Californian Ronald

Reagan was sworn in as the nation's 40th president. As other parts of the country got caught up in a conservative renaissance, Pelosi lashed out at Reagan's assault on the social safety net. She held a news conference at which she decried Reagan's cuts in social spending and accused Republicans of caring only about the wealthy. She wanted it known that not all of California was Reagan country.

When Republicans complained about the new district boundaries drawn by Burton after the 1980 census, Pelosi assumed the role of junkyard dog.

"What we're hearing from the Republicans are the squeals of sore losers," Pelosi said. "If the Republicans wanted to draw the redistricting plan, they should have won the last election."[3]

Pelosi immersed herself in party politics and was in her element.

"There were ten crises a morning. It was wonderful," she said with delight.[4] "[It's] like being in a campaign all the time."

Pelosi was often underestimated. She was a young, attractive woman. Her voice was soft; she dressed stylishly; and she was often retiring, almost shy. If the caricature of a big-state party boss was a cigar-chomping, balding man, Pelosi never fit the role.

"I had a few persons say to me, 'Oh, do you work for the committee?' It was pretty exciting to say, 'I am the chair,'" Pelosi said.[5]

The post of state party chair was less magnificent in the early 1980s than it would become a decade later, when the advent of soft money campaign contributions built state operations into mighty forces. Still, California was a behemoth, with 11 more members in Congress than New York, its closest rival, and 18 more seats than Texas, the nation's third most populous state.

At the time of her election, no other large state had a woman at its helm. Some states, like Illinois, had no women at all on their central committees. The nation was still getting used to women assuming executive roles.

"We have been good Democrats all our lives," Pelosi told an interviewer in her first week on the job. "I knew I could win the chair, and as a woman, I want to do the job better." Even in the *San Francisco Chronicle*, chief political writer Larry Liebert explained that Pelosi was the state party "chair"—"the awkward term adopted by the Democrats to eliminate sexist titles."

If her demeanor was retiring, her determination was not. Jaicks remembers Tom Hsieh, an ambitious architect who was an official with the state party, going to talk to Pelosi, apparently intent on becoming the chair himself. Hsieh was a Chinese immigrant who would go on to serve on the San Francisco Board of Supervisors and run for mayor.

Hsieh went into Pelosi's office to tell her of his plans. Jaicks, whose office was next door, couldn't make out the exact words, but the tones grew sharper and sharper. By the time he left the office, it was clear to everyone that Pelosi, not Hsieh, would be running the party.

"That told me one thing: Don't mess with Nancy," Jaicks said.

As she would during her years as a leader on Capitol Hill, Pelosi regularly pushed party unity. "We are what we are—very diverse with many opinions," she said. "We could learn from the Republicans, who agreed on certain matters and set the others aside. That's a good lesson for us."[6]

Democrats responded to her enthusiasm, and the responsibilities kept coming. Without diapers to change and strollers to push, Pelosi was able to devote more and more energy to the party.

Pelosi told a reporter for *San Francisco* magazine that she tried to be home every day by 3:00 p.m. when the kids arrived home from school. She said she found that if she woke up before 6:00 a.m., she could begin making calls to the East Coast before the family was out the door. There was no downtime.

The 1981 interview was most notable for its final two paragraphs. Pelosi discussed her interest in helping the symphony, museums, and other organizations. Then she added: "I won't be running for office. I enjoy the Democratic Party, but it has enough good candidates. I am better as a chair, because I am not building for any office. This is it.

"Our oldest child will soon be going to college, and the others just behind her," she explained. "I will have to get a job—a paying job."

Those who knew her didn't doubt that she meant it. Pelosi never seemed to pine for elected office. She was still a bit reserved and told people she was shy. She could be friendly and gracious, yet she did not seem to draw her energy from crowds the way other politicians did. She got that energy from her kids.

IT WAS DURING HER TERM AS PARTY CHAIR that the career of John Burton—Phil's younger brother—suddenly crashed.

Like Phil, John was a heavy drinker. But John was also getting into drugs. While serving in Washington—a town he said he hated—Burton started to use cocaine. The experimentation became a habit and then an addiction. He would disappear for days at a time, leaving his staff wondering when he'd show up for votes.

Stories of Burton's drug use began to spread. John Fogarty, the *San Francisco Chronicle*'s Washington Bureau chief, got a call from his editors telling him that they'd heard the rumors of Burton's cocaine use and wanted him to confirm it. Fogarty tried with little success to follow Burton, and then settled on a straightforward approach.

Fogarty sat down with Burton over lunch and told him of his assignment.

"You'll never catch me," Burton told Fogarty. But he appreciated his candor, and he pledged to let Fogarty know first if he was going to leave Congress. It would not be long.

Burton was a mess. He needed help for his addiction. His brother had drawn a hideously contorted district to help John win reelection (asked how he could justify the district, which spanned five counties and crossed the San Francisco Bay, as a single, contiguous entity, Phil bellowed, "It is at *low* tide"). Now John wouldn't even be able to take advantage of it. John was so afraid of his brother's reaction that he enlisted his friend George Miller, a congressman from the East Bay, to tell Phil he was leaving the House.

The older Burton had two days to find someone to fill his brother's seat before the filing deadline. He turned to Agnos, who had been his eyes and ears in the district.

"I want you to take his place," Burton told Agnos.[7]

Agnos told him he didn't want to run for Congress. Burton didn't understand.

"You'll have a free ride. Nobody's going to run against you. You'll have labor, you'll have environmentalists. You'll have everybody. I want you to be there to take [John's] place."

Agnos refused. The conversation went around in circles.

"Give me a reason," Burton demanded.

Finally Agnos pulled two pictures of his young boys from his wallet. He put the pictures on Burton's desk and said, "Here's reason number one. And here's reason number two."

Burton picked up the pictures and stared at them. He put them down and sighed.

"What am I going to do for a candidate?"

Unbeknownst to Agnos, Burton had also reached out to Pelosi. Agnos had two kids. Pelosi had five. Now was not the time. Agnos suggested Marin County supervisor Barbara Boxer, who had worked in John's district office. Boxer went on to hold the seat for 10 years before winning election to the Senate.

The Burton legacy was changing chapters. It was only a matter of months before Phil would be gone.

On a visit to San Francisco, Burton talked about running once again for a House leadership post. He knew that Speaker Tip O'Neill would retire after the 1986 election. He was torn between challenging Jim Wright for the post of majority leader following the next election or waiting until 1986 to challenge Wright for the speakership.[8]

Shortly after midnight on April 10, 1982, at his familiar suite at the Sir Francis Drake Hotel, Burton turned to his wife, Sala.

"Jesus, Sala. I don't feel good."[9]

Moments later he collapsed. An ambulance raced him to the hospital. He was dead by the time it arrived. The cause of death was a ruptured artery in his abdomen.

The city had lost its most powerful political figure.

Agnos went to the hotel, where the first person he saw was Agar Jaicks. Jaicks told him immediately that Sala was going to replace Phil in Congress.

"Put my name down. I'm for Sala," Agnos told Jaicks, remembering his pledge to Burton.

No one would challenge Burton's widow, and Sala won easily.

PELOSI'S TIME AS STATE CHAIR coincided with the term of Chuck Manatt, a gregarious attorney from Los Angeles, as chair of the Democratic National Committee (DNC). Under Manatt, Pelosi had a chance to shine.

Manatt named Pelosi to oversee delegate selection for the 1984 convention, making her a referee in the squabble over which state would hold the first primary. New Hampshire, which had held the distinction for half a century, threatened to move its election to February to stay ahead of Vermont, which had decided it would take New Hampshire's spot in early March. Pelosi traveled to New Hampshire to express the party's displeasure over such an early primary.

Under the golden dome of the state capitol in Concord, Pelosi told New Hampshire secretary of state Bill Gardner that the party would not tolerate a February election. If his state persisted, their delegates would not be seated at the convention.

Gardner told her state law required that New Hampshire go first, and if Vermont persisted, his state had no choice. It was apparent that neither would budge, and 25 years later Gardner vividly recalled Pelosi's words as she left his office to make a similar pitch to the state's governor.

"You're a young man and you probably think you have a political future. If you do this, you won't be elected again."[10]

It was no threat. It was merely an observation that New Hampshire's voters would not forgive him if he did not yield. In this instance, Pelosi was wrong. New Hampshire proceeded with its February primary, and the national party relented a few weeks before the convention. Gardner was still serving as secretary of state when Pelosi became Speaker two decades later.

As state chair, Pelosi was instrumental in bringing the 1984 Democratic National Convention to San Francisco. California was the nation's largest state, home to far more Democrats than anyplace else, and it would make a nice backdrop for voicing opposition to President Reagan, who had served two terms as the state's governor.

Democrats had last come to California in 1960, when they nominated John F. Kennedy in Los Angeles. Los Angeles was consumed with hosting the 1984 Summer Olympics, so San Francisco was the logical choice. Pelosi teamed up with Walter Shorenstein, a wealthy developer and major contributor to the Democratic Party, and California Assembly Speaker Willie Brown to push the idea.

The first step was to convince Mayor Dianne Feinstein. Pelosi, Brown, and Shorenstein paid a visit to Feinstein in her second-floor office at City Hall. She was skeptical. A political convention meant raising lots of money. It meant scrubbing the city, paying police overtime, and putting on a program.

"I don't want to say that Dianne is not gung ho, but we have to make the case to her," Pelosi said at the time. "It hasn't been one of her crusades, let's put it that way. The mayor is a very frugal lady, and there's money involved."[11]

At Feinstein's office, Shorenstein assured the mayor he would get the convention center—named after Mayor Moscone—in shape. Brown told her a convention would position San Francisco as a significant player. And Pelosi assured her the money would be raised.

THE CHOICE FOR THE CONVENTION'S LOCATION was announced at a tense gathering in April 1983 at the party's Washington headquarters. San Francisco was in competition with Chicago, New York, Detroit, and Washington, DC, which had just completed its own convention center. Pelosi was there along with Hadley Roff, Feinstein's trusted deputy mayor and a bear of a man perhaps three times Pelosi's size.

When the words "San Francisco" were pronounced, Roff remembers hugging Pelosi in what he recalls must have looked like King Kong embracing Fay Wray.

The 1984 convention showcased the rising political influence of women. The mayor of the host city was Dianne Feinstein. The convention's executive director was Roz Wyman, the former Los Angeles city council member and Southern California Democratic powerhouse. Pelosi was named chair of the convention's host committee. And presidential nominee Walter Mondale, for the first time in history, named a woman, Geraldine Ferraro, as his running mate.

Pelosi's task was to take care of the 3,923 delegates, 1,310 alternates, and 10,000 journalists coming to San Francisco.

Hotel and seating assignments were based on a lottery, with state names being drawn from a hollowed-out loaf of stale sourdough bread placed on a silver platter. The first state drawn received its first choice of hotels and the last seating assignment. When delegations inevitably complained, Pelosi told them about her father's memory of the 1960 Democratic Convention in Los Angeles. He had been promised the nicest hotel and closest seats. While the Biltmore Hotel was posh, it was isolated. And the seats were so close that members of the Maryland delegation had to crane their necks to get a view of the podium. Pelosi's message was the same one she'd delivered to her children many times: Stop whining.

DAYS BEFORE THE CONVENTION, Pelosi was a guest on a Sunday talk show on KRON-TV, the NBC affiliate in San Francisco. Cohost Belva Davis, at the time one of the few female political reporters on a local TV station, asked another guest—a man—questions about Mondale, the city's standing, and the Democrats' position heading into the campaign. She then turned to Pelosi to ask about the week's parties. Pelosi answered politely. When they went to commercial break, Pelosi's eyes were flaming. She approached Davis just outside the studio.

"Don't you ever do that to me again," she scolded Davis in anger. "Why would you, Belva, do this to me? You haven't done your research."[12]

Davis could hardly miss Pelosi's point: I am a substantive Democratic official, not some party girl.

"She was right," Davis acknowledged many years later. "I learned my lesson.

"One of the facts of life is if a woman is nice and dresses nice, she can't be a powerhouse. Nancy was always so nice. She always looked great, and [was the] mother of all these children. She just wasn't the image of someone you'd think would be willing to be playing hardball in politics," Davis said. "There obviously has been a brainwashing in this country of what power should look like."

As the convention arrived, Pelosi drew grumbles from some locals for pledging "to portray San Francisco as an all-American, family-oriented city." Advocates for the homeless complained they'd been rousted from their downtown perches in an effort to hide the city's underside.

There was also some talk about whether San Francisco was a poor choice because of its large gay population, providing fodder for their opponents, who would try to cast the party as outside the mainstream.

On this Pelosi gave no quarter. Foreshadowing arguments she'd make to her conservative critics a quarter century later, the devoutly Catholic Pelosi reminded those who criticized homosexuals that San Francisco's embrace of alternative lifestyles was a badge of honor.

"Who are these gays? They're somebody's child, brother, sister, friend, that's who. They're not from another planet. The fact that they're here means that the rest of the country is not as hospitable to them as we are," Pelosi told an interviewer.

"People have brought this up in connection with the convention, make no mistake about it. But I think the Democrats have made a good choice, and I certainly don't think we shouldn't have had the convention here because of our large gay population. This is a city of equal rights and all God's children, and one of the reasons San Francisco is the way it is is because other places out there don't practice what they preach."[13]

The 1984 election produced two enduring stories. The first was Mondale's selection of Ferraro as his running mate. Through 195 years of American history, no woman had ever been on a major party's national ticket.

"Ladies and gentlemen of the convention, my name is Geraldine Ferraro," the exuberant nominee told the crowd at the Moscone Center as she accepted the nomination. "I stand before you to proclaim tonight: America is the land where dreams can come true for all of us."

Standing with the California delegation on the floor of the Moscone Center, Pelosi could not have imagined that she would be Speaker of the House before either party would nominate another woman.

The other big story was Mondale's crushing defeat. After liberals asserted themselves in San Francisco—Mario Cuomo gave the keynote address, Jesse Jackson fired up the crowd—UN ambassador Jeanne Kirkpatrick used the phrase "San Francisco Democrats" at the GOP convention a few weeks later. It was an epitaph that Republicans would use against Pelosi many years later.

PELOSI'S NEXT OPPORTUNITY CAME before summer was over. On the eve of the convention, Mondale tried to dump Charles Manatt as the national party chair and replace him with Bert Lance, the jowly Georgian who had served as

President Carter's budget director. Mondale backed down after Californians rallied to Manatt's defense, but Manatt decided he would not run for another four-year term. Pelosi quickly dismissed rumors that she would seek the post.

But Democrats took a beating in the 1984 elections, with Mondale winning just 10 electoral votes. By November, Pelosi was one of seven candidates seeking the ultimate political insiders' job.

The quest to become DNC chair would contain many of the story lines of Pelosi battles to come. But this was one she would not win. At a Democratic gathering in the Virgin Islands, Pelosi made her case to hundreds of committee members who were still licking their wounds from the Mondale debacle.

She was already serving as chair of the largest state in the union; she could raise lots of money; she possessed a record of modernization and competence; she was unaffiliated with any candidate, unlike the front-runner, Paul Kirk, a longtime aide to Senator Ted Kennedy (D-MA); and she boasted of having a "western outlook."

"I come from the West, where we address individual aspirations. Westerners aren't bound to any kind of group ideology and are more likely to ask, 'What does this mean for me?' We're a little more independent," Pelosi said.

Pelosi had the backing of the California Democratic establishment, including Manatt, Leo McCarthy, who was by then the lieutenant governor, and Willie Brown, who was Speaker of the California Assembly. She had support from her friend Mario Cuomo, who had won election as governor of New York and become the toast of the party after a spellbinding speech at the San Francisco convention.

"She has a nice pragmatism to her," Cuomo told CNN.

And she still had some juice from Baltimore, where her father and brother—both out of office for years—retained considerable clout.

This was the big time. Pelosi planned a campaign budget of $100,000 to win over the 378 members of the DNC and rented a suite of offices in Washington to serve as her headquarters.[14]

Upon returning from the Virgin Islands, Pelosi confidently asserted that she had the lead. "I believe I am number one at the moment. I think I have more committed votes than anyone else," Pelosi said.[15]

By early January, less than a month before the balloting, Pelosi claimed to have 125 votes—enough to guarantee her a spot in a runoff in a large field. Her chances appeared to be further boosted a few days later, when fellow Bay Area Democrat Duane Garrett dropped out, leaving Pelosi the lone westerner in the race.

As Pelosi drew more and more attention, some of the same questions were asked that would be raised years later about her run for Speaker.

"Can a 42-year-old mother of five with an Italian name from ultra-liberal San Francisco persuade the good ol' boys in the South and Midwest that she can and should run their Democratic Party for the next four crucial years?" political writer Carl Irving wrote in the *San Francisco Examiner*.[16]

Just as they would when Pelosi made a run for the House leadership 15 years later, party elders and pundits questioned whether a moderate, perhaps one from the South—in this instance, North Carolina governor Terry Sanford, who was pursuing the DNC post—might better steady the party and recoup its losses, particularly among white men.

Front-runner Kirk had advantages. Organized labor, which controlled 40 of the DNC votes directly and many more indirectly, was in his corner. Kirk was the party's treasurer and a former administrative assistant to Senator Kennedy and also had been political director for Kennedy's 1980 run for president. And in Pelosi's eyes, Kirk had something else going for him: He was a man.

Pelosi suspected that some of the delegates did not take her seriously. They all knew she was a great fund-raiser. They knew she was gracious, attractive, and a wonderful hostess. But after losing 49 states in the presidential election, the party wanted someone who would raise hell and topple the party structure. Pelosi sensed that many did not think a woman could fill that role.

"The party at the time was saying, 'We need a strong, firm leadership. We need an authoritative voice. Someone who can really take on the Republicans in Washington.' And they just couldn't envision a woman being able to speak in an authoritative voice," recalls Rose King, who worked with Pelosi on the race.

"It was a real awakening for some of us who thought these things got decided on merit," King said.

And so Pelosi was furious when she heard that an AFL-CIO official had dismissively referred to her as an "airhead."

An "airhead"? An "airhead"!

After raising hundreds of thousands of dollars for candidates, helping Jerry Brown win the Maryland primary, working tirelessly behind the scenes to bring voter registration files up-to-date, opening a Democratic Party headquarters in Sacramento, conducting the first statewide party polls, relentlessly attacking Reagan's presidency, helping to bring the Democratic National Convention to San Francisco, and running it without a hitch—they were calling her an airhead?

"I can take the knocks. But [that] made me angry," Pelosi said.[17]

Pelosi arrived in Washington during the week of the vote aware that Kirk had the lead. She sat down with a group of mostly male reporters for eggs, bacon, and sausage in a wood-paneled room at the Capitol Hilton, just blocks from AFL-CIO headquarters, and asserted that she had the credentials, while all Kirk had was links to labor and Kennedy.

"Everywhere I go they tell me, 'If you were a man this would have been over a long time ago—slam dunk.' I have all the credentials," Pelosi said.[18]

Pelosi told reporters at the breakfast that John Perkins, head of the AFL-CIO's Committee on Political Education, had referred to her as an airhead in a conversation with a Cuomo aide and that she took it as a personal and sexist assault.

"I don't think that's looking to the future. I would tell that to Ted Kennedy right here and now."

Perkins denied he ever made such a comment. Cuomo's aide didn't back off.

Heading into the final weeks, Pelosi and Kirk each claimed to have more than

100 commitments among the delegates. However, it soon became apparent to Pelosi that she could not win, and she dropped out the day before the vote. She had invested heavily in the race and lost. It was something that rarely happened. In leaving the race, Pelosi made her displeasure apparent.

"It is clear to me [that] many of you did not think the right message would go out if a woman was elected chairman of this party," she told the committee when she withdrew.[19]

"If we send out a message from here that says we elected a chair from the Northeast, a 15-year staff person for Kennedy, with the support of organized labor—have we learned anything?" she asked. "The Republicans can use this to the hilt. It's yesterday; it's not the message of tomorrow."[20]

Pelosi learned some bitter lessons. She learned to be relentless in pursuit of votes. And she learned that the Democratic Party had a long way to go before it would be ready to be led by a woman.

Neither Manatt nor Kirk remembers gender playing a role in the contest. Manatt, the Los Angeles attorney who backed Pelosi, said the deck was stacked against her in part because she was unknown to labor, the single most important voting bloc at the time, and in part because there was no way committee members were going to choose two California chairs in a row.

Kirk, who served for four years, recalls party members believing that he was the guy who was "going to really rearrange the furniture."

"The woman issue was not an issue," Kirk said, recalling the race two decades later. "We had had a woman before."

That was true. In the 137-year history of the Democratic Party, there was a five-month stretch in 1972 when Jean Westwood of Utah, who had been George McGovern's campaign manager, chaired the DNC. The other 37 chairs since the party's inception in 1848 were men.

In 1985 it was apparent that the image of a political boss was a browbeating, cigar-chomping bull—perhaps a Tommy D'Alesandro—and not, as Pelosi's own hometown paper described her, the "beguiling and dynamic operative in a size 4."[21]

BY NOW PELOSI WAS well known in national circles. Maine senator George Mitchell tapped her to be the finance director of the Senate Democrats' campaign committee. Pelosi was thrilled to be working with a prominent senator on a national campaign.

Democrats had high hopes. Twelve new Republican senators had been pulled in on Reagan's coattails in the 1980 election. However, Reagan was now in his final years, and the Iran-Contra affair had sapped much of his popularity. Pelosi traveled the country raising money, including events in her home state of Maryland and a fund-raiser at Barbra Streisand's home in Malibu, California, where the singer crooned 14 songs to the assembled guests. Among the Senate candidates she helped raise money for was a 46-year-old member of the House from Nevada named Harry Reid, who would become the Senate majority leader the same year Pelosi became Speaker.

The election was a smashing success for Democrats, who grabbed the majority back from Republicans by netting eight new seats. It was the first time since 1918 that the Senate had changed hands in the sixth year of a presidency.

A week after the election, Pelosi presented Mitchell with a white frosted cake in the shape of the Capitol dome. The incoming majority leader, Senator Robert Byrd of West Virginia, presented Pelosi with a silver platter thanking her for her help, a memento she proudly displayed in her office for many years.

When Pelosi arrived at Congress as a member just a year later, it would amaze people how quickly her calls to Democratic senators were returned.

CHAPTER FIVE

CANDIDATE PELOSI

*"She had everything. She had the political background.
She had a strong commitment to her issues, a husband who
was nothing but supportive, she had great kids, she was smart,
and of course—I don't want to sound sexist—she was attractive."*
—FORMER NEW YORK GOVERNOR MARIO CUOMO, 2007

"She is, in the best sense of the term, a political animal."
—*SAN FRANCISCO EXAMINER EDITORIAL*, 1987

MARIO CUOMO HAD TRIED to convince Pelosi to run for office. So had Leo
McCarthy and Agar Jaicks and numerous other local Democrats.

Her kids were getting older—all but Alexandra had left for college—and with her connections, her political smarts, her ability to raise money, and her thirst to win, she would be formidable.

Pelosi repeatedly rebuffed the prompting. She had never pictured herself as the candidate. She sometimes told people she had imagined herself married to a politician, but not becoming one. She understood her political activity was laying a groundwork, but for what, it wasn't clear. Serving on the Board of Supervisors— San Francisco's equivalent of a city council—seemed too parochial. Being mayor interested her, but she knew firsthand from watching her father how difficult that job would be to win, let alone to perform. Pelosi had never seen herself as a politician. Her older brother Tommy—*he* was bred to be mayor. Pelosi was comfortable in her role as a party operative, raising money and supporting others.

And then an opportunity came.

Representative Sala Burton had been conspicuously absent from her fall campaign for Congress. Aides knew she was sick. But almost no one knew how sick Burton was.

In early 1986, Sala Burton secretly entered the hospital with colon cancer. One of her top aides in Washington, Judy Lemons, accompanied her to the hospital and waited all day for the doctor to give his prognosis. It was bleak.

"She'll be lucky to live another year," the doctor told Lemons. They had removed almost her entire colon.[1]

Burton didn't want to hear it. She ordered Lemons, who had begun working for Phil Burton in 1974 and then continued for Sala, not to tell a soul. Burton recovered from the surgery and returned to Capitol Hill as if nothing had happened.

Lemons helped her cook. She helped her walk. She helped her hide the disease that was eating away at what was left of her colon and sapping her energy. Other Burton aides who didn't know the severity of the sickness grew angry. She seemed to be ignoring her reelection bid. Sure it was a safe district. But it was an election year. She wasn't campaigning! Where was she? Some were racked with guilt when they found out later that she wasn't campaigning because she was dying.

In August Burton returned to the hospital. Lemons practically had to carry her down the stairs. She refused to call an ambulance for fear one of her neighbors, several of whom served in the House, might spot it. The secret was growing impossible to hold.

In September Burton told reporters she'd had a tumor removed from her colon during the August recess and was making a full recovery. She received a standing ovation from her colleagues when she returned to the floor.

Burton was not recovering. In October, the only people who knew Burton's true condition were Lemons, her daughter in Spain, her housekeeper, and her doctor. Burton was having a hard time making it up and down stairs, let alone functioning as a member of Congress. Lemons felt someone else had to know. She phoned John Burton back in San Francisco and told him Sala's condition was inoperable.

Sala kept up a brave front. On election day, she strode into San Francisco's Washington Square Bar and Grill, a favorite North Beach hangout for politicos, for lunch.

"How ya doing?" a familiar patron called out.

"I'm in better shape than you," she responded, and then shot a smile at balding *San Francisco Chronicle* columnist Herb Caen, who had printed rumors she was undergoing chemotherapy.

"And you will notice that I have more hair than you!"[2]

San Franciscans reelected Burton with 75 percent of the vote. The Burtons had won their 14th consecutive election to represent San Francisco in Congress. No one knew she wouldn't last a month into her term.

Jaicks learned sometime over the holiday season that the illness was terminal. He approached Pelosi to propose the unthinkable.

"Nancy, Sala Burton is not going to live out the rest of her term," he told her, broaching the awkward topic. "I know that sitting here and talking about a woman that you care about—and I care about—and then talking politics about it is uncomfortable," he said. "Let's put all that aside. This is something you could do."[3]

For the first time, unlike her responses to all of his previous entreaties, Pelosi nodded her head in approval.

"That *is* something I'd be interested in," Pelosi told Jaicks.

Pelosi may have already given it some thought. She was close to Sala and spoke to her regularly. She stayed at Burton's townhouse when she visited Washington. Her eldest daughter, Nancy Corinne, had interned for Burton, and the two had developed an almost mother-daughter relationship. It would have been surprising if she did not already know of Sala's grave condition.

But Pelosi had always regarded herself as someone behind the scenes, not a potential candidate. Pelosi would later tell people that when she first heard Burton was interested in having Pelosi run for her seat, she assumed Burton meant Paul.

Pelosi had been in politics long enough to know what was at stake. As finance director of the Senate Democrats' campaign committee, host of the 1984 Democratic convention, former California party chair, and daughter of a mayor and former member of Congress, Pelosi knew that to run for the seat would be difficult and that a victory would change life as she knew it. She talked it over with Paul, who was game. And she approached Alexandra, who was still a junior in high school.

"I said, 'Alexandra, Mom has an opportunity to run for Congress. But since you have just one more year in high school, if you don't think that's a good idea, then don't worry about it because I'm not invested into this. It would be easy for me just to say no,'" Pelosi recounted years later.

"Mother," Alexandra said, "get a life."[4]

Pelosi knew that to win a seat that had been occupied for the past 23 years by Sala or Phil, she would need the Burton family blessing. She asked Jaicks to feel out Phil's younger brother John, who had served in Congress, finished rehab, and was now considering his own political revival.

Jaicks met Burton at a coffee shop on Montgomery Street in the heart of San Francisco's financial district and asked him straight up if he could support Nancy.

"I said, 'Great. Nancy is my buddy. I'd be happy to help,'" Burton recalled.

But Burton thought Jaicks was talking about Nancy Walker, a close friend and a four-term member of the Board of Supervisors.

"Not Nancy *Walker*," Jaicks corrected him. "Nancy *Pelosi*."

Jaicks recalls Burton letting out a groan.

Burton remembers practically choking on his coffee.

"What!? Why!? I didn't get it," Burton recalls thinking. "My first thought was, she hadn't earned her spurs."

If a woman was going to run, Burton thought, Walker made sense. Why this woman who'd never run for office should go for his brother's seat was lost on him.

To Jaicks the explanation was simple. Pelosi was a savvy political operator who understood how Washington worked. She could raise far more money than Walker. She was a winner. He returned to Pelosi and told her that she needed to speak to John himself.

Pelosi returned to the same coffee shop, which was just downstairs from Burton's office. Burton never forgot what Pelosi told him.

"If you think that my running would be any embarrassment to you or your family's name, I will not run," Pelosi said.[5]

Burton was impressed by her graciousness, but still he was not persuaded. He did not see the qualities that could make Pelosi a winner, let alone the future Speaker. He saw her as a money raiser. He saw a woman who organized Democratic affairs and threw parties. He didn't see her as a politician. He told her he needed to think about it.

"I went home and said, 'What the fuck do I care? If this is what Sala wants, it's good enough for me.' So I called her and said, 'I'm in, for what the hell it's worth.'"

It would be worth a hell of a lot.

Meanwhile, Sala Burton was dying.

She showed up for work on January 6 to be sworn in to the 100th Congress but was so weak she retreated to her apartment three blocks away, where fellow California representative Don Edwards administered the oath of office in her living room.

In the newspapers, speculation had already begun over who might run for Burton's seat in the 1988 election—or sooner if she couldn't make it through her term. In the second week of January, the *San Francisco Chronicle* ran a story naming seven potential candidates. The list did not include Pelosi. Rose King—Pelosi's former top aide at the California Democratic Party—told her she'd better get her name out there if she was interested. Within days, Pelosi released a statement signaling that she was looking to run in 1988 if Burton did not.

Burton's colon cancer forced her back to George Washington University Hospital in mid-January. She would never leave. Weak and unable to care for herself, she knew she was dying.

Burton sent word to Pelosi, Jaicks, her longtime aide Susan Kennedy, and her brother-in-law John to come to Washington to see her. They knew what was coming.

The foursome flew into a winter storm that dumped nearly a foot of snow on the Capitol, closing businesses and emptying streets. On a Saturday morning, they gathered a block from the White House, in the ornate lobby of the Willard Hotel—the lobby where influence peddlers seeking favor a century before had inspired the term "lobbyist."

They went together to the hospital, several blocks beyond the White House. The scene inside George Washington Memorial Hospital was a jarring contrast to the Capitol's corridors of power. Sala, once a robust and vivacious force, looked like a ghost. Jaicks recalled that, pale, gaunt, and hooked up to IV tubes, she looked like death.

"If I hadn't known this was Sala Burton, I would have thought I was in the wrong room," Jaicks recalled.

Propped at a 45-degree angle in her hospital bed, the matriarch of the Burton machine was all business. Burton had summoned four visitors to the room, but it was Pelosi she wanted to talk to. The others were there to bear witness.

In a frail voice, speaking over the beeps of the hospital equipment and the scurrying of medical personnel outside the room, Burton asked Pelosi if she understood the demands of the job, if she appreciated what it would do to her marriage and family, and if she could imagine what it would be like to spend her life traveling from coast to coast for as long as she held the seat.

"You know, Nancy, I would like to see you run, but you should not run unless you want to run," Burton told her. "You have to want that office."

"You know you're a wife. You have five children. You have a husband. You're going to have to take that into consideration," Burton said.[6]

Pelosi didn't do much talking for several minutes. She seemed reluctant to join in the conversation, perhaps not wanting to engage a dying woman in a discussion about her demise. Pelosi waited. Finally, she spoke.

"I expect you to get well. I want you to get well. And I want you to be able to finish out your term," Pelosi said carefully. "But if you decide at some point that you are not going to run for it, I'd be honored to be able to run for the Congress of the United States."

There were no tears. This was business. They all understood.

After less than half an hour, Burton's cousin entered and told them that was enough. Sala told each of them individually how much they had meant to her and to Phil. And she said good-bye.

The four left the room, shaken.

"We all knew that she was very ill and it would not be long," Jaicks said.

Burton's congressional office had already prepared a statement in Sala's words recommending Pelosi for the job. But that would wait. Instead, John Burton went downstairs and told the assembled press that his sister-in-law "has no intention to resign. She intends to finish out her term."

But he added, "She has decided not to seek reelection in 1988. She has had a serious operation. She wants to be able to recover."[7]

The flight home was filled with mixed emotions. A dear friend was dying. A great political opportunity was at hand.

Pelosi sat in an aisle seat. Jaicks was across the aisle, one row ahead. He spent much of the five-hour flight craning his neck, talking over the potential race with Pelosi. John Burton was seated in first class, and he came back periodically to talk. He was fully on board.

On Tuesday John summoned reporters to Sala's office on the 14th floor of the San Francisco federal building and read a statement from his dying sister-in-law.

"Based on doctors' advice, I shall undergo further treatment and recuperation for a period of six to eight weeks," Burton said in the statement. "After this period of treatment and recuperation, I will consult with physicians and make a public statement concerning my condition and my future plans.

"As many of you have said all too often, I am a very private person during the best of times, and I remain a private person during these times that are not the best," the statement said.

It went on to recommend Nancy Pelosi as her successor.

Burton died Sunday evening, five days later.

NANCY PELOSI WAS 46 YEARS OLD when she began her first campaign for public office.

By the time her father was 46, he'd won five elections to Congress and was serving as mayor of Baltimore. When Sam Rayburn, the legendary House Speaker, was 46, he'd already served as Speaker of the Texas House of Representatives and been elected to the US Congress nine times.

Pelosi had spent her twenties having babies and her thirties raising a family. She had spent the last decade entwined in the inner workings of the Democratic Party. She was now ready to run.

The competition to replace Burton holds an important place in San Francisco history and was decided by just a few thousand votes. It also provides a fascinating glimpse at the political abilities of the winner, who would never again face a serious challenge at home during her long congressional career.

ON FEBRUARY 12, SIX weeks shy of her 47th birthday, Pelosi declared her candidacy for Congress at the Jack Tar Hotel on Cathedral Hill. She stood with former mayor Joseph Alioto; her neighbor, John Burton, who was named campaign chairman; Del Martin and Phyllis Lyon, pioneers of the lesbian movement; and other local leaders.

It was a place she had never pictured she would be. She had stood at her father's side at hundreds of political events. She had offered her skills to dozens of men who had sought public office. She had been embroiled in Baltimore politics since she could remember and San Francisco politics for more than a decade. She had licked envelopes, walked precincts, mobilized neighbors, raised money, plotted campaigns, and even hosted a national political convention. She was perfectly familiar with the game, but she was now playing a role she had never imagined for herself.

She was a behind-the-scenes operator who needed to become comfortable being out front. She was a political tactician who needed to master enough policy to win election to Congress.

At her declaration, she spoke of banning offshore oil drilling and ending foreign military interventions and called the battle against AIDS a "very top priority." She called herself the front-runner, though the polls indicated something else.

In reality, Pelosi began her first campaign for public office an underdog. By 1987, San Francisco was beginning to more closely resemble the far-left outpost for which it became renowned. The Reagan presidency had bred activism among many residents who resisted the notion of a conservative revival or a return to "traditional values."

AIDS was killing more than 100 San Franciscans a month, and Reagan remained silent. The death toll in the city was approaching 2,000, with nearly all the victims being gay or bisexual men. By one estimate, as many as 20,000 of the city's 56,000 gay men had been exposed to the virus. Reagan, answering a question at a news conference in 1986, had pledged to battle AIDS, but he had not publicly uttered the word since.

Meanwhile, opposition to aid being given to the Nicaraguan Contras had mobilized the city's peace groups. Republicans were all but shut out of city offices. Even as Vice President George Bush won California's electoral votes in the following year's presidential election, San Franciscans voted against him by a four to one margin.

Pelosi was not the obvious choice for the city's emerging radical class. She was a political operator who threw pricey parties for the political elite at her Presidio Terrace home. She was the wife of a wealthy businessman and real estate investor. She had never held elected office.

Political insiders were moved by Sala's deathbed endorsement, but few people outside political circles had ever heard of Pelosi. Many who heard the name still thought it was her brother-in-law Ron Pelosi, who had left the Board of Supervisors after failing to win reelection a decade earlier.

And the once-mighty Burton machine was staggering. It had been devastated by Phil's and Sala's deaths, John Burton's drug problems, and the murder of Mayor Moscone. Some suspected that Sala's "anointment" of Pelosi had been hyped. Some even suggested it had been manufactured. No matter; a congressional seat was not something that could be bequeathed, and the nod from the San Francisco Democratic establishment was no guarantee of victory.

It was against this backdrop that Pelosi prepared to display the skills and political instincts that had made her a force among party insiders for the previous decade. She had now lived in San Francisco for 18 years—not a lifetime, but long enough in a town of transients and newcomers. The campaign would foreshadow the energy, determination, and raw political skill Pelosi would exhibit during her subsequent years in Congress and rise up the leadership ladder.

California's Fifth Congressional District hadn't held a competitive election in a generation. Since 1964, Phil Burton and then Sala had dominated San Francisco politics. No one anticipated that either would die so young—Phil was 56, Sala was 61—let alone both. So the special election that was set for April 7 touched off a frantic scramble and attracted 14 candidates, none of whom had had any reason to give serious thought to running for Congress just a few months before.

Pelosi's own polling showed Supervisor Harry Britt, an eight-year veteran of the Board of Supervisors, in the lead.

Britt was a reluctant politician, far more comfortable at the horse track than City Hall. Britt had been thrust into the contest by circumstances dating back to the 1978 Milk-Moscone murders. He was deeply committed to progressive causes, but politics was his profession, not his passion.

Just days before he was killed, Harvey Milk had recorded an eerily prescient video discussing his wishes in case of his death; in effect, it was a political will. Desperate to keep leadership out of the hands of those he considered acquiescent gays—those who would not shake up the power structure—he named four people he'd want to replace him. Britt was on the list.

Britt was a handsome, heavyset man with more hair on the top of his head than along his closely cropped sides. Easily approachable, he was often seen in City Hall in a rumpled suit and tie, a minimal gesture to his unlikely standing.

Britt in many ways had led an all-American life. Raised in Texas, he had idolized Doak Walker, the Heisman Trophy winner from Southern Methodist University who went on to run, kick, and catch passes for the Detroit Lions. Just as Pelosi's father had hung a portrait of Franklin Roosevelt in their living room, Britt had grown up seeing an FDR portrait hanging at his grandparents' house, and he revered the tradition of Democratic politics. He was president of his fraternity at Duke University, got married, was ordained as a minister, and moved to Chicago to work with a congregation on the South Side.

It was there that he met the Reverend Martin Luther King Jr., and he spent much of the 1960s working on civil rights issues. Britt had known he was different from the time he was a little boy, and the 1960s helped him confront his sexuality, leading him eventually to move to San Francisco, where his long-closeted homosexuality would no longer need to be hidden. There he met Harvey Milk and was stirred by Milk's passion to make gays an unapologetic political force. Britt became president of the San Francisco Gay Democratic Club, which was later renamed for Milk.

When Mayor Dianne Feinstein named Britt to replace Milk on the Board of Supervisors, he accepted the position dutifully but not without reluctance. It made him perhaps the most visible gay politician in the country, a responsibility he felt obliged to fulfill until two lesbians were elected to the board in 1990 and Britt felt he could walk away.

"I'm not a politician and I never was. And I knew that before I went in," he said.[8]

Nevertheless, when Burton's seat became available in 1987, Britt and many around him felt he owed it to the community—the gay community, the progressive community, and Harvey Milk—to chase after it. With the exception of Representative Gerry Studds of Massachusetts, who acknowledged that he was gay after he was caught soliciting sex from a congressional page in 1983, no one who was out of the closet had ever run for Congress. Britt hoped to come to Congress as the first openly gay nonincumbent, and gay leaders considered this a momentous occasion.

"The sense for many of us was that this was the most important campaign we'd ever been involved in. Win this and we'll be on the map," recalled Britt strategist Jim Rivaldo.

Britt had some advantages. He was well known from his work on the Board of Supervisors, which had included advocating rent control for residents and businesses, calling for limits on downtown growth, and a strong push to address the exploding AIDS crisis.

He had a built-in constituency in the city's gay community, which by some estimates constituted as much as 25 percent of the city's voting population. Britt had the endorsement of Burton's friend Nancy Walker, president of the Board of

Supervisors; four members of the school board; the chair of the San Francisco Democratic Party; and many others.

Pelosi also had some advantages. She was very well known in Democratic circles. She had the backing of the city's most powerful political machine—Lieutenant Governor Leo McCarthy, House Speaker Willie Brown, Assemblyman Art Agnos, and John Burton—and, of course, Sala's deathbed endorsement. She had money and the ability to raise much more. She had influential friends on the East Coast, like Governor Cuomo and Senator Mitchell, in addition to every newly elected Democratic member of the Senate willing to help.

The conventional wisdom in San Francisco was that Britt and Pelosi were the front-runners—and that the election was Britt's to lose.

The first thing Pelosi needed to do was move. The district included 75 percent of the city, but not Presidio Terrace. Phil Burton had carved out parts of the city during the 1980 reapportionment to shape a district for his brother.

The Pelosis found a large redbrick home roughly a mile east of Presidio Terrace. It did not have the same grandeur, but it was located in posh Pacific Heights, and the second and third floors had stunning views of the Marin headlands, Alcatraz, and the Golden Gate Bridge.

Pelosi opened a downtown campaign headquarters at 666 Mission Street, which later became home to the California Historical Society (with a change of address). Assembling a professional staff was easy. Pelosi knew everyone. She enlisted veteran organizers Marshall Ganz and Fred Ross Jr., whose father had helped Cesar Chavez form the United Farm Workers. The pair's innovative grassroots and get-out-the-vote tactics had been instrumental in Mayor Feinstein's landslide victory in a recall election three years before.

For a strategist she turned to Clint Reilly, who was among the state's premier political consultants. Britt had also contacted Reilly about using his services, a prospect that had excited some on Reilly's team who cherished the idea of working for the insurgent. But with McCarthy and Brown pushing him to help Pelosi, Reilly signed on with her.

There were many ways to run the campaign. She could be the mother; the woman; Burton's choice; the well-connected Democrat; the pragmatic liberal; the competent tactician; the straight, family values–embracing Catholic. In the end, she touched on each of these themes. But it was decided early on that the one quality that would separate her from the pack was her ability to get things done.

Though she had never held office, she declared in her first speech as a candidate, "I believe the No. 1 issue in the upcoming campaign will be who can accomplish the most for San Francisco."[9]

After all, Senators Kennedy, Mitchell, and Hart came to her house for dinner. She was known to the entire California delegation. She had worked at the DNC and helped win the Senate for Democrats. The campaign would show where Pelosi could succeed while the others would not.

Themes are important in a campaign. Slogans are essential.

Reilly was on an airplane from San Francisco to Washington to visit some clients when it came to him. He got off the plane and immediately rushed to a pay phone to call his creative director, Eric Jaye.

"I've got it," Reilly said, ready to test his idea for a campaign slogan: "*A voice that will be heard.*"

Jaye was taken aback.

"You want to run a woman who never held elective office as a candidate with connections and stature and effectiveness?" he asked incredulously.

Reilly laughed.

"That's exactly right."[10]

The theme was repeated everywhere: *A voice that will be heard.* The Pelosi campaign, which spent more money than all of her competitors' campaigns combined, even ran a television commercial, a rare luxury in the expensive pre-cable Bay Area market.

In the commercial, Handel's "Hallelujah" chorus plays behind sweeping shots of the US Capitol, the Golden Gate Bridge, a missile being fired, and children playing on swings, and a deep voice strikes the theme.

Four hundred and thirty-five men and women to decide America's fate. In Congress, San Francisco has just one voice. One voice to speak for our hopes. The future of our land. One voice for today. One voice for tomorrow. One voice for San Francisco. *Nancy Pelosi: A voice that will be heard.*

The slogan was printed on so many campaign brochures, mailers, and billboards, with the word HEARD in such big letters that it became a running joke among Pelosi staffers. They didn't want anyone to miss the point: Pelosi would be able to get things done in Washington. The others wouldn't. Pelosi may never have held office, but she was a mover and a shaker.

In retrospect, the strategy seems prescient. Pelosi was a dynamo who would indeed be loudly heard in Washington. But to many at the time, Pelosi's boast seemed less prescient than presumptuous. How could a mother of five who had never held elective office be expected to represent San Francisco, to force the federal government to pay attention to the AIDS crisis, to carry on the Burton legacy?

AMONG THE MOST MEMORABLE MOMENTS of Pelosi's first campaign was a live debate on public television station KQED that included all 14 candidates and captured the election's circuslike atmosphere.

The number one topic was Nicaragua. Tom Spinoza, one of four Republicans in the field, opened the forum by volunteering that he'd drop a bomb and wipe out President Daniel Ortega.

"Wouldn't that cause war?" inquired moderator Spencer Michels.

"How could they fight after they'd been bombed out of existence?" Spinoza responded.

Pelosi, wearing a conservative blue knee-length skirt, licked her lips nervously as she answered questions thrown to the candidates seated on three levels of risers. Her answers were stiff yet thorough.

Michels was addressing a question to Pelosi when the debate unraveled.

"Harry Britt has charged in several forums that you don't represent the struggling people in San Francisco—" Michels began before he was cut off by Ted Zuur, the Peace and Freedom Party candidate, who leaped to his feet and assumed a spot in the middle of the stage.

"This show is a fraud!" Zuur bellowed. "The most important issue is that Reagan . . . "

Michels tried to end the outburst. "Okay, could you sit down."

Zuur, one hand in his pocket and the other hand flailing, wasn't going to stop there.

". . . and Bush and the Contras and . . ."

"Ted, Ted," implored Michels.

"Nobody is addressing the issues," Zuur shouted. "I think the president must resign!"

"Could you sit down," Michels demanded.

"I think everyone here should take a stand on it," Zuur resisted.

At that point Michels called over a heavyset security guard who—quite aware he was on live television—sheepishly placed his arm around Zuur to escort him out.

"*Excuse me!*" Zuur bellowed. "I'm not finished here."

With that, Zuur was forcibly removed from the stage as most of the participants watched in stunned disbelief.

Pelosi did not look ruffled.

"If I could address those two things," Pelosi volunteered.

But Pelosi was quickly cut off by Carol Ruth Silver, a bespectacled member of the Board of Supervisors, who immediately complained that Pelosi had written a $250,000 check to her own campaign.

"How can she relate to people like me, a single parent, working mother. She's never had to meet a payroll. She's never had to worry about child care. She's never had a kid in the public schools. She's never worried about the things that most of the people of San Francisco have."

Pelosi was ready. She attacked right back. Pelosi first asserted that her wealth provided independence that none of her opponents shared.

"Especially the four supervisors who were reported this week to have received $1,000 each from the Embarcadero Center, and then voted to give them a street," Pelosi responded icily. "So if you want to talk about independence, let's talk about independence.

"Second of all, I don't think you have to be sick to be a doctor or poor to understand the problems of the poor. I have spent my life committed to the ideals of the Democratic Party, and I believe that I have recognition in Congress for my commitment to the principles of the Democratic Party, for my determination to get the job done, and in my skill in getting the job done. I don't think it hurts [that] Democrats in the United States Congress recognize me as the person most responsible for winning the Senate for Democrats."

The sense in the Pelosi camp was that she had survived but not done particularly well. The others were ganging up on her. Britt had been quite articulate, and there was concern over how she'd fare as a candidate.

THE STORY LINE FOR THE NATIONAL MEDIA was Britt's homosexuality versus Pelosi's party connections. News organizations from around the country picked up on the race in part because it was the only election going on that spring and in part because San Francisco is a wonderful place to visit. It also offered a historic story line.

If being a woman in Congress was still rare, being openly gay and running for Congress was unheard of. In the 200-year history of Congress, Representative Studds was the only member open about his homosexuality. Another Massachusetts congressman, Barney Frank, was rumored to be gay, and his appearance wearing a tank top at a District of Columbia Gay Pride Day festival in the mid-1980s seemed to confirm the not-so-hidden secret. But Frank would not publicly discuss his sexuality until later that year.

Certainly many gays had served in the House. Yet none had been out of the closet when they'd first sought election. Harry Britt and a sizeable number of gay advocates set out to change that.

"We can do it. We must do it," read a Britt mailer aimed at gay and lesbian voters. "Because we need a leader, not just a friend."

THE MEMORY OF HARVEY MILK hung heavy over the campaign. His murder was not yet nine years past, and there was an urgency to Britt's candidacy.

"Harvey Milk taught us not to depend on others. . . . Some things we have to do for ourselves—no one can do them for us," read a brochure.

The Britt campaign enlisted scores of volunteers to stuff envelopes, walk precincts, and work the phones. Banners at rallies read: "Harvey Milk Would Be Proud!!"

"Ten years ago we made history by electing Harvey Milk to the Board of Supervisors," read another campaign mailer. "His election inspired our brothers and sisters throughout the nation. Today we can send the same message of hope and pride across America by electing the first openly gay non-incumbent candidate to Congress. WE MAY NOT HAVE THIS OPPORTUNITY AGAIN FOR DECADES."

No one could accuse Pelosi of failing to support AIDS research and prevention, protections against discrimination, and other gay causes. But it was one thing to support gay causes; it was another to be gay.

"For Harry Britt, gay and lesbian issues aren't just topics for election year rhetoric. Every moment of his life, Harry Britt confronts the reality of being gay. He feels the pains and problems of our community in his heart and that fires his determination to correct the injustices we face," read yet another mailer.

Pelosi worked hard to cut into Britt's gay support. She had gay supporters, some of whom were ostracized for not supporting Britt. The Pelosi campaign knew it would lose the gay vote but felt that if they could win 25 to 30 percent, it would be enough for victory.

While parts of the city would vote for Britt because he was gay, others would vote against him for the same reason. Phil Burton had built a coalition that included gays and cops, but that didn't mean that the socially conservative residents west of Twin Peaks were going to vote for a homosexual to serve in Burton's seat. For a sizeable number of voters, the images that came from San Francisco's Gay Pride Day Parade, Sister Boom-Boom, the Sisters of Perpetual Indulgence, and the Exotic Erotic Ball were as unsettling as they were to many around the country.

There is no evidence that Pelosi played to those fears. She never alluded to Britt's sexuality, questioned how Congress would treat a homosexual, or suggested that his being gay might make him any less effective. Pelosi never made morality a part of the campaign. When some of her advisors suggested that she make an issue of Britt having left his wife, she refused.

But that didn't mean she couldn't promote her own family. It is a time-honored tradition for those seeking office to showcase their families, even if some gays took it as a way of saying, "I'm straight and he's not."

Most of the Pelosi campaign brochures included pictures—some spread out over two pages—of the entire family wearing sweaters, closely cropped hair, and warm smiles. They looked like a 1980s version of the Brady Bunch.

The clean-cut family brochures were sent to the western side of the city, where many households sent their kids to Catholic schools and felt alienated from San Francisco's progressive downtown. The campaign was aware that it was benefiting from some antigay votes.

Burton remembers getting a call one morning from an old-time San Franciscan who called to say he wanted to help Pelosi.

"I love my city," the man told Burton, who many years later recalled that he knew exactly what that meant.

"Enough said. This was his way of saying, I guess, he didn't want a fucking gay in Congress. People weren't ready," said Burton, who included gays among his own most loyal supporters.

The gay divide was apparent to Pelosi. Art Agnos, who was then running for mayor, told Pelosi he would endorse her. The two had been close since their days helping Leo McCarthy, and Pelosi had already endorsed Agnos for mayor. Pelosi wouldn't let him return the favor.

"She said, 'No, no. I don't want you to support me. I'm grateful for your support, but you are not to support me,'" Agnos recalled.

"I said, 'Why not? You supported me.'

"She said, 'I know, that's okay. But you're in a tougher campaign than I am. If you support me, it's going to hurt you with the gay community. I don't want you to risk your campaign.'"

Agnos was stunned. "I brought a liberal progressive thing, which she was accused of not being. She was the Pacific Heights party girl. Britt was the darling of the left. She didn't want to do me any harm."

Agnos was struck by Pelosi's selflessness.

"I kept telling everybody, I told Leo [McCarthy]. He said, 'That's the way Nancy is.'"

THE GAY ISSUE WAS a favorite for out-of-town journalists. But there was another, more subtle story line that better captured the campaign and echoed 20 years later in Pelosi's role as Speaker. This was about progressives battling the mainstream.

When it came to policy, there was not much difference between the front-runners. To win a congressional seat in San Francisco, it went without saying that a candidate supported labor, women, gays, abortion rights, gun control, the environment, and social spending and opposed President Reagan, aid to the Contras, drilling off the California coast, and other Republican priorities.

"By any traditional standard there are three liberals running in this race:

liberal, very liberal, and liberal with hot fudge sauce," observed candidate Bill
Maher, a Democrat and member of the Board of Supervisors who was running to
the right of both Pelosi and Britt.

In fact, there were more than three liberals. Besides Pelosi, Britt, and Maher,
there were three other Democrats, as well as members of the Humanist, Peace
and Freedom, and Socialist Workers parties. The four Republicans in the race
were never a factor.

What distinguished Britt and Pelosi was their approach to politics and governing. Britt was an activist in the San Francisco progressive tradition. His mentor,
Harvey Milk, had been a renegade who forced the political establishment to
rethink the way it did business. As a supervisor, Britt had worked to carry on
Milk's legacy.

Liberal politicians from the suburbs used to tell Britt how jealous they were of
the political freedom he had in representing a place like San Francisco.

"I could stand up for injustices in ways that they couldn't. To me, that's the
function of the San Francisco seat," Britt said.

If demanding that city workers have the right to share employment benefits
with their gay partners and standing up to wealthy developers—let alone riding
in the annual gay pride parade along with half-naked men displaying pierced
genitalia—was political suicide for most elected officials, in San Francisco it was
a way of doing business.

Britt believed that the same envelope-pushing mind-set was a prerequisite for
the city's representative in Congress. The mainstream would become more
progressive only when progressives imposed themselves on the mainstream.

"I am proud to take all of the flavor of San Francisco back to Washington,
because I think the country needs a good healthy dose of San Francisco right
now," Britt said.

"Yes, we're different from other American cities. And I'm not going to go back
there and say, 'You know, we're just like Wichita only farther west.' That's not the
role of San Francisco in the political process. We are the center of the peace

movement, of the women's movement, of the environmental movement."

The premise of Pelosi's candidacy—that she was a mover and shaker who would get things done—rang hollow to Britt, who believed that anyone who came up through the party establishment and the Presidio Terrace fund-raising circuit couldn't shake up the order and attract new constituents.

Change could not happen from within.

"Nancy Pelosi says her 'voice will be heard.' But to whom would she listen, and for whom would she speak?" the Britt campaign charged in one brochure.

Britt wanted to disrupt the political order. Pelosi *was* the political order. He wanted to rearrange the power structure. She *was* the power structure.

She was a "party girl," a phrase that the Britt campaign used with a double meaning: She was the Democratic Party establishment, as well as a socialite who was more comfortable at high-end parties than fighting for working stiffs.

In San Francisco it was a battle more divisive than the gay-straight divide and one that the city would struggle with in many elections over the coming decades.

Britt didn't do all the attacking. His campaign enlisted the help of fellow supervisor Bill Maher. Britt's polling showed the best he could do on election day was draw slightly more than one-third of the vote, maybe 36 percent at best. But in a crowded field, that might be enough. Britt's strategists figured that if there were conservative voters who couldn't bring themselves to vote for Britt, they needed to offer them an alternative besides Pelosi. Under the special election rules, if no one received more than 50 percent of the vote, there would be a runoff between the top vote getter from *each party*. That meant that if Britt could win 36 percent of the vote and keep Pelosi at 35 percent, Britt would advance to a runoff against a Republican.

So as the campaign entered its final month, Britt's campaign struck a deal with Maher. They steered tens of thousands of dollars to Maher that he was to use to attack Pelosi.

Signs began to appear around town: "Dilettante" and "Debutante." Many of them said nothing about Pelosi, but voters knew whom they were talking about. Maher took on Pelosi and the Burton endorsement.

"We used to have a system like the one she wants. It was called 'lords and vassals,'" Maher sniffed.

The attacks on Pelosi were effective, and the race tightened. But her opponents failed to realize that she was less a creature of Presidio Terrace than of Albemarle Street. Pelosi was neither a dilettante nor a political fool.

One Saturday morning at campaign headquarters, Pelosi was addressing volunteers before they were dispatched to the neighborhoods, armed with clipboards and ironing boards, to sign up supporters.

"I have to admit, I didn't really know what an ironing board was," Pelosi told the campaign workers.

Catherine Dodd, a nurse who had organized dozens of volunteers for the campaign, flinched. She couldn't believe Pelosi was going to admit to a crowd of volunteers that someone else did her ironing.

"I'm a mother of five," Pelosi continued. "All I do is take clothes out of the dryer, shake them off, and put them on the kids."

Dodd, who would later serve as Pelosi's district director, understood at that moment that she was working for a pro.

BRITT FELT THAT HIS BRAND OF POLITICS was closer to the Burton tradition and bristled when people described his campaign as being "against" the Burton machine. Britt had been close to Phil Burton. He'd ridden with him in the gay pride parade. Many around Britt felt that Burton—with his fondness for sticking it in the eye of the political establishment—might just as likely have endorsed Britt in the race as Pelosi.

"I just felt like when Phil Burton died, it was time for the new demographics of San Francisco to step forward. And it didn't happen with Nancy," Britt said.

Even Pelosi, reflecting on Burton in an interview 15 years later, said, "He was a strong force. I respected what he did. Sala's endorsement meant a great deal in that race. I don't know if Phillip would have done it."

Shaking up the political order—even if it is Democrats who are being rattled—is a potent message in San Francisco, and the Britt campaign sought to exploit it.

"FEAR," read the cover of one Britt brochure. "What are the political bosses, Washington lobbyists and big businessmen so afraid of? They know Harry Britt's record and they know Nancy Pelosi. That's why they're spending a fortune to stop Harry Britt's election to congress and to elect Nancy Pelosi. Nancy Pelosi has spent her lifetime doing favors for the rich and powerful. Now they're returning the favor."

For much of her congressional career, Pelosi was branded by opponents in Washington as a representative of the liberal fringe. Beginning with her first campaign, Pelosi was branded by opponents in San Francisco as a representative of the establishment.

"Harry Britt doesn't have a million dollars for a slick campaign," read another typical Britt brochure featuring a simple black-and-white picture of the supervisor. "Oil companies, highrise developers, Washington lobbyists and other special interests are pouring a million dollars into San Francisco to elect their candidate to Congress and to defeat Harry Britt. We can't let them buy our seat in Congress."

"Activists want to change power arrangements," Britt said, looking back decades after the race, still unconvinced that Pelosi can consider herself a progressive.

"I do not have any lingering dislike of Nancy Pelosi. We just come from different worlds. I wanted to push the discourse within the Democratic Party forward in terms of progressiveness . . . trying to come up with legislation that wouldn't pass anywhere but San Francisco. Nancy is not going to do that. Nancy can't do that. She's too connected to too many networks of money."

"I am a politician representing Haight-Ashbury. . . . You don't want a Lyndon Johnson, a sort of Great Compromiser–type person, representing the Haight-Ashbury. They should be representing Kansas City or somewhere."

Pelosi took offense when the Britt campaign hired a private investigator to look into her finances. And she resented the *party girl* label as a not-so-subtle dig at her intellectual heft.

Unlike the race for Democratic Party chair two years earlier, Pelosi didn't need to convince San Franciscans that a woman was capable of leading. Dianne Feinstein had been mayor for eight years; Nancy Walker was president of the Board of Supervisors, presiding over a body that included four other women; and Representative Barbara Boxer represented portions of San Francisco, a city that had elected two women to Congress in the 1920s.

Being a woman candidate in San Francisco was not a disadvantage, even if being part of the party establishment was. Pelosi could hardly shed her insider image. Instead she set out to convince voters that her connections were a big advantage.

MANY YEARS LATER, AS she ascended the House leadership ladder, Pelosi presented herself as a doer, an accomplished political professional who could get things done. It was the same argument she made in her first run for office. Britt may have supported rent control, but Pelosi had battled Ronald Reagan and Republicans coast-to-coast.

"Nancy Pelosi was honored as the person most responsible for the new Democratic majority—a first step in altering the legacy of Ronald Reagan," boasted one Pelosi brochure that named her "Ronald Reagan's No. 1 opponent."

Another had a picture of a smiling Pelosi and a grimacing Reagan with the headline: "Nancy Pelosi Fights the Reagan Agenda."

"Ronald Reagan has no compassion. Ronald Reagan has no vision. For the past two decades," the letter read, "I have battled Ronald Reagan whenever he has attempted to disenfranchise people, jeopardize our environment or risk our future. . . . Now as a candidate for Congress, I want to bring my longtime battle with Ronald Reagan to the floor of the House of Representatives."

Even as a rookie, Pelosi's campaign materials made her look like a long-standing incumbent. One listed 35 accomplishments that dated back to her service on the Library Commission.

One Pelosi mailer that went to more conservative neighborhoods made an unlikely claim for a San Francisco Democrat: "The individual tax burden is too high. We need a representative who will fight all efforts to raise the personal income tax."

PELOSI CALLED IN CHITS WITH NATIONAL LEADERS, including fellow Institute of Notre Dame graduate and Baltimore native Senator Barbara Mikulski, who told a large gathering about her own pitched battle for the Senate the previous year against Republican Linda Chavez.

"She had Ronald Reagan, and I had Nancy Pelosi," Mikulski roared to an approving crowd.

After spending more than a decade impressing party officials, Pelosi needed to introduce herself to voters. She showed up at roughly 200 house parties, socials, church gatherings—wherever people met. Pelosi would speak for 20 minutes, take questions, and move on to the next one. A staff member would stay behind and enlist volunteers. The pattern would be repeated several times a night.

She drew mixed reviews. Some people found her savvy and well informed. Others found her stiff, relying on clichés and campaign jargon. But she earned credit for showing up. She may have lived in Presidio Terrace and Pacific Heights, but she appeared quite comfortable in living rooms from the Mission to Hunters Point. Nancy Pelosi had listened to people from all walks of life since she was a little girl, and it showed.

Like her father a generation earlier, Pelosi campaigned with fierce intensity. If she was unsteady before cameras and still absorbing policy, she made up for it by meticulous organization. She displayed a cool confidence as polls began to show her passing her competitors and she became the focus of the others' attacks.

"They started off nasty. They warned us it would be brutal, that it would be a bloodbath and I'd be sorry I ever got in the race, but I wasn't frightened by any of that," she said. "My attitude is they'll take the low road, I'll take the high road, and I'll get to Congress before them."

Many of her campaign brochures told her Baltimore story, featuring pictures of her at her father's knee on Albemarle Street.

"It was a life of serving people and their needs. Each of us was blessed with a burdensome conscience," Pelosi said in one mailer. "My parents would not allow us to ignore injustice."

Meanwhile, the field operation was state-of-the-art.

By the time Pelosi became Speaker, "microtargeting" was the buzz word denoting complex computer programs that could figure out individual voting preferences based on information ranging from where people bought groceries to what magazines they read. In 1987, targeting was in its infancy.

Campaign strategist Clint Reilly's firm was in the vanguard, using tech-niques that were ahead of their day. For example, there is no computer program that distinguishes gay and straight voters. So Pelosi's campaign looked at first names. If two men within 20 years of age lived in the same house, they were regarded as highly probable to be gay, and a brochure aimed at gay voters went to their house. Previous campaigns had spent precious resources on comprehen-sive get-out-the-vote drives. Reilly's firm ignored voters who'd voted in each of the four previous elections, who would need little encouragement, or in none of the past four, figuring they would be more difficult to motivate. Instead they focused their get-out-the-vote efforts on voters who *sometimes* showed up at the polls.

John Burton bridged the gap with labor. Britt had a perfect pro-labor voting record on the Board of Supervisors and had counted on labor's support. Burton went to union halls and talked to union leaders, convincing some to support Pelosi and others to remain neutral. Labor should have been a slam dunk for Britt. Instead, it was a wash.

Burton would later say that with the exception of George Moscone's run for mayor in 1975, working on Pelosi's congressional bid was the most fun he ever had in politics.

By the time the campaign was over, Pelosi had spent about $1 million, which was more than the other 13 candidates combined. Pelosi was endorsed by both daily newspapers.

"She is, in the best sense of the term, a political animal," the *San Francisco Examiner* wrote in an editorial.[11]

A week before election day, Pelosi's father in Baltimore dispatched his eldest son to see how things were going. Young Tommy remembers his little sister inviting him to join her on the stump as long as he made one promise: "You can't say a word."

He looked over the headquarters, the precinct maps, the lists of volunteers, the voter registration files, and the get-out-the-vote operation.

"I called my father and told him, 'She's better organized than we ever were,'" he said.

Election day was a dead heat between Pelosi and Britt. But Pelosi's field operation had given her a several thousand–vote advantage in absentee ballots, and Pelosi triumphed with 36 percent of the vote to Britt's 32 percent. Of the 105,000 ballots cast, Pelosi received 3,990 more than Britt.

The runoff election was no contest. Pelosi received 62 percent of the vote, while her Republican challenger received 30 percent. It was the closest any Republican would ever get.

On the night of her victory over Britt, Pelosi stood beside Burton and McCarthy on the large stairway that descended to the middle of the open first floor of her campaign headquarters and told her troops, "I had the best endorsement possible. I had Sala, and that was the biggest factor in my campaign. I'll tell them in Washington I was sent by the people of San Francisco, and Sala Burton sent me."

The next day Eric Jaye was at his desk at 7:00 a.m. when the phone rang. It was Pelosi calling to thank him. She clearly was going through a long list and personally thanking everyone on the campaign.

The vote breakdown showed a tale of two cities. Britt handily won the liberal neighborhoods closest to downtown—the Castro, the Mission, Noe Valley, Twin Peaks, Potrero Hill, South of Market, and the Tenderloin. He was virtually shut out in the more distant neighborhoods—the Sunset, Ingleside, the Outer Mission, and west of Twin Peaks. Had Burton not cut liberal areas such as the Haight out of the district after the 1980 census, Britt almost certainly would have prevailed.

But there was an even richer irony in the results: Pelosi would never have been elected to Congress if not for the support of conservatives and Republicans.

PART III

WASHINGTON, DC

A WOMAN IN A MAN'S HOUSE

"I am no lady, I'm a member of Congress."
—REPRESENTATIVE MARY NORTON, 1925

*"The day I wore a pantsuit onto the floor you'd
have thought I asked for a land base for China."*
—REPRESENTATIVE PAT SCHROEDER, 2003[1]

WHEN NANCY PELOSI ARRIVED AT CONGRESS in June 1987, she already knew 200
members by name.

Between her involvement with Maryland politics and the California
Democratic Party and her work on the 1984 convention and the 1986 Senate

campaign, she had a personal connection to nearly half the elected Democrats in Washington.

She had never expected to become a member. Before Sala Burton's illness, she had never anticipated running for office. But she understood the institution. She had always been involved in politics. And she planned to get things done.

Her entire family, including her mother and father, was on hand to see her sworn in by Speaker Jim Wright (D-TX). Tommy D'Alesandro Jr., dressed in a dark jacket with a white kerchief in his front left pocket, sat beside her in a wheelchair. As he wheeled past the Speaker, Pelosi's father told Wright, "She ought to be on Appropriations."

The Appropriations Committee, which D'Alesandro had served on 50 years before, is where all spending bills originate, making it a prized power center that Pelosi also desired. But Pelosi was at the bottom of the seniority list, and her seat on the committee would have to wait.

Instead, she asked for and received assignment to two less heralded committees.

On the Government Operations Committee, Pelosi would have a hand in getting the Food and Drug Administration to speed up its approval of AIDS drugs. On the Banking, Finance, and Urban Affairs Committee, Pelosi could push for housing for those dying from the disease.

The House is an institution built on seniority, and typically it is unkind to its newest members. Before her swearing in, Pelosi recalled asking "how much time will I get to speak, and they said none."[2]

So she was rather surprised after taking her oath that the presiding officer suddenly recognized "the gentle lady from California."

Pelosi spoke before the House for the first time on June 9, 1987. For years her supporters would tell the story of how Pelosi began her tenure with a crisp 11-word introduction: "My name is Nancy Pelosi and I'm here to fight AIDS!"

In fact, Pelosi packed more than 300 words into an impromptu two-minute address. She thanked her colleagues, her family, and her constituents.

"Never did I think that I would be a member of the House of Representatives.

But that happened because of another proud tradition, and that is the tradition of the Burton tradition in the Fifth Congressional District," she said.

"We are very proud of the Fifth Congressional District and its leadership for peace, for environmental protection, for equal rights, for rights of individual freedom, and now we must take the leadership, of course, in the crisis of AIDS. And I look forward to working with you on that.

"I would change the circumstances under which I came if I could, but I cannot. I wish Phillip were here, I wish Sala were here, but they are not, and I cannot do anything about that except to follow in their tradition of excellence, of commitment, and of making government work for people."

Pelosi showed no ambivalence toward her new bicoastal life or serving in public office. She appeared to have pent-up determination to get things done professionally after spending 23 years raising a family.

The US Capitol is a daunting complex: six enormous office buildings connected by circuitous tunnels and subways; more than 10,000 workers, its own police force, and two newspapers; and the majestic House and Senate chambers situated on each side of the historic dome. A code transmitted by buzzers and bells alerts members to votes as tiny speakers on portable pagers bark out staticky instructions to members of each party. Members juggle hearings, committee assignments, news conferences, constituent meetings, fund-raisers, caucus meetings, and votes at a frantic pace.

The pace matched Pelosi's tempo. Short bursts of information. Competing demands. Quick decisions. Long hours. A never-ending collision of politics and policy. She had seen it all as a kid. A year into the job, she remarked that she enjoyed it even more than she'd imagined.

The 100th Congress had 24 women, half of them Democrats and half Republicans. Although they were outnumbered 411 to 24, the women of the House were a vocal and well-known group, including Geraldine Ferraro of New York, Republican Lynn Martin of Illinois, and Democrat Pat Schroeder of Colorado.

The culture was unmistakably male, but it had evolved since Schroeder had arrived in the early 1970s. At that time there no women pages, no women on the Capitol police force, and virtually no women reporters. Schroeder learned her place after she won a seat on the Armed Services Committee along with fellow freshman Ron Dellums from Oakland, over the objection of Chairman F. Edward Hébert of New Orleans.

Hébert didn't like the idea of a woman or a black, let alone a pair of anti–Vietnam War activists, being on his committee. As the two arrived at the panel's first meeting, Hébert announced that he may have lost power over who served on his committee, but he still had control over the number of chairs. He provided a single seat. Schroeder and Dellums sat cheek to cheek for the rest of the meeting. Not a single member of the committee offered a word of protest.

Barbara Boxer, who had taken over John Burton's seat, remembers making remarks at a meeting of the House Merchant Marine Committee shortly after she arrived in 1983. When she finished, a fellow Democrat followed with the traditional phrase "I want to associate myself with the remarks of the gentle lady from California."

Then he added with a smirk, "As a matter of fact, I'd like to associate with the gentle lady."

Another member chirped that he'd also like to associate with Boxer as the men snickered at their little joke. Boxer remembers walking out feeling humiliated.

If Pelosi received such treatment, she didn't discuss it. She had been operating in a man's world from the day she was born. She seemed quite at home among the good old boys of the House.

Being a woman in politics was less and less of a novelty. By 1987, there were 1,168 women serving as state legislators, three women governors, and two women in the Senate. It was still only a tiny slice of the pie, but the political desirability of reaching out to women was evident in the selection of Representative Ferraro as Walter Mondale's running mate (even if the 1984 election results suggested that other factors were more potent than gender when it came time to vote). In

1977, the Congresswomen's Caucus was founded with 15 members. When men were invited to join in 1981, more than 100 chose to do so.

The culture of the House was still dominated by men. Many women in Congress had succeeded their husbands. No woman chaired a prominent committee. Though Lynn Martin was elected to be vice chair of the GOP caucus, the number four post in her party's hierarchy, no woman of either party would rise higher until Pelosi was elected minority whip in 2001. Democrats had a long tradition of elevating women to the position of caucus secretary. Men had defeated them each time they'd tried to move higher.

Pelosi appreciated how underrepresented women were. Two days before she was sworn in, Pelosi delivered the commencement address at Mount Vernon College in Washington, where her eldest daughter was graduating.

"Twenty-three out of 435, 5½ percent," the soon-to-be congresswoman told the graduating class. "Certainly not enough. Not even close."[3]

Pelosi knew how to fit into a man's world. If the old guard felt threatened by the assertiveness of the new women members, Pelosi put them at ease. She was gracious, respectful, and a touch flirtatious at times. She was also sharp and could be trusted. She understood the institution. She understood its members.

During Pelosi's first months in Congress, the House voted to reprimand Representative Austin Murphy, a veteran lawmaker from near Pittsburgh. Murphy was charged with having enlisted someone to electronically cast a pair of votes for him while he was out of town, and for keeping an aide on his payroll who no longer showed up for work. Murphy was adamant about his innocence, insisting that he was baffled about how the votes had been cast and that he hadn't been aware that his employee had been absent while tending to his ailing mother.

Pelosi was one of only 56 Democrats to side with Murphy and vote against the reprimand, which nevertheless passed overwhelmingly. The vote caught the attention of Representative John Murtha, whose steel and coal district outside Pittsburgh neighbored Murphy's.

"You got a hell of a lot of guts for a freshman," Murtha told Pelosi.

She and Murtha developed a long and close relationship. Pelosi had a black coal doll that had been a memento of her father's from his struggle on behalf of union miners. She made certain the doll was on her desk when Murtha visited the office, and he was charmed. Murtha would later be instrumental in Pelosi's rise though the leadership, running her first bid to become whip and teaming up with her in the fight to end the war in Iraq.

Pelosi was regularly underestimated. Her scripted speaking style led some to believe she didn't know the material. Her San Francisco district led others to believe she was a liberal ideologue. Her good looks and social graces led many to believe she was a pushover. Pelosi was usually able to smile in the face of such slights, as long as she got what she was after.

Several years into her tenure, her former campaign manager, Fred Ross, was running an organization called Neighbor to Neighbor that was promoting a boycott of Salvadoran coffee. The group had produced controversial television ads, narrated by actor Edward Asner, that warned consumers that buying Folgers or Hills Bros. coffee brings "misery, destruction, and death" in El Salvador and ended with a coffee cup spilling blood.

Pelosi had already helped convince San Francisco–based Hills Bros. Coffee to participate in the boycott. Ross noticed that the chief executive of Procter and Gamble, which owned the Folgers Coffee Company, was sponsoring a reception on Capitol Hill for members of Congress. He told Pelosi he wanted to confront the executive.

After the two walked into the Rayburn Building reception, Ross recalled, the executive quickly noticed the congresswoman from San Francisco.

"Miss Pelosi, I want to tell you about a new fragrance that just came out," he told her.

Pelosi neither scowled nor kicked the executive in the shin. Instead, she smiled and introduced her guest.

"I want you to meet my good friend and the leader of Neighbor to Neighbor— you've probably heard of him—Fred Ross."

The executive's face turned ashen.

"I must say," he told Ross, who had his hand extended, "I find some of your tactics reprehensible."[4]

A meeting was arranged between Ross and Folgers officials, who eventually suspended coffee purchases from El Salvador. Ross and Pelosi would later joke that the new fragrance must have been named "Reprehensible."

PELOSI WAS ASSIGNED AN OFFICE on the fifth floor of the Longworth Building, named after 1920s House Speaker Nicolas Longworth of Ohio. It was possibly the worst office in the Capitol complex. Most members' offices include an anteroom with space for a receptionist and a couch, hiding the cramped conditions where senior staff work. Pelosi's office had no anteroom, with the door opening directly into the work area. Veteran lawmakers on the other side of the building gazed out upon the Capitol dome. The view from Pelosi's window was of I-295.

Pelosi had been around politics for too long to have expected glamour. She moved into an apartment about two miles from the Capitol, on Pennsylvania Avenue close to Georgetown, with enough spare rooms for her children, several of whom were attending college on the East Coast. Paul remained in San Francisco. She was now living a cross-country existence that would take her from coast to coast as many as 40 times a year.

The men of the House had their habits and institutions. Sometime in the 1970s, East Bay representative Pete Stark, who had made millions as a banker, began inviting members to his Capitol Hill apartment, where he had a cook. It had been an all-men's club not because Stark wanted to keep out women but because there were so few women around. Representatives Barbara Boxer and Barbara Kennelly (D-CT) integrated what had become a Tuesday night tradition in the mid-1980s, and Pelosi fit right in when she was elected.

On October 17, 1989, the group gathered at New York representative Tom

Downey's home on C Street to watch the San Francisco Giants and the Oakland A's in game three of the World Series. They couldn't get a signal. Downey had a satellite dish primarily so he could get New York news and sports. They tinkered until they brought in the San Francisco station. It was then that they learned that a major earthquake had struck Northern California, one that killed 63 people and devastated homes in San Francisco's Marina District, not far from where Paul Pelosi had grown up. Paul was at Candlestick Park for the game, which was postponed for 10 days. TV crews came to Downey's house to get the reactions of the Bay Area representatives.

Pelosi took a military plane back to her district and toured the damage with Mayor Agnos and President George H. W. Bush. Agnos remembers her serving as almost a "Washington chief of staff," cutting through the bureaucracy to obtain federal dollars for rebuilding the American Conservatory Theater company's Geary Theater, tear down the Embarcadero Freeway, and fulfill other local needs.

As a working woman, Pelosi could be quite scattered. She constantly left her purse behind, lost her wallet, and regularly misplaced envelopes of cash that her staff had prepared for her. She brought piles of constituent mail on airplanes, rarely allowing herself enough time to get through the stack, and would end up lugging it back and forth, trip after trip. She lost expensive jewelry, including a Bulgari necklace, on her cross-country flights.

As a legislator, Pelosi was intensely focused. She had a clear idea of how many votes she had on a particular piece of legislation and where she could find more. It was all about putting together coalitions. She'd urge her staff to get as many reporters and television cameras as possible to show up at news conferences, which was not unusual for a member of Congress. But in Pelosi's case it had nothing to do with ego. Pelosi was not compelled to hear her voice or see her name in print. It was about impressing the members who stood beside her. As the cameras rolled, she would thank each member who had joined her, by name, for their leadership and involvement. Such comments made journalists' eyes roll, but

Pelosi believed it solidified her coalition. If other members knew that working with Pelosi meant publicity and shared credit, they'd be more likely to join forces with her.

Pelosi warned her staff not to write press releases that appeared to take too much credit. That was not how you built coalitions.

Pelosi's reputation as a San Francisco liberal is richly earned, based on her home and her voting record. She was consistently rated as being among the most liberal members of the House, though she was typically more conservative than some of her neighbors from across the Bay. Over the course of her first 20 years in Congress, the only vote of consequence on which Pelosi disappointed the left was her 1994 vote in favor of the North American Free Trade Agreement.

She traveled back to San Francisco most weekends. Paul made the trip east about once a month. Over the course of her first 20 years in office, Pelosi figures she flew roughly 800 round-trips or 4 million miles, the equivalent of 160 trips around the world. The five-hour flight offered Pelosi some downtime to do crossword puzzles or occasionally watch a movie. More often, she'd spend the time poring over binders of legislative material or trying to answer an endless supply of constituent mail, which she insisted on reading herself.

Once she arrived in San Francisco, Pelosi typically raced from one community event to another, often being driven by Michael Yaki, who ran her district office.

"By the third year doing it, she stopped giving me directions," he recalled.

CHAPTER SEVEN

GAY PNEUMONIA

"It's our problem now. Don't you think it's going to be your problem?
It's a communicable disease."
—NANCY PELOSI, LATE 1980s

"You'd think we're having a meeting of the flat earth society.
How can we turn our back on science?"
—NANCY PELOSI, 1998

THE FIGHT AGAINST AIDS was in its infancy when Pelosi arrived at Congress.

It had been seven years since the first cases of "gay pneumonia" had shown up in San Francisco, Los Angeles, and New York, and only four years since scientists had isolated the human immunodeficiency virus (HIV) as its cause. Fear, ignorance, and shame still clouded the public health response to an epidemic whose victims were primarily gay men and drug addicts who shared syringes.

By 1987, AIDS had killed roughly 20,000 Americans, more than six times the number who died in the terrorist attacks of September 11, 2001. About 1 in 10 of the dead was from San Francisco, where a thriving gay community, with its accommodating bathhouses and culture of promiscuous sex, had contributed to the spread of the virus. Most San Franciscans knew of at least someone who had died or was dying of AIDS. In the Castro, the human toll was overpowering.

President Reagan had just begun to publicly broach the topic. He delivered his first speech on AIDS during Pelosi's 1987 congressional campaign, vowing to find a cure, urging compassion for victims, and calling on young people to abstain from sex as the best way to avoid the disease.

Congress faced a slew of AIDS legislation, much of it based on fear, including proposals for mandatory testing, to keep foreigners with AIDS out of the United States, and to impose criminal penalties on doctors with AIDS who performed surgery without disclosing their condition.

Pelosi had pledged during her campaign to make Washington appreciate the horror that had befallen her community and to add urgency to the way the federal government confronted the disease.

"We've got to make them understand it's an emergency situation—almost as if we've had an earthquake in San Francisco," Pelosi said the day after winning her primary.[1]

Federal spending on AIDS had started slowly—just a few hundred thousand dollars for the Centers for Disease Control—but it had more than doubled in each year since the early 1980s. The 1987 budget contained $766 million for research and prevention but left those battling the disease, their health care providers, and the cities in which they lived entirely responsible for their care, which could cost thousands of dollars a week.

Pelosi would spend much of the next decade, particularly her first several years in Congress, making certain that Washington confronted the crisis and seeing to it that the federal dollar commitment went up.

In her first week on the job, Pelosi hired a noted San Francisco AIDS expert to work from her Washington office, making him the first congressional staffer hired to work primarily on AIDS issues. Steve Morin brought impressive credentials to the Hill; he was a psychologist and professor at the University of California at San Francisco, president-elect of the California State Psychological Association, and a member of the California Assembly's AIDS Budget Task Force and of the state's AIDS Strategic Planning Commission. His presence brought not only expertise but also credibility to an issue in dire need of attention.

"We were in an epidemic. There was no higher-priority issue in San Francisco than AIDS," Morin said. "If you lived here, you knew that."[2]

Horror stories would flood in from Pelosi's district office, demanding attention: Men with AIDS were losing jobs and unable to find health insurance, losing apartments and left with nowhere to spend their final months, being cut off from disability programs that hadn't been designed for terminally ill men in the prime of their lives.

Much of Pelosi's AIDS work involved wrestling with complex bureaucratic formulas to make sure that benefits were reaching a new class of dying constituents. COBRA laws, for instance, provided individuals who lost their jobs with a chance to purchase up to 18 months of group health coverage from their previous employers. However, it took 29 months before individuals with disabilities were eligible for Medicare coverage. That left a devastating 11-month gap when people with AIDS faced tens of thousands of dollars in medical expenses, and no insurance company was willing to offer them a policy. Pelosi introduced the COBRA-Continuation Tax Disabilities Amendments of 1989, which allowed people with AIDS and other disabilities to maintain group health insurance coverage for the full 29 months until Medicare coverage became available.

Similarly, Pelosi worked to adjust Social Security requirements to allow people with AIDS to qualify for disability payments, expanded definitions of AIDS so that those suffering from AIDS-related complex—the precursor to AIDS—would qualify for benefits, and worked to make federal benefits available for home care as well as for care given in hospitals.

Pelosi was not shy about using her lifelong familiarity with some members to get things done. Her network of contacts from her Democratic Party work meant her phone calls got returned. During her first months in Congress, she wanted to offer a pair of AIDS-related measures on the floor and was told that her prospects as a freshman were slim. Pelosi appealed to the chair of the Rules Committee— 88-year-old Claude Pepper of Florida, who knew her father from their days together in Washington during the 1930s—and both measures were introduced.

Pelosi represented the city hardest hit by the disease, but she understood that her best chance to boost the allotment of federal dollars was to include as many members as possible in the fight. The more representatives who could take credit for the effort, the more allies she would have. She invited fellow members to San Francisco for field hearings on AIDS. At every opportunity, she thanked her colleagues for their leadership and support on the issue.

She appealed to other members' mercy, citing the charitable work of St. Francis of Assisi, the revered Catholic patron saint of San Francisco. She also regularly made a more pragmatic argument: "It's our problem now. Don't you think it's going to be your problem? It's a communicable disease."

She was at times obsessively hands-on. During her first year in Washington, she was enlisted by Cleve Jones, a constituent and the founder of the Names Project, to negotiate an agreement with the National Park Service to bring the AIDS Memorial Quilt to the National Mall. The enormous tapestry contained original artwork with thousands of panels honoring the lives of those who had died from AIDS. The park service protested that the football field–size quilt would smother the grass. Not a problem, Pelosi insisted, proposing that the panels be lifted every 20 minutes to give the grass a chance to breath. Pelosi was among those who read the 1,920 names on the quilt as some onlookers wept. The AIDS quilt would return to Washington four more times and grow to more than 40,000 panels. By its last visit in 1996, it covered the entire Mall.

There were other members out front on the AIDS issue, most notably Representatives Ted Weiss from Manhattan and Henry Waxman from Los Angeles. Pelosi's work often required her to wade deep into the thickets of the federal health bureaucracy, and her efforts often went unnoticed as the goals eventually were accomplished as part of a larger reconciliation bill or an executive order.

When her hometown paper quoted a congressional aide's complaint that Pelosi was a "backbencher" who had disappointed some by being too cautious, she responded that on matters like AIDS, she intended to work within the system rather than confront it.

"I want to get a job done. I'm not here to grandstand," Pelosi told the interviewer.[3]

Pelosi kept pushing. She had heard stories of young men spending their final days in cheap residential hotels because AIDS had cost them their jobs and they had no means to pay rent. From her perch on the banking committee, she cowrote the bill creating the Housing Opportunities for People with AIDS program, which provided billions of dollars in housing subsidies.

Some of the initial steps that consumed Pelosi's early days seemed so basic only a few years later, such as a bill to set up a way for cities with large AIDS populations—San Francisco, Los Angeles, New York—to share data with each other. She mailed every home in her district a copy of the surgeon general's 36-page, 1986 report on AIDS, which used graphic explanations of safe and unsafe practices, called on parents to have "frank, open discussions" about AIDS with their children, and counseled that the disease is not spread by "sitting on toilets, shaking hands, hugging, crying, coughing or sneezing."

When Republicans pushed a measure that barred federal money from being spent on distributing clean needles to drug users, Pelosi complained, "You'd think we're having a meeting of the flat earth society."[4]

Perhaps her most lasting contribution to the early AIDS effort was legislation approved in 1990 that finally provided for the care of those afflicted by the disease. The staggering cost of caring for the sick was bankrupting families and the cities in which they lived. Yet there was strong opposition in the Bush administration to creating an entirely new, disease-specific entitlement program that would guarantee federal benefits to a rapidly rising number of victims. Pelosi was among those who pushed for a compromise under which the federal government sent money to the state and local municipalities hardest hit by AIDS, which would then disperse the resources to victims. The comprehensive AIDS funding measure was regarded as a breakthrough and named after Ryan White, an Indiana teenager who had been barred from attending his public school after being diagnosed with AIDS in the mid-1980s and who died in 1990, just weeks before the measure was passed.

In 1990, the Ryan White Act—which Pelosi coauthored—distributed $220 million to the cities hardest hit by AIDS, including San Francisco. By the time she became Speaker 17 years later, more than $20 billion had been distributed, providing services to more than 500,000 recipients a year.

The gains in federal spending on AIDS came amid a backdrop of fear and prejudice about a deadly disease that targeted gay men and intravenous drug users but, with each passing month, threatened to spread to a larger population.

Representative Dan Burton of Indiana introduced a bill to make AIDS testing mandatory for all Americans. California representative William Dannemeyer proposed that state health agencies keep records of the identity of anyone testing positive for AIDS. Another measure sought a prison term for any AIDS-infected doctor, dentist, or nurse who performed "invasive procedures" without disclosing their aliment. Senator Jesse Helms of North Carolina introduced legislation to prohibit the Centers for Disease Control from funding AIDS programs that "promote, encourage or condone homosexual activities."

Pelosi repeatedly provided medical advice, data, and anecdotes from her district to encourage her colleagues to embrace "reason rather than hysteria."

When Republicans won control of the Congress in 1994, Pelosi found herself playing defense, trying to maintain programs. The first budget under the GOP majority chopped $23 million from HIV prevention funds and $13 million from the Ryan White Act. Now seated on the Appropriations Committee, Pelosi was able to restore the money.

Pelosi argued that cutting financing for basic medical care and prevention would eventually end up costing taxpayers even more.[5]

Pelosi became more and more closely associated with the effort against AIDS. In April 1993, gay rights advocates organized a rally in Washington. President Bill Clinton chose not to appear, citing a conflict. But he sent a letter and asked Pelosi to read it at the rally.

"Where's Bill, where's Bill," chanted some members of the crowd as Pelosi read Clinton's letter, which pledged his commitment to increasing spending on AIDS.

By the time Pelosi became Speaker, AIDS had killed more than 18,000 San Franciscans, 529,000 Americans, and 20 million people around the world.[6] The federal government was spending more than $20 billion a year to battle the disease.

CHAPTER EIGHT

THE PRESIDIO

"Losing is not an option."
—NANCY PELOSI, 1995

"Without her work, I would guarantee you
this would not be in front of us today."
—REPRESENTATIVE JAMES HANSEN (R-UT), 1995

PROBABLY THE GREATEST DISPLAY of Pelosi's pure legislative skills came after the Pentagon decided to close the two-century-old Presidio Army Base, which sprawled over 1,488 acres of prime San Francisco real estate.

The army base in the shadow of the Golden Gate Bridge was arguably the

133

most picturesque green space in any American city. Nearly twice the size of New York's Central Park, its fog-shrouded forests and chaparral slopes offered sweeping views of the Golden Gate to the north and the rocky Pacific coast to the west. Its prized golf course abutted homes on Presidio Terrace, where Pelosi had raised her family.

The land was first claimed for the king of Spain in 1776, as American colonialists were declaring their independence from England on the other side of the continent. Its location at the opening of the San Francisco Bay made it a natural military outpost, and for many years it was the westernmost perch of the Spanish empire. The United States took the base over from Mexico in 1846, four years before California joined the Union.

The grounds were rife with American history. African American cavalry regiments known as Buffalo Soldiers were stationed there during the Spanish-American War at the turn of the century. General John Joseph Pershing dispatched troops from the Presidio in 1915 to chase after Pancho Villa in Mexico. Troops dug foxholes near the Presidio's beaches in 1941 after the Japanese attacks on Pearl Harbor.

It was also the fifth-largest employer in San Francisco. However, it cost the Defense Department $50 million a year to maintain, and with the cold war over and threats from the Pacific no longer a priority, a panel commissioned by the Pentagon included the Presidio on a list of 86 bases to be closed early in Pelosi's tenure.

The late representative Phil Burton had foreseen the possibility two decades earlier and inserted language in a 1972 bill stipulating that if the military ever abandoned the Presidio, the land would revert to the National Park Service. Burton was no outdoorsman, but he had visions of protecting the Pacific coast from Canada to Mexico, and he wanted to be certain that the land wasn't built upon.

When the Presidio showed up on the Pentagon's hit list, Pelosi and Representative Barbara Boxer, whose district then included the northern tip of San

Francisco, went to see Representative John Murtha, who chaired the sub-committee that doled out money to the Pentagon. The two Californians were enthused about carrying out Burton's vision to turn the military post into a park.

Murtha told them to slow down. He knew Burton and he knew the plan. He also knew that the costs of cleaning up a centuries-old military base would be astronomical and that the Department of Defense could afford it far better than the National Park Service. Murtha told them that the longer the Department of Defense held on to the property, the more the Pentagon would have to contribute to its cleanup.

"She saw immediately what I was doing," Murtha recalled. While other park enthusiasts insisted that the Presidio immediately become a park—an approach that was "completely amateurish," Murtha said—Pelosi understood.

So she and Boxer went to work fighting the closing of the Presidio, producing studies, charts, testimony, and whatever evidence they could get their hands on to prove that it would cost taxpayers more to shut it down than keep it open. They petitioned other members to have the Presidio removed from the base closure list, held news conferences, and rallied local leaders.

"The facts and figures don't add up to justify closing the Presidio," Pelosi maintained, at one point producing a study that claimed that, rather than saving $74 million a year, as the base closure commission had estimated, turning the land over to the park service would end up costing taxpayers $26 million a year.[1]

Congress eventually voted to close the Presidio along with the other bases. But by then the military had agreed to commit more than $65 million toward its cleanup.

Meanwhile, some members of Congress were beginning to balk at the idea of turning prime real estate—which *Forbes* magazine conservatively estimated to be worth $4 billion—into a national park.

"It's not Yosemite," noted Representative Craig Thomas of Wyoming.

Even Interior Secretary Bruce Babbitt sounded skeptical when one of the initial estimates for the cost of running the park came in a $45 million, more than the park service spent to operate Yellowstone, Yosemite, and the Grand Canyon national parks combined.

"I've learned that in San Francisco, there are 2 million experts on the future of the Presidio," Babbitt said wearily. "The Presidio undertakes a scope and complexity which we have never approached in the National Park Service."[2]

Pelosi knew Washington well enough to know that even a Democratic Congress would never approve such an expensive park. She knew San Francisco well enough to know residents would never accept selling the land to developers.

Pelosi was no more an outdoorsperson than Burton. But like her predecessor, she was driven by her determination to forever preserve such a unique setting as a park.

Pelosi seized upon a novel idea to lease parts of the Presidio—its hospital, its golf course, some of its 571 buildings—in order to maintain the rest as a park. The concept, first proposed by a firm commissioned by the Department of the Interior, was mired in complex bureaucratic obstacles that made it difficult for an agency like the National Park Service to directly engage in leasing its property. But that could be fixed with creative legislation.

In November 1993, Pelosi introduced legislation to create the Presidio Corporation, a quasigovernmental agency that would be charged with collecting rent on parts of the Presidio and providing the money to the park service to run the rest.

The proposal drew protests from some in San Francisco who accused Pelosi of selling off a national treasure. Some advocated that the entire 1,488 acres be a park, regardless of cost. Others suggested the buildings could house the city's enormous homeless population. Still others suggested that the area simply be fenced off and left as natural, open space.

On Capitol Hill, some Republicans doubted that the government could be an effective landlord. Representative John Duncan of Tennessee introduced legislation that would have allowed all but 200 acres to be leased or sold off and lined up 72 cosponsors. Others insisted that if the park was so important to San

Francisco, the city should either take it over or contribute millions to its annual upkeep.

Pelosi pushed her proposal as a sensible middle ground that would maintain the Presidio as green space while it paid for itself.

After five years of work, the House approved Pelosi's bill to create the quasi-governmental agency. The 245 to 168 vote split mostly along party lines, with Democrats voting in favor and Republicans voting against. The bill allocated $25 million a year to run the park and was immediately hailed by Pelosi as a "big victory."

Then things got tougher.

Senate Republicans balked at the measure, and Democrats were focused on passing another big California parks bill, authored by Senator Dianne Feinstein, to create a national park in the Mojave Desert. The Presidio bill was held for the following year.

Then Republicans won control of Congress. The members who had complained that millions were being spent on a playground for Bay Area residents were suddenly running the committees.

Pelosi instructed her staff that "losing is not an option." She personally visited every Republican member of the House Resources Committee, which had jurisdiction over national parks. She invited them to the district, told them why the Presidio was so special, outlined the free market leasing plan that would offset the price of the park, and warned that San Francisco's arduous planning process made the notion of selling the land to developers entirely unrealistic.

She personally escorted members through the Presidio. She enlisted California's Republican governor, Pete Wilson, to join the fight.

"This is a national park. It is a federal responsibility. This is not a city park for San Francisco. It is a park of national stature," Pelosi said.

Pelosi offered the GOP concessions. Her new bill gave the Presidio Trust more autonomy from the park service and adjusted the composition of its board of directors to encourage those with financial and real estate backgrounds to join.

And perhaps most important, she inserted a clause that said that if the Presidio was not self-sufficient in 15 years, it would be deemed surplus and taken over by the General Services Administration, offering comfort to those who doubted that the leasing plan would work. (What Pelosi didn't tell her opponents was that by then her staff had unearthed the 150-year-old treaty that had granted the United States possession of the Presidio and believed the property couldn't be sold off even if it became surplus.) Pelosi's relentless lobbying efforts on behalf of the bill drew praise even from Republicans.

"I don't know if people in the Bay Area realize the hundreds of hours that she and her staff have put into this," said Representative James Hansen of Utah, marveling at Pelosi's doggedness. "They should be very proud of her work. Without her work, I would guarantee you this would not be in front of us today. There is no question [she is] a very persistent legislator."[3]

On September 19, 1995, nine months into the first year of the new Republican majority, the House passed Pelosi's Presidio bill in a 317 to 101 vote.

"I feel like I've just been in a marathon run," Pelosi said.[4]

The Senate followed suit, and one week after President Clinton won reelection he signed the bill, calling the Presidio a "sanctuary of nature and history" and hailing Pelosi's legislation as "a blueprint for national parks."

Pelosi, as she began her 10th year in Congress, had managed to get a Republican Congress to create the nation's most expensive national park in, of all places, Democratic San Francisco.

CHAPTER NINE

The Butchers of Beijing

*"I cannot say one thing about George Bush's policy
and another about Bill Clinton's when they are the same policy."*
—NANCY PELOSI, 1994

*"I'm Gary Bauer with the Family Research Council, and I'm proud
this morning to be here with . . . Congresswoman Nancy Pelosi."*
—CHRISTIAN CONSERVATIVE GARY BAUER, 1997

IT WAS THE EVENTS OF JUNE 4, 1989, half a world away, that thrust Pelosi onto the national stage.

After nearly two months of pro-democracy demonstrations in Beijing's

Tiananmen Square, the People's Liberation Army violently dispersed the crowd, rolling tanks and firing machine guns into the enormous plaza the size of 90 football fields. Exactly how many students were killed is a matter of debate. Eyewitnesses reported seeing hundreds of bodies, and by some estimates as many as 2,700 died. The Chinese government said that no one was killed in the square itself but acknowledged that as many as 300 died in the surrounding violence. Footage of a sole protester standing before a row of moving tanks, played repeatedly on television, provided a searing image of courage and defiance.

Pelosi's district had deep cultural ties to China dating back to the mid-1800s, when Chinese began arriving in North America via the Pacific Ocean in search of gold. San Francisco's Chinatown, which produced big numbers for Pelosi's 1987 and 1988 elections, was the biggest and best-established Chinese community in the United States.

Something had to be done. Pelosi chief of staff Judy Lemons watched pictures of the Tiananmen crackdown from her Washington, DC, home in horror. Lemons locked her senior staff in Pelosi's personal office and told them not to emerge until they had a plan. Phone conversations with immigration attorneys in the Bay Area revealed widespread concern among Chinese students in the United States whose visas required them to return home immediately after their studies were done.

There were as many as 40,000 Chinese students in the United States, including thousands in the Bay Area. Pelosi's staff recommended the visa requirement be waived so that Chinese students would not have to fear returning in the midst of such oppression and turmoil.

Pelosi dove into the issue with characteristic tenacity. She quickly introduced legislation waiving the visa requirements. She then systematically charged through a list of phone calls and "dear colleague" letters to build support. She enlisted the help of House Judiciary Committee chairman Jack Brooks (D-TX), who had been close to Phil and Sala Burton. By the end of June she had 100 cosponsors.

Over the next decade her battles with the Chinese government would force leaders in Washington and Beijing to take note and built her reputation as a relentless advocate of human rights.

"Given the allegations of official harassment of Chinese students and the videotaping of demonstrations in the United States, we simply cannot force these students to go back to China," Pelosi said.[1]

President Bush offered to waive the requirement for a year, but Pelosi insisted that that was insufficient. Her legislation would have given the Chinese students at least four years to return and set out conditions that would allow them to remain in the United States permanently. It also could not be reversed by executive order. By midsummer the relatively new congresswoman had solicited 258 cosponsors, and with Brooks's help it cleared the House Judiciary Committee on a voice vote. The House passed the bill unanimously in November.

President Bush had diplomatic concerns. The Chinese students were guests, granted permission to study in the United States on the condition that they return. Bush worried that if the United States suddenly waived the requirement, the Chinese would retaliate by ending all exchange programs. The State Department issued a statement opposing the bill, and Bush threatened to veto it.

Pelosi was undeterred by the threat. The violent images from China had prompted widespread outrage, particularly in her district. Pelosi was moved by the youth of the protesters. She had college-age kids herself. The notion that the Chinese government would jail, torture, and shoot at students was more than she could take.

"It's up to the president to sign the bill and tell the Chinese government that as long as it continues to massacre its young people, the United States will not send them back," Pelosi said. If Bush vetoed the measure, she warned, Congress was "definitely ready to override."[2]

When Bush followed through on his veto threat, Pelosi was blunt and swift in her criticism. She called the veto a "slap in the face to the forces of democracy" and "an encouragement of a tyrannical regime."[3]

It didn't faze her that Bush had been in public office for nearly a quarter century, having served as a member of the House, ambassador to the United Nations, chair of the Republican National Committee, US representative to China, director of the Central Intelligence Agency, and vice president. Pelosi had been in Congress two years, but she was no newcomer to politics.

She spent hours lobbying on the House floor. She called as many as 30 House members a day, including scores of Republicans. She traveled to Mexico on vacation over the Martin Luther King Jr. Day holiday only after seasoned congressional hands warned her that she'd lose more votes than she'd gain by lobbying through the recess. While on holiday, she reread books on the history of US-China relations.

"He has the power," she said of Bush as the vote approached. "I have the issue."[4]

Pelosi's feverish pace was evident the day before the House took up the vote, when she held a news conference with Chinese students on the Capitol lawn, testified at a Senate hearing, appeared on PBS's *MacNeil/Lehrer NewsHour*, took charge of allocating speaking time to her allies on the House floor, and delivered her own speech in which she launched a blistering assault on the Chinese government.

"The fact of the matter is that everything we do in Congress sends a message, and overriding this veto will send a very clear message to the butchers of Beijing that it was entirely wrong for them to kill their people for speaking out for democracy in China," she said.[5]

On January 24, the House voted 390 to 25 to override Bush's veto. Pelosi's success prompted Bush to defend his China policy at a news conference later in the day.

"When Congress passed the Pelosi bill last fall, I was faced with a choice. If I signed the bill, the students would still be safe, but China would retaliate and cut off future student exchanges," Bush said. "If I vetoed the bill, I could take action to provide the students with even greater protection while keeping the door open for more Chinese scholars to study here. And the price of the Pelosi bill is lost opportunity for the Chinese scholars of tomorrow. And people should understand that very, very clearly. The bill is totally unnecessary."

Pelosi had a powerful ally in the Senate in George Mitchell, her mentor from the 1986 campaign, who was now the Senate Majority Leader. Sixty-two senators rejected Bush's argument. But it took 67 votes to override the veto, and the legislation was lost. Pelosi's bill had failed.

Nevertheless, Bush had pledged to issue an even stronger executive order that would keep enough senators on his side. And Pelosi had now established herself in Washington as a force to be reckoned with. The skills she had exhibited as a party operative in San Francisco were becoming evident on Capitol Hill. Members who had hardly noticed her arrival in 1987 took notice.

"I had this confidence when I came to Congress," she told *San Francisco Chronicle* Washington Bureau chief Larry Liebert. "I always believed I could do this job very well because I'm relentless in pursuit of my colleagues, and I know how to mobilize people. I've been doing it my whole life."[6]

With the student fight behind her, Pelosi searched for another vehicle to keep pressure on the Chinese government to honor human rights. A few weeks before the override vote, a couple dozen Chinese students, scholars, and congressional staffers attended a human rights conference at Harvard University. Pelosi was the lone member of Congress in attendance.[7] The idea of challenging China's trade status was raised. It was a fight Pelosi would keep up for a decade.

China had received "most favored nation," or MFN, status since 1979, which enabled it to export goods to the United States with the same low tariffs as most countries. However, a cold war provision aimed at the Soviet Union required the president to renew the status each year for nations that did not let their citizens freely emigrate, which included China. Without MFN, tariffs on some goods would rise as much as eightfold, making it a grave threat to the Chinese economy.

Pelosi embraced the idea of conditioning trade on human rights in order to make the Chinese pay attention. To Pelosi it went beyond politics. This was a moral issue.

"Frankly, I don't see how we can face ourselves in the mirror if we just extend the benefits without any new conditions," she said.[8]

Pelosi was a coalition builder, and she put together an eclectic alliance. Some were devoted to human rights, some were staunch anti-Communists, and still others saw the provision as an opportunity to stick it to the Bush administration.

The House overwhelmingly passed a measure in 1990 to condition trade on human rights, but the measure died in the Senate. Pelosi introduced a similar bill the following year, calling "the old men who rule China . . . more intransigent than ever. They haven't demonstrated improvement in any significant way."[9]

Pelosi's bill was less punitive than other measures that sought to shut down US-China trade. It would allow China to keep its trade status so long as it released its political prisoners and made "significant progress" toward advancing human rights.

For Pelosi, revoking China's trade status was not a goal. It was a tactic. If angry denunciations from American politicians had no impact in Beijing, perhaps threatening to cut off billions of dollars worth of trade would. Pelosi was dogmatic about the issue but pragmatic about the legislation.

"I would prefer to ask my colleagues to take a principled stand on something that has a reasonable chance of success," Pelosi explained.[10]

This time both the House and the Senate approved the measure, which was vetoed by President Bush.

Pelosi's profile on the issue grew after she led a nine-member delegation in September 1991 on a contentious trip to China that would garner international headlines.

The group included human rights leaders and two other members of Congress. They started in Hong Kong, where they met with Martin Lee, a prominent member of Hong Kong's Legislative Council and the future founding chairman of Hong Kong's Democratic Party. Lee handed them a small black banner with stitched silver letters and asked if they would make a small gesture in Beijing to remember those who had died at Tiananmen Square. The banner, smaller than the length of Pelosi's outstretched arms, read in both Chinese and English: "To Those Who Died for Democracy in China."

Pelosi and Representatives John Miller of Washington and Ben Jones of North Carolina looked at each other and, without discussion, nodded their heads.

In Beijing, the delegation had hoped to meet with jailed dissidents but was told upon arrival that there would be no jail visits. They were also told that there were no political prisoners or restrictions on speech. Pelosi raised the specter of revoking China's trade status at a news conference attended by foreign journalists and called on China to release dissidents arrested in the 1989 crackdown.

After several days of royal treatment, the delegation was scheduled to spend its final afternoon visiting the Great Wall of China several hours outside Beijing before dining with the Chinese foreign minister. Pelosi and her two congressional companions said they were tired and begged off the excursion. Instead, they snuck out the back door of their hotel, hoping to elude their handlers, and jumped into a car that took them to Tiananmen Square.

Before he left the hotel, Jones, a second-term congressman who was better known for his role as Cooter on the television show *The Dukes of Hazzard*, placed a call to a Beijing-based TV producer he knew from CNN. Figuring his room was bugged, he simply told his friend they'd be going to the square and he might want to show up. He also brought the banner, which he had smuggled into China in his underwear.

By the time Pelosi, Jones, and Miller showed up at the enormous plaza, several news crews had gathered. They walked toward the Monument to the People's Heroes in the center of the square, each carrying a white rose made of cloth. As a growing crowd of Chinese passersby stopped to watch and the news crews filmed, Jones read a statement in memory of the slain: "Those who died here on June 4, 1989, did not die in vain."

Pelosi, Jones, and Miller then placed their flowers on the pavement, and Jones unfurled the banner for the TV cameras. Uniformed guards suddenly appeared. They confronted the members of Congress and began shouting loudly in Chinese. They grabbed the TV cameras and began shoving the journalists. One policeman grabbed Miller by the arm and gave him a slap. Jones contends that another policeman was about to grab him when he shot him a menacing look that made him back off.

"I think there's an international sign that says, 'I will hit back,'" Jones recalled years later.

The officials were shouting in Chinese, and the Americans were shouting back in English. The journalists took pictures. So did Paul Pelosi, who had accompanied his wife on the trip. The delegation turned and briskly walked to the square's edge. They jumped into the car that had brought them. They were shaken. They thought they were going to be arrested.

The news crews were not so fortunate. Chinese authorities confiscated their equipment and marched them to a nearby police station. Seven journalists— from CNN, CBS, and ABC—were held for about an hour, some of them bruised from the scuffle. They were told it was a violation of health regulations to place flowers on the square and that they had no permission to film.[11]

Dinner that night with the Chinese foreign minister was chilly. The incident was news around the world. Jones recalled that they had all been nervous. However, fear is not an emotion Pelosi shows in public.

"She was almost regal throughout the trip. Unflappable," Jones recalled. "An iron fist and a velvet glove."

Pelosi called the police response an "overreaction" and said the incident seemed to contradict the assurances they had received from their handlers that China embraced free speech.

Pelosi remained unapologetic when she returned to Beijing as a member of the House Intelligence Committee two years later, insisting that the action was necessary to let those in prison know they were not forgotten.

"It was one of the proudest moments of my life," Pelosi told reporters on the return trip. "I have absolutely no regrets about it."[12]

THINGS WERE ALSO CHILLY between Pelosi and the Bush administration. Many Democrats saw Bush's friendly relations with the Chinese as an opening to attack his foreign policy in advance of the 1992 presidential election. The administration grew defensive.

When Secretary of State James Baker testified before a House panel that progress in China's human rights policy was due to the president's dialogue with China, Pelosi barked, "It's not your policy but the debate in Congress on MFN that forced change. I don't think you would have made progress if our MFN bill didn't exist."

Baker responded testily, "You say it's what *you've* done. I say it's what *we've* done."[13]

Many critics assumed Pelosi's harsh words toward the Bush administration were motivated by partisanship. It was a reasonable assumption based on Pelosi's aggressive approach to politics and her dismissive attitude toward Republicans. They would soon be shown wrong.

The following year brought a Democratic president and optimism for Pelosi. Bill Clinton had campaigned against Bush's China policy, accusing him of "coddling dictators from Baghdad to Beijing."

As president, Clinton assured Pelosi and Mitchell that he would attach conditions for renewing China's MFN status in an executive order. He told them their legislation—which would have easily passed—was unnecessary. Pelosi smiled triumphantly as she stood over Clinton's left shoulder at the White House while he signed the executive order, handing her one of the signing pens as a gesture of his gratitude.

She would later remark ruefully that Clinton's signature "was not worth the paper it's printed on."

An intense fight took shape early the following year over whether China was making enough progress to fulfill the requirements of the executive order. Some House members, including Pelosi allies like Representative Bob Matsui of Sacramento, began an early effort to push for MFN renewal. Pelosi was appalled by these efforts, figuring the Chinese would interpret any divisions in Congress as a sign that the United States would not back up its threats.

"I don't know what purpose it serves to send China the message that the demand for human rights is wavering," Pelosi said in an interview. "We don't think they are anywhere close to the kind of progress that would lead to renewal of [MFN]. It's like a high-stakes game of poker, and the Chinese want to see if we're going to blink. We're not going to blink."[14]

The threat of revoking China's trade status was a tactic. Pelosi said prisoners had told her that the conditions in Chinese jails miraculously improved each year when Congress debated MFN status. And the tactic would be much more effective if the Chinese believed the Americans would not fold.

Pelosi used the same relentless techniques that had been effective in pushing for AIDS dollars and the Presidio. She perpetually tried to build a coalition to keep pressure on China. When Democratic allies like Matsui wouldn't stand with her, she looked across the aisle for votes among Republicans. This was at a time when Republicans hadn't been in the majority since the Eisenhower administration and books were being written about the GOP being a "permanent minority." They were neither influential nor in agreement with Pelosi on most other issues. But they each held a vote, and many were as appalled by the Chinese government as Pelosi was.

Pelosi struck a bond with conservatives like Chris Smith of New Jersey and Frank Wolf of Virginia. They, in turn, were impressed that a Democrat with a reputation as a money person, a fund-raiser like Pelosi, would turn against business interests in the name of human rights, and they stood beside her at numerous news conferences.

She also became increasingly disparaging of big business as it spent millions of dollars to exert whatever influence it could to keep the booming trade business alive. She pointedly suggested that if the business community wanted to keep its financial interests afloat, it should persuade the Chinese to improve human rights, not its own government to ignore them.

"What a laugh for the Chinese government to see these businesspeople groveling for favor among the Chinese to the point of being openly critical of the secretary of state," Pelosi said when business leaders criticized Clinton's secretary of state, Warren Christopher, for suggesting that human rights had not improved in China.

"Many who oppose conditioning MFN for China characterize this debate as one of values versus jobs," she said. "They are wrong. It is better characterized as a debate about ideals versus deals."[15]

In her office she kept a replica of the Goddess of Democracy—the makeshift statue constructed by pro-democracy demonstrators in Tiananmen Square— photographs of herself with prominent Chinese dissidents, and a large Chinese quilt signed by grateful constituents.

The issue, which had not even been on Pelosi's radar screen when she'd run for Congress a few years earlier, became a staple of her identity. She was a regular guest on national television shows and the subject of profiles around the globe.

"How do you give an American businessman trading with China heartburn?" asked the lead sentence in an article appearing in Singapore's *Straights Times*. "Just mention United States Congressman [sic] Nancy Pelosi's name."[16]

Some in the business community said she was doing it only for the publicity. In Washington, many characterized Pelosi's vehemence as political fealty to her Chinese American constituents. "She has to do it because of her district" was a common refrain. Such sentiment reflected a fundamental misunderstanding of Pelosi's district.

San Francisco did indeed have a large and influential Chinese population. But it was the Chinese community that had the strongest business ties across the

Pacific and therefore the most to lose in a US-China trade war. Many of Pelosi's own Chinese constituents were among those pushing hardest for engagement. It was San Francisco's liberal base, not the Chinese, who most strongly supported her stance on human rights.

The Chinese community had backed Pelosi over Britt in 1987 in part because she seemed friendlier to business interests. They had supported Pelosi's efforts on behalf of Chinese students, and they supported her immigration stance and other positions. But they felt that her pragmatism had suddenly abandoned her as she embarked on an ideological human rights crusade that they believed threatened San Francisco's position as the "Geneva of the West," the trading capital of the Pacific Rim for the 21st century.

"Everyone was very puzzled," recalled Rose Pak of the San Francisco Chinese Chamber of Commerce and a strong Pelosi supporter. "On social issues and immigration, everyone was behind her. How can you fault her caring for seniors, education, child care. They loved her for it. She had never been an ideologue. That's what surprised us on China."

To Pelosi, such arguments were overstated. The economic impact would be manageable. And to allow profits to dictate morals was unacceptable.

"I rue the day when our economic stability as a city would depend on our relationship with a country which represses its citizens," she said in an interview. "You're saying that the 'Geneva of the West' should be built on the backs of slave labor?"

Clinton was under great pressure as decision time approached. Human rights by any reasonable measure were not improving. Yet most favored nation status was withheld from only six countries: Cuba, North Korea, Vietnam, Cambodia, Laos, and Azerbaijan. The United States and China had a $40 billion a year trade relationship. Inside the White House, many believed that revoking MFN would be a foreign policy disaster and that engagement—the policy Bush had pursued—might just as quickly lead to political reform.

Clinton asked his chief of staff, Leon Panetta, who, as a former member of

Congress from California, had known Pelosi for years, how much of a problem she would be.

"A big problem," Panetta advised the president.

Pelosi met with Clinton and knew the decision wasn't going her way. She crafted compromise legislation with her friend George Mitchell in the Senate to give the Democratic president an out. To avoid an all-out trade war, she called on Clinton to raise tariffs only on items made by state-run enterprises, like the People's Liberation Army. The goal was to punish the Communist state without harming its emerging entrepreneurial class.

On May 27, exactly one week before the deadline, Clinton phoned Pelosi in the middle of the lunch hour. She knew the news was going to be bad, but she had no idea how bad. Over the course of a 50-minute phone call, Clinton told Pelosi he intended to not only renew MFN for the following year but also permanently abandon the policy of linking trade to human rights.

Pelosi was furious. She felt betrayed. It was Clinton who had attacked President Bush for "coddling dictators." It was Clinton who had convinced her the previous year not to pass legislation because he would act unilaterally. And it was Clinton who had signed an executive order—with Pelosi standing behind him—calling on China to improve its human rights or lose its trade status.

Pelosi had spent her entire life supporting her party. But she didn't see how she could be taken seriously if she refrained from attacking the president.

"I cannot say one thing about George Bush's policy and another about Bill Clinton's when they are the same policy," she said shortly after the phone conversation.[17]

Using phrases she knew would be fighting words back in her district, she accused Clinton of distorting the facts to protect the business community and compared his statement on China to President Reagan's declaration that El Salvador had lived up to human rights standards despite sponsoring death squads.

Publicly she attacked Clinton for protecting the "butchers of Beijing." Privately she fumed that she'd made a big mistake by trusting him.

Pelosi remained in Washington a few days later, over the long Memorial Day weekend, in order to attend the White House wedding of Hillary Clinton's brother and Senator Boxer's daughter. However, relations between Pelosi and Clinton remained chilly for years. In 1996, at a United Nations anniversary session in San Francisco, Pelosi was seated next to national security advisor Tony Lake when Clinton said, "We will not limit our enthusiasm for human rights just because of the almighty dollar."

Pelosi turned to Lake.

"How could he possibly say that?"

Lake did not respond.[18]

Pelosi understood the importance of having a Democratic president, and though she abhorred his China policy, opposed his welfare reform proposal, and no longer trusted him, she dutifully stood behind his reelection.

"President Clinton is all that is standing between us and the Republican agenda," she said as the 1996 election approached. "Rather than say 'The era of big government is over,' I'd rather he say 'We want a government that is lean, not mean,' because government does have a role. But make no mistake, there is no doubt in my mind that President Clinton has done great things as president."[19]

PELOSI BECAME INCREASINGLY HOSTILE toward the business community, which earned billions from trade and spent millions of dollars lobbying to make sure that no obstacles stood in its way.

As the Clinton administration faced withering press scrutiny and a congressional investigation for accepting thousands of dollars worth of what turned out to be illegal campaign contributions from Chinese citizens, the Chinese were engaged in a much more ambitious and perfectly legal form of influence buying. The government in Beijing spent billions of dollars on products and services from US companies including Boeing, Ford, Time-Warner, and IBM. The

Chinese knew that in order to keep the lucrative relationship alive, the US companies would spend millions to keep MFN alive.

Pelosi ruefully observed that big deals with American companies seemed timed to influence the annual MFN fight and that big donations flowed to members who stood against her legislation.

And she made it clear that her position was not based on political calculations, decrying the China policy of her own party's president as "dictated by US businesses."

"That's why the president changed his view. Because big business weighed in," she said. "They have enormous resources. They are willing to spend an unlimited amount. And the money not only speaks, the money rules."[20]

She accused Clinton of selling out to America's "exporting elites" and said his policy "is being driven by the heavy, heavy lobbying effort of the business community."

Meanwhile, Pelosi formed an unlikely bond with social conservatives.

At one news conference in May 1997, Pelosi found herself standing with Republicans Smith and Wolf and Gary Bauer, a former policy advisor to President Reagan and president of the Family Research Council, which advocated constitutional bans on abortion and gay marriage.

"I'm Gary Bauer with the Family Research Council, and I'm proud this morning to be here with . . . Congresswoman Nancy Pelosi," he began his remarks, uttering words many would have a hard time believing were ever spoken.

Wolf, at the same news conference, gushed that "Nancy has done probably more on this issue than anybody else in Congress."

Pelosi flat-out rejected the argument that engagement—the term the business community used to describe open trade—would open up Chinese society and in the end lead to greater reforms.

"I don't believe in the concept of trickle-down liberty," Pelosi said.

Pelosi's vehemence on the issue was apparent when Chinese president Jiang Zemin came to Washington in October 1997 for a state visit. As guests inside the White House State Room, including Pelosi's old San Francisco neighbor Dianne Feinstein, dined on chilled lobster with corn leek relish and a Mandarin tea tartlet, Pelosi spoke to protesters through a tinny amplifier across the street at Lafayette Park.

"The Chinese know that money rules in Washington, DC," Pelosi charged.

Pelosi did not criticize Feinstein. Pelosi had led a delegation of California House members into Feinstein's Hart Building office just three days earlier for a private meeting to urge the former San Francisco mayor to run for governor. But in an interview during Jiang's visit, she was particularly scornful of Clinton, calling the state dinner "the ultimate coffee," a cruel reference to the fundraising events hosted by Clinton for wealthy contributors before his reelection.

"For the president to be rolling out the red carpet for a head of a regime that has slaughtered its children in Tiananmen Square is hard to understand . . . is totally inappropriate," Pelosi said in an interview.[21]

"As [Clinton] was toasting this tyrant at this event, he should remember that President Jiang controls the torture of [political prisoner] Wei Jingsheng and other prisoners of conscience in China. And he and his guests ought to think about it over dinner."

And in a glimpse of the depths for her disdain for the president, she added, "There is nothing more dangerous than a leader whose policy has failed and now he has to justify it. Clinton is very good at it. He can do it without blinking."

Pelosi opposed Clinton as he secured permanent trade relations with China a few years later, doing away with the annual MFN fight and allowing China to join the World Trade Organization.

"I lost that fight," Pelosi said after becoming Speaker, looking back on her efforts to use trade as a weapon to promote human rights in China. "It didn't seem like people cared so much about human rights after a while."

But she noted that the White House policy of engagement had not only failed to improve conditions in China, it had cost America jobs. Despite the insistence of presidents Bush and Clinton and the business community that trade sanctions would harm the domestic economy, she noted that the US trade deficit to China had grown 50-fold since she began the fight.

"So it didn't achieve any of the goals," she said of her opponents' policy. "It was a big success for K Street."

Each year on the anniversary of the Tiananmen Square massacre, Pelosi issued a statement to honor the students' sacrifice and call on the Chinese government to address human rights issues. She remained an outspoken critic of China, promoting freedom in Tibet, condemning China for providing military aid to Sudan, and warning Chinese leaders to allow open dissent during the 2008 Summer Olympics in Beijing.

CHAPTER TEN

LIFE IN THE MINORITY

"No. No, no, no, no. San Francisco? No."

**—NANCY PELOSI, WHEN ASKED WHETHER HER HOMETOWN HAD GROWN
MORE CONSERVATIVE AFTER REPUBLICANS TOOK OVER CONGRESS, 1996**

*"At the start of this Congress, the Republican majority gave you,
Mr. Speaker, the highest honor this House can bestow—the speakership.
The Republican majority did this after you, Mr. Speaker, were charged
with and admitted to lying under oath to the Ethics Committee about the
conduct of your political affairs. How inconsistent, then, Mr. Speaker,
for this same Republican majority to move to an impeachment
inquiry of the president for lying about his personal life."*

—NANCY PELOSI TO SPEAKER NEWT GINGRICH ON THE HOUSE FLOOR, 1998

THE REPUBLICAN SWEEP OF 1994 hit many Democrats like a two-by-four between the eyes. The GOP picked up 54 House seats to win control of the chamber for the first time since 1955. In the half century since Pelosi's father had left the House, Democrats had been the majority party for all but four years. Not a single member of the 104th Congress had ever served under GOP rule.

Pelosi had won 82 percent of the vote in San Francisco, but she returned to a decidedly more conservative Washington. Republicans captured eight seats in the Senate to take a 52 to 48 majority, a majority that swelled to 54 votes after Democrats Richard Shelby of Alabama and Ben Nighthorse Campbell of Colorado switched parties.

President Clinton's ambitious health care plan was dead, and the talk of the town was incoming House Speaker Newt Gingrich, who would be named *Time* magazine's "Man of the Year."

Pelosi hated losing the majority, but she loved life in Congress. She refused to accept that the country had rejected the core principles of the Democratic Party. Like her parents, she was working on the side of angels. Democrats were trying to help people. Republicans would do anything to protect the rich. She attributed the loss to tactics. Democrats had failed "to present a clear message to energize our base," and Republicans had "flooded the election with money."

"Being in the minority among moderate Republicans who share some of our values would be one thing. But being in the minority among the radical leadership we have in the House of Representatives is intolerable," Pelosi said after getting a taste for being in the minority.[1]

Years later she theorized that President Clinton's election had greatly enhanced Gingrich's hand by giving him a Democratic target to rail against.

"Newt Gingrich for a long time wanted to run against Washington. He couldn't, because Republicans were in [the White House]. The minute Bill Clinton was elected, through no fault of his own, he provided the environment for the [GOP] success. Now Newt Gingrich had an open field."

In a lengthy conversation a year into Gingrich's speakership, Pelosi said she felt sorry for her Republican friends in the Bay Area.

"They thought they were going to have their day with Republicans coming in. But I don't believe that many of them identify with the radical agenda of Newt Gingrich, which is anti-environment, which cuts investments in people, in their education, their health, and their job opportunities."

Pelosi seemed most put off by the conservative ideologues who had been swept in by the 1994 election, the ones who "speak of the word *compromise* as unprincipled—when it is, indeed, an art. If you compromise your principles, that is not a good thing. If you compromise in order to say, 'On every issue I understand that I can't have it my own way,' then that is trying to make progress."

Asked whether her own district was turning more conservative, Pelosi was incredulous.

"No. No, no, no, no. San Francisco? No."

She acknowledged that the tide had moved to the right on Capitol Hill, but only for the moment.

"Today. Today. We have another election [next] November. I always tell people, never confine your hopes and dreams to what is necessarily possible today. I'm not going to tell people to diminish their dreams. I love dreams. A politician likes to see a roomful of dreamers—an auditorium full of dreamers—because that's what this is about, about using imagination to make things better."

During her first five years in the House, with Democrats in control, Pelosi had built a record of legislative accomplishment and begun to stake out a national profile.

She followed her father's advice—and footsteps—and secured a seat on the Appropriations Committee during her third year, after beating back complaints that California already had too much clout on the powerful panel where all spending bills originate.

"People would say directly, 'I think California has too much and I don't want to vote for any more Californians,'" Pelosi complained after losing out on her first attempt for a seat.[2] (A decade later it would be California's clout and large numbers that would boost her efforts to break into the even more rarified air of the House leadership.)

The Appropriations seat put Pelosi in position to push for more spending on AIDS and other projects important to her district, boosted her ability to raise money, and solidified her relationships with veteran lawmakers who would be crucial to her future, such as Representatives John Murtha and David Obey (D-WI).

In 1992, Speaker Tom Foley tapped Pelosi to serve on the House Select Panel on Intelligence, which had jurisdiction over the nation's secretive intelligence community, and the Ethics Committee, which investigated complaints of wrongdoing by other members.

Pelosi made the argument that each assignment was right for her constituents—Appropriations would be good for AIDS, Intelligence helpful for relations with China—but she hardly needed to explain herself. After the bruising 1987 special election, Pelosi was left mostly unchallenged at home, winning reelection by huge margins that freed her to pursue battles in Washington. After edging out Harry Britt in 1987 by barely 4,000 votes in the primary, Pelosi compiled a remarkable string of 10 consecutive victories in which she won at least three-quarters of the vote. Despite the large margins, she paid close attention to the numbers and set a goal of winning at least 80 percent of the votes, something she did in every election after 1990. When a reporter casually mentioned her 80 percent tally in one election, she quickly corrected him: "Eighty-four percent."

The committee assignments also signaled her interest in playing a leadership role down the road. The Appropriations Committee is a prized perch for raising money and doling out favors. Intelligence Committee members receive classified briefings, and its members are well regarded for their foreign policy heft. And the Ethics Committee is a thankless insider's job that earns members the gratitude of their fellow members.

There were no obvious openings in the House leadership, yet Pelosi understood that fortunes change quickly on Capitol Hill. If the chance arose, Pelosi would be ready.

Pelosi was also named cochair of the 1992 Democratic Platform Committee, stepping in for Representative Mary Rose Oakar (D-OH) after it was revealed that she had bounced 213 checks at the House bank. Pelosi had 28 overdrafts herself, but that paled in comparison to the records of many of her colleagues.

Oakar was a friend, and Pelosi had campaigned for her in Ohio. During one campaign swing, Pelosi arrived in Cleveland after an overnight flight, but her baggage did not. She had worn sweats and a long coat on the red-eye and had planned to change into more formal attire upon landing. The event was first thing in the morning, and there was no time to go to a store to buy appropriate clothing. Pelosi calmly pulled her sleeves and pants legs up and draped her coat to conceal her outfit. No one at the rally had any reason to wonder why Pelosi's coat was buttoned so tightly.

Pelosi was thrilled by the platform committee appointment, which gave her national stature and allowed her to step beyond her fund-raising role and focus on policy.

"I've spent my life as a political organizer and, of necessity, have become a fund-raiser of some reputation, so now to get to be able to get to the heart of the matter, to the issues, is a source of satisfaction. I'm really unabashedly pleased," Pelosi said.[3]

For years she kept the California pylon that had identified her state's delegation on the convention floor as a memento in her office.

Presaging what would be the most successful year for women candidates in American history, Pelosi said at the start of the Democratic convention: "I think this is the year of the woman the way 1776 was the year for our country's declaration. I feel quite certain that it's real and it has staying power and it's going to change public policy forever."[4]

The 1992 Democratic platform reflected Bill Clinton's economic centrism.

Pelosi said she would have preferred a more liberal document, though her influence was apparent from planks declaring a war on AIDS and prohibiting discrimination against gays and lesbians.

"It's a platform about jobs, jobs, jobs," Pelosi told reporters, using the word seven times in her opening remarks on the first day of the convention. Clinton dispatched Pelosi as part of a small delegation to meet with billionaire Ross Perot in Texas about his on-again, off-again presidential campaign, trying unsuccessfully to persuade him that Clinton's economic policies addressed his concerns.

Pelosi's star was high enough that she had been mentioned as a possible vice presidential candidate for Clinton, a notion she laughed off.

"The perception of a Democrat from San Francisco is so far afield from where people across the country think the party should be," she said dismissively.

Despite Clinton's success in winning the White House, Democrats looked flummoxed as the GOP took control in 1995, passing their "Contract with America" and essentially shutting out the party that had been the majority for most of the past half century.

"It's appalling, and we have a responsibility to get the message out," Pelosi said of the Republicans' first budget in 1995, which Democrats decried for its effects on children, the elderly, and the poor. "When the American people understand what this GOP majority is about, they will reject them."

But that would not come for more than a decade. Pelosi had to adjust her tactics to find a way, even under a GOP majority, to remain *a voice that will be heard.*

Pelosi's language grew sharper. She could work with Republicans on China, the Presidio, and even on AIDS. But when it came to the Republicans' spending priorities or their socially conservative agenda, Pelosi grew increasingly confrontational.

On a hot July afternoon in 1997, as the House took up a foreign aid bill, Pelosi became angry when the GOP-controlled Rules Committee decided that only two abortion-related amendments—both written by Republican men—would be considered. One amendment would have denied money to any family planning organization that performed or promoted abortions, while the other would have forbidden any US dollars from being used to pay for abortions. Pelosi opposed both and grew livid when she was not allowed to present her own measure.

Pelosi took to the floor and accused the Republicans of cutting a "backroom deal . . . with not one Democrat or one Democratic woman present."

Ignored by Republicans, Pelosi enlisted the support of all 34 Democratic women, who essentially shut down the House proceedings by demanding roll call votes on routine matters to prevent Republican leaders from concluding the week's business.

"I am the ranking member of the Foreign Operations Committee," Pelosi said, her voice rising in anger. "There are not many women ranking members, and I insist on the respect the ranking member should receive."

The Democratic women of the House erupted in cheers as Pelosi finished speaking. Representative Rosa DeLauro of Connecticut gave her a hug and a kiss.

Pelosi's unwavering support for keeping abortions legal prompted some religious conservatives to question her Catholicism and others to call on priests to deny her communion during Mass. Like President Kennedy a generation before, Pelosi insisted that her faith—something she rarely talked about publicly—did not dictate her positions on public policy.

At the same time, Pelosi bristled whenever she was described as pro-abortion. Like many Catholics, Pelosi found abortion immoral. She never advocated abortion. She was pro-choice. Pelosi disapproved of the government imposing that moral judgment on all women.

After delivering a speech to NARAL—the National Abortion and Reproductive Rights Action League—during her first week as whip many years later, CNN host Robert Novak asked her, "Does that mean we can expect the Democratic Party in Congress to stress the abortion issue more than previously?"

"I don't think I made a speech on abortion," Pelosi responded coolly. "I made a speech on freedom of choice: choose to have a baby, choose not to have a baby. It was about reproductive freedom. And the generation that I'm in and that we're in, gentlemen, we hardly ever would use that word. So I didn't make a speech on that."

Pelosi's prickliness was well known to reporters.

Carolyn Lochhead, a longtime writer for the *San Francisco Chronicle's* Washington Bureau, wrote a column in 2001 detailing boorish comments made by Representative Pete Stark, Pelosi's neighbor from across the Bay. Stark had made a crack about Oklahoma representative J. C. Watts having had a child out of wedlock and had come close to getting punched out by the former University of Oklahoma quarterback.

Lochhead noted that it was not the first time that Stark's mouth had gotten him in trouble, pointing to past episodes in which Stark had called Republican representative Nancy Johnson of Connecticut a "whore" for the insurance industry and former Bush cabinet secretary Louis Sullivan, an African American, for being a "disgrace to his race."

Noting the silence of Stark's fellow Democrats, Lochhead wrote in the final paragraph of her column, "One can imagine the reaction if a rich white male Republican called Rep. Nancy Pelosi a whore, or Rep. Maxine Waters a disgrace to her race."

Pelosi did not like the analogy. In fact, she hardly spoke to Lochhead again. Pelosi expressed her anger to *Chronicle* publisher John Oppedahl, who ordered his editorial page editor, John Diaz, to phone Pelosi with an apology.

"I miss my parents every day," Pelosi told Diaz. "But the day that column appeared is a day I was glad they weren't around."

Lochhead sent Pelosi two written apologies. She never received a response.

While friends marveled at Pelosi's warmth, graciousness, and sense of humor, she was much more guarded with reporters. She stuck close to her talking points, a quality politicians find admirable and journalists find frustrating. She was often ill at ease with journalists and uncomfortable in front of a camera. Her brain was often so far ahead of her mouth that she'd frequently trip over her own lines, offering long paragraphs that seemed in need of periods, commas, or dashes.

She sometimes grew impatient with questions.

"Why are you even asking me this?" she asked another hometown reporter who inquired whether her move into the House leadership was good for her San Francisco constituents.

"Because some will complain that you are spending time on national issues rather than local ones," he responded.

"You find me that person and then we'll talk about it," Pelosi shot back.

At the same time, Pelosi devoured several newspapers a day and paid close attention to what was written. She was sometimes up as early as 5:30 a.m., frustrated that her papers hadn't yet arrived.

"I keep checking, checking, checking," she said.[5]

PELOSI TOOK UMBRAGE AT Gingrich's contempt for New Deal politics, as well as what she viewed as his lack of respect for the institution. Gingrich had arrived in Washington at about the same time that C-SPAN began airing gavel-to-gavel coverage of House proceedings, and he was the first to figure out how to best use the airtime to his advantage. Gingrich regularly requested speaking time at the end of the legislative day in order to challenge Democrats in fiery speeches broadcast across the country on cable television. Gingrich's taunts so enraged Speaker Tip O'Neill that one evening he ordered the cameras to pan the room as the Georgia lawmaker was speaking, revealing a near empty chamber and prompting a new rule that C-SPAN not stray from the speaker in the middle of speech.

Gingrich directed many of his speeches at O'Neill's successor as House Speaker, Jim Wright of Texas, leveling ethics charges that ultimately led to Wright's resignation in 1989. Democrats returned the favor when Gingrich became Speaker six years later, filing dozens of charges that ended up before the Ethics Committee. Pelosi spent hundreds of hours sifting through evidence in a process so secretive that she once had to kick Paul out of their bedroom at 3:00 a.m. so she could conduct a candid conversation by phone.

The investigation and its subsequent handling in the House hardened Pelosi's contempt for her GOP counterparts and once again thrust her into the role of a high-profile Republican antagonist.

The most serious charge against Gingrich involved his use of tax-exempt contributions for a college course he taught entitled Renewing American Civilization, which the panel determined was primarily aimed at advancing Gingrich's political goals. There was nothing wrong with using tax-free dollars to teach a college course and nothing wrong with pursuing political goals, but it was not permissible to use tax-free dollars to promote partisan causes.

In late 1996, the ethics panel concluded that Gingrich had acted either "recklessly or intentionally" to disregard House rules. More seriously, it concluded that he had provided "inaccurate, incomplete and unreliable" information during his testimony. Pelosi thought he had flat-out lied. Congress was in recess, and the findings would not be announced until January.

The politics of the situation were explosive. Gingrich was already a divisive figure whom Democrats had used during the election to try to drag down moderate Republican candidates. Republicans held a slim 22-seat majority, and the vote to elect Gingrich Speaker—typically the first order of business for a new Congress—was not automatic. Pelosi and other Democrats sought to postpone the vote until after the Ethics Committee presented its findings and recommended its punishment. Under House rules, a member who has been censured is ineligible to become Speaker.

Pelosi was stunned to learn on New Year's Day that GOP whip Tom DeLay had distributed a letter written by two Republican members of the Ethics Committee that stated that they intended to vote for Gingrich for Speaker.

"We know of no reason now, nor do we foresee any in the normal course of events in the future, why Newt Gingrich would be ineligible to serve as Speaker," the letter read.

Pelosi was furious. The letter in essence was tipping off GOP House members that the committee was not going to recommend censure for Gingrich. What the letter did not say was that the committee had agreed to a reprimand—backing down from a censure only because Democrats believed it would prolong the fight—in addition to a $300,000 fine. It would be the first reprimand or financial penalty ever levied against a Speaker. Gingrich had been told of the committee's recommendations and had agreed not to fight them.

For Republicans to claim that Gingrich was in essence not facing a serious penalty was a lie. For Pelosi to complain publicly would have violated the Ethics Committee's code of secrecy. All she could do was urge Republicans to hold off on their vote for Speaker, which, not surprisingly, they ignored. When the 105th Congress convened two days later, all but nine Republicans voted for Gingrich, who narrowly held on to his post.

Pelosi was appalled that Gingrich, who knew he faced penalties, would offer himself up for election. Two weeks later, when the ethics matter was brought before the full House, the GOP leadership rallied around their Speaker. DeLay, who was now majority leader, argued that Gingrich was being held to an impossible standard and concluded his speech by declaring, "Let's stop this madness, let's stop the cannibalism."

There was some irony to the phrasing. When Speaker Wright had resigned his post in May 1989 after an ethics investigation brought by Gingrich, he had called on his fellow lawmakers "to bring this period of mindless cannibalism to an end."

Pelosi stood on the floor and told her colleagues that their Speaker "is not to be believed.

"Others have said it's a sad day. I say it's a tragic day," she said.

The House voted 395 to 28 to impose the penalty that Gingrich had agreed to. By stopping short of censure, it allowed Gingrich—who remained off the floor in his private office during the proceedings—to keep serving as Speaker.

"The question is not whether he is technically qualified but whether he is ethically fit," Pelosi complained when the vote was complete.

It was not until the following day, when her term on the Ethics Committee officially came to an end, that she could openly vent her anger. Gingrich had shamed the institution, and Pelosi voiced her fury in an interview.

"What happened to the soul of the Republican Party?" she asked in disgust.

"If a person loved the House of Representatives, if he loved his party, he would step aside," she said of Gingrich. "Most of us have more respect for the job of Speaker than the Speaker himself."

She was further appalled that Gingrich had remained in his personal office rather than facing his accusers during the proceedings, which she called "a cowardly act."

"I never believed that he would step aside," she added derisively. "I know him a little better than that."

PELOSI WOULD DIRECTLY CHALLENGE GINGRICH in an extraordinary confrontation on the House floor the following year, when Republicans were seeking permission for an impeachment inquiry into President Clinton's lies about his sexual relationship with intern Monica Lewinsky.

Members of Congress rarely address each other directly during floor speeches, typically referring to "the gentleman from Georgia" or "my friend from California" to avoid the appearance of antagonism. But not this time.

Pelosi, speaking from an aisle on the House floor, looked squarely up at Gingrich, who was sitting at the Speaker's podium.

"At the start of this Congress, the Republican majority gave *you*, Mr. Speaker, the highest honor this House can bestow—the speakership," Pelosi said sternly. "The Republican majority did this after *you*, Mr. Speaker, were charged with and admitted to lying under oath to the Ethics Committee about the conduct of your political affairs.

"How inconsistent, then, Mr. Speaker, for this same Republican majority to move to an impeachment inquiry of the president for lying about his personal life.

"We all agree that lying is wrong. But why the double standard?"

Republicans jeered as Pelosi spoke. Democrats exploded in applause when she had finished.

Pelosi's reputation as a partisan bomb thrower grew during the Gingrich years. Her pointed attacks on the Speaker, her far-left voting record, her San Francisco district—all fed into a caricature of her as a liberal ideologue.

In fact, Pelosi's governing was very much following in Phil Burton's footsteps. Burton, in his two decades in Congress, had never served under a Republican majority. But both sought alliances between liberals, minorities, labor, and working-class Democrats to build broad coalitions. Both were willing to cut deals and bend legislation to pick up votes.

Pelosi didn't look the part of a backroom operator like her father. But with the exception of China—and even there to a certain degree—Pelosi was willing to seek out middle ground if it expanded the base of her support.

"I don't consider myself a moderate. But I certainly reach out to them," she said during one interview, seated on the leather couch of her Rayburn Building office. "There are plenty of reasons to vote against every bill that comes up here. You vote for nothing if you are an absolute, 100 percent purist—you would vote for no bill."[6]

She pointed to a statue of Burton that was sitting on her desk.

"I think Phillip Burton was a great deal maker. He knew that to get something done you had to get votes. And how do you get votes? You get votes by giving votes, get votes by educating people to what you are trying to achieve, and if there is something in your proposal that they couldn't accommodate, you had to see if that was part of your bottom line, if it was not something you could live without. You can deal with it later. There's always tomorrow, after all."

Her liberal voting record and biting rhetoric at times made it hard to see, but Pelosi was quite proud of her pragmatism.

When asked during the interview what was in her future, Pelosi said, "I have no plans to leave my job. My work is not finished."

"Do you have any interest in running for mayor of San Francisco?" she was asked.

"I never say never," Pelosi responded, offering that she didn't "have any personal ambition to run for mayor. As a little girl, I knew what it meant to be mayor. My father loved it and thrived at it, and my brother after that. But it was not something that I desired."

And what about in Washington? "Do you see yourself running for a leadership position in the House, such as Speaker or whip?"

"I don't," Pelosi responded unhesitatingly.

Pelosi explained that she anticipated rising to become the ranking member of the Foreign Operations Committee, a subcommittee of the House Appropriations Committee, which distributes dollars and has wide influence on foreign policy matters. When Democrats win back the majority, she said, she would be the chair of the subcommittee, a privileged position known as an Appropriations "cardinal," which would make her the first woman to hold that post.

"I would feel very successful at increasing the leverage of the people in my district to get that chairmanship."

In addition, she said, she enjoyed her work on the House Intelligence Committee.

"When you come here there are different avenues. You can get on the leadership track. Or you can work on your issues," she said. "I'd rather have a vote from my colleagues on an issue I'm interested in than a vote in a position for leadership. I like to spend my time legislating."

CHAPTER ELEVEN

THE PATH TO LEADERSHIP

"The sooner the public sees a woman in a leadership position,
the sooner we will get a woman in the White House."
—NANCY PELOSI, 1999

"It was like I had been hit in the head by a sledgehammer
and kicked in the stomach by a mule."

—NANCY PELOSI, AFTER LEARNING THAT GEORGE W. BUSH HAD BEEN
PROJECTED TO BE THE WINNER ON ELECTION NIGHT 2000

"FIRST, WE EAT."

Pelosi used those three words to open dozens of meetings that would take her
from lawmaker to the House's number one Democrat.

Typically it was gourmet sandwiches and a chocolate dessert in her office. Sometimes it was General Tso's chicken and sesame beef at the nearby Hunan Dynasty. The scent of chocolate replaced cigars, but these were very much the smoke-filled rooms of her father's day. Food was served. The doors were closed. Then Pelosi and her lieutenants would get down to the business of seizing power.

The House is a place with 435 overachievers: class presidents, city council presidents, state senators and assemblymen, business leaders, military officers, and successful community organizers. They are all winners by definition. Unlike the Senate, whose members until 1913 were elected by state legislators and can still be appointed by a governor to fill a vacancy, the only way to serve in the House is to win an election.

House leadership positions provide a chance to rise above the pack. Each party elects a leader, a whip, and a chair to run its caucus. In addition to the Speaker, who is chosen by the full House, it is these few members whose voices are heard above the din and who shape their party's agenda. Many have spent careers trying to win these positions. Many fewer have succeeded.

Sometime in the mid-1990s, Pelosi saw a path to the top.

Barbara Boxer recalled Pelosi telling her after only a few years in Washington that she wanted someday to be Speaker, though Pelosi has no recollection of saying any such thing. (Boxer said her reaction at the time was "You've got to be nuts.") Some of Pelosi's associates saw her positioning herself on key committees—Appropriations, Intelligence, Ethics—with an eye toward bolstering her credentials for a leadership run. And admirers noted early on that her money-raising skills, energy level, and comfortable relations with other members made her a natural for a leadership post, a notion that seemed to please Pelosi.

But the event that thrust Pelosi into openly seeking such a role was the retirement of Sacramento congressman Vic Fazio during Pelosi's 11th year in Congress. Fazio was an amiable consensus builder who had tirelessly worked his way from being a legislative aide in Sacramento to holding a seat in the California Assembly and eventually to serving in the US Congress. Adept at putting together coalitions, he had quickly moved up the leadership ladder, running the House Democrats' campaign committee during the 1994 and 1996 elections and being elected chair of the Democratic caucus, the party's number three post.

Speaking from the couch of her Rayburn Building office just a year before, Pelosi had said she did not envision herself ever running for either whip or Speaker, naming Fazio as a main consideration.

"He's our horse in the race. I don't see any reason in competing within our California delegation on the leadership track. And I'm not particularly interested."

But Pelosi knew that congressional life was taking a toll on Fazio. His Sacramento-area district had grown increasingly competitive. Fazio was a regular target for Republicans, and commuting between coasts was a terrible burden. His daughter was battling leukemia, and Fazio was rethinking his priorities.

Pelosi and Fazio were part of the same "reflection group," a small gathering of House members who, through the Faith and Politics Institute, met weekly with a member of the clergy for an hour-long private discussion. Pelosi was unwavering in her support of Fazio. No one suspects that she would have tried to replace him. But Pelosi knew that an opportunity might come.

On November 17, 1997, at age 55, Fazio announced his retirement from the House, saying, "I have come to the season in my life when I believe it is time to prioritize what matters most to me: the need to put aside the relentless pace of congressional service so I can give more time to family life."

The retirement touched off a flurry of activity in the Capitol, where ambition is more plentiful than opportunity. Pelosi looked at the composition of the House and its leaders in 1998 and saw the path.

Dick Gephardt of Missouri was the Democratic leader, and David Bonior of Michigan the whip. If Democrats won back the majority, Gephardt would become Speaker, Bonior would become majority leader, and the position of whip would be open. Democrats could hope, but few thought that with President Clinton facing an impeachment inquiry in the sixth year of his presidency, a Republican collapse was likely. That, however, was the short view. Even if

Democrats failed to win the majority, Gephardt had his eyes on the presidency and might well step away from the House. Bonior faced the possibility of Michigan Republicans redrawing his district. And there was always the prospect of Democrats winning back the House in 2000.

There had been no new faces in the Democratic leadership since Bonior was elected whip in 1991. Democrats were in the minority and ready for change.

Pelosi's path was cleared by Fazio's departure, leaving no Californian in the line of leadership. Pelosi talked to her old friend George Miller, who had represented the East Bay since 1975, to see if he was interested. He told her she should go for it.

"When Vic left, it was clear we had to have somebody run [from California]. I came here to do my issues and represent my district. I had not ever been plotting or planning for this," Pelosi said in an interview after Fazio's departure. "People said, 'You should run for leadership.' I always thought that Vic would be here, and he would go all the way. . . . California provides a strong base for someone to go forward."

The path was widened by the departure of Representative Barbara Kennelly, Pelosi's good friend and vice chair of the Democratic Caucus since 1994, who was returning to Connecticut to run for governor.

The top leadership of the House consisted of a Tom, a David, a Dennis, and two Dicks. Everyone could see that there was a serious lack of women among the ranks of leaders.

For a party that drew well over half of its support from women voters, clearly there was a powerful incentive to put a woman in charge.

If the Democrats were in the doldrums, Pelosi was ready to provide some oomph. She had the confidence, the energy, the fund-raising connections, and the hunger to push the Democrats back into the majority. House Democrats had now lost consecutive elections, and Pelosi believed that she was in a strong position to end the streak.

The uncertainty among Democrats set the stage for a long period of fighting and repositioning, the effects of which would be felt for at least another decade. For 50 years Democrats had taken their majority for granted. Now they needed to find someone to lead them back to power.

Many names were discussed: Steny Hoyer of Maryland, who had led the caucus and run against Bonior for whip in 1991; Martin Frost of Texas, head of the House Democrats' campaign committee; and deputy whips Chet Edwards of Texas, Robert Menendez of New Jersey, Rosa DeLauro of Connecticut, and John Lewis of Georgia. Conservatives felt they needed one of their own to steer the party back to the center, and John Tanner of Tennessee, Charlie Stenholm of Texas, Gary Condit of California, James Moran of Virginia, and Tim Roemer of Indiana were put forward as potential leaders. Maxine Waters and Xavier Becerra of California and Louise Slaughter of New York were all discussed as leaders who could potentially broaden the party's appeal.

But no one was better situated to pounce on the opportunity than Pelosi. She had arrived at Congress on a higher plane, able to use the connections she'd built during years of service at Democratic functions, as chair of the California Democratic Party, in her work at the party's 1984 convention, and in her role in the 1986 Senate election. Her committee assignments gave her standing.

Pelosi's stature had continued to grow. She was once again being talked about as a potential vice presidential candidate, something she again dismissed as far-fetched given her liberal reputation and voting record. ("Compatible with my district, but maybe not compatible with a presidential nominee," she said. "No way I could mold my thinking to another person.")

And on top of all of that, there was the money. Only a handful of House members were able to raise as much money as Pelosi. Members would come through San Francisco, where Pelosi would arrange a gathering with some of her vast network of friends. Sometimes a reception would be held at Pelosi's home, sometimes at a friend's. Other times Pelosi would just phone people and ask them to contribute to colleagues in tough campaigns. Members would leave tens of thousands of dollars richer and extremely grateful.

It was money that ultimately convinced Pelosi to run for a leadership position. After raising thousands of dollars for Lois Capps, who won a special election in early 1998 to replace her husband after he died of a heart attack at Dulles airport on his way back from his district, Pelosi was increasingly asked, "What are you getting out of this?"

Pelosi for years had worked on behalf of the party. Even as an elected official, she had used her Northern California connections to distribute hundreds of thousands of dollars to needy Democrats. In early 1998, Pelosi brought President Clinton to her friends Bill and Sally Hambrecht's home for a $10,000-a-head dinner and atop Nob Hill for a $500-per-person reception.

"When Nancy Pelosi almost drank my water," Clinton told the overflow crowd at the Fairmont Hotel, "I thought to myself, she has carried so much water for me she ought to drink some of it."

So if Pelosi was raising the money, why wasn't she calling the shots?

In the D'Alesandros' home on Albemarle Street, the favors were eventually called in. Now there were scores of elected officials around the country who owed Pelosi.

"She raised the fucking dough, she ought to be able to get something for it," said her good friend John Burton. "My theory in life is those who pay the piper call the tune. That's why she decided to run for leadership. Because her friends are saying, 'You're raising all this money, and where are you in the picture?'"

In Washington, there was enormous interest in Pelosi taking over the Democratic Congressional Campaign Committee, the DCCC, which would have been a natural use of her skills as a fund-raiser and strategist. Democratic leader Dick Gephardt approached Pelosi about taking the position, and many of her supporters thought it made great sense.

But Pelosi had loftier ambitions. She was good at raising money, but she didn't want to be limited to doing that.

"I hate it," she said in an interview several years later. "I don't know anybody who enjoys it. I admit this. I am good at it."

Pelosi said her fund-raising ability came from carefully listening to people and having a strong sense of what they were interested in. She was known for her incredible attention to detail, for sending her donors gracious notes, their favorite flowers, or, in one case, a bottle of pomegranate bath oil to a supporter passionate about the fruit. She would set specific targets for potential donors and ask them only to contribute to candidates she felt were good matches.

"People rarely say no. They'll [give] something," she said.

But the money was a means to an end. Pelosi wanted to be making decisions that would bring Democrats back to the majority.

Pelosi would no more challenge Gephardt or Bonior than she would Fazio. She said so publicly, and no one doubted her sincerity. But she was enough of an inside player to have identified the longer path. The first step would be whip, but those who knew her understood that Pelosi was aiming to become Speaker.

"The time has come. The opportunity is there," Pelosi said in conversation as she began her pursuit. "Being in leadership strengthens your hand in every issue you are involved with. You are more than a member. Anything you are interested in becomes more important. Anything you say is important because you are a leader.

"I love the House," she said. "I have no statewide ambitions. I don't want to be appointed to any cabinet positions. I'm not into derivative power. I like to get it on my own. People have asked me, 'What will you do next? You have to move up and do something.' Now I see my path, which is to do that in the House."

REPRESENTATIVE STENY HOYER HAD gone through a different set of calculations and reached a similar conclusion.

Hoyer was the very picture of a House leader. His long, chiseled face, large frame, and backslapping arms could easily have been transposed onto the portraits of statesmen that adorn the Capitol. He had been in politics since his days at the University of Maryland, where as a young Democrat he'd gone by the

D'Alesandro house on Albemarle Street to pay his respects. He'd worked in Maryland senator Brewster's office with Pelosi, and when she left to marry Paul, he'd stuck around and become one of the senator's top aides. He won election to the Maryland Senate at age 27—at roughly the time that Pelosi was giving birth to her fourth child—and eight years later became the body's youngest president. Like Pelosi, he'd won a seat on the House Appropriations Committee, and in Pelosi's second term—with her support—he became the chair of the Democratic Caucus.

Hoyer was well liked. He had a friendly, easygoing manner, was extraordinarily articulate, and was comfortable with members who supported different ideologies. He was the image, drawn from stereotypes dating back hundreds of years, of what a congressional leader looked like. Anyone who knew him understood that he aspired to become Speaker, and many assumed he'd succeed. Hoyer had lost his wife, Judith, a high school sweetheart, to cancer in 1997, but he was not backing away from the House.

Pelosi and Hoyer were friends. They had known each other for nearly 40 years, had served together on the Appropriations Committee's labor and health panel, and helped each other raise money. When Hoyer had run for whip in 1991 against Bonior, Pelosi had seconded his nomination in a speech before the Democratic Caucus.

"She was a Marylander. I was a Marylander. We were friends. We had known each other a long time. She and I got along well," Hoyer recalled.

So it came as a shock when, during a congressional recess in the summer of 1998, Hoyer received a phone call from Pelosi in which she bluntly announced that she was running for whip.

There was an awkward silence on the phone as Hoyer collected himself. Most people had assumed that Hoyer would try for the position when it became vacant, and he had thought she'd be with him. Instead, Pelosi was putting Hoyer on notice that she would be standing against him.

"It was not 'Are you running again?' or 'What would you think of my running?' or 'Would you have any objections?'" Hoyer recalled.

"*Hurt* might be the right word, coupled with *disappointment*," Hoyer said, reflecting on the conversation seven years later. "But you know, I've been around a long time as well. I got the message."

Pelosi made it known to her colleagues a few days later, distributing a letter that read: "If we expect to win we must act like winners. . . . I, therefore, want you to know that I intend to run for a leadership position in the new Congress. It is my assumption that we will win, that Dick Gephardt will become Speaker and that Dave Bonior will become Majority Leader, leaving the Whip position as the highest opening for new leadership in the 106th Congress."[1]

Pelosi's ambition didn't make headlines in the summer of 1998, in part because almost no one expected the Democrats to win the majority. The political world was far more caught up in President Clinton's testimony in front of a grand jury and televised admission of having an "inappropriate relationship" with 24-year-old intern Monica Lewinsky.

Pelosi, who had been sharply critical of Clinton for his China policy, was steadfast in her defense of his presidency.

"The president's actions are cause for embarrassment but not for impeachment," Pelosi said the day of Clinton's public confession.

The sixth year of a presidency is historically a rotten time for the president's party in Congress (as Republicans would learn a few years later). Democrats didn't win a majority, but anger over Republicans' zeal for impeachment cost the GOP five seats, shrinking their advantage to 223 to 211 with one Independent, the narrowest House margin since the Eisenhower administration.

"The position of whip is not available," Pelosi said after election day. "We'll have a hat in the ring for the next time."[2]

A week later Democrats returned to Washington to pick their leaders. Martin Frost edged out Rosa DeLauro as the head of the caucus. That meant there were no women in the Democratic leadership, not even in deputy positions. Party leaders knew it was a problem and quickly named Bay Area Democrat Ellen Tauscher to a deputy post at the DCCC. It was clear a woman needed to step forward.

Pelosi was focused on being that woman. Dismissing the chatter about placing her on a national ticket, Pelosi made it plain that she intended to make her contribution in the House.

"Think of me in terms of a majority whip or whatever comes after that," she said in an interview in early 1999. "The sooner the public sees a woman in a leadership position, the sooner we will get a woman in the White House."[3]

Sensing that Republicans would struggle to hold on to their thin majority, Democrats began preparing to take over. Pelosi moved into a penthouse apartment, with sweeping views of the Potomac and plenty of room to entertain.

She began a series of casual dinners. They ate at Barolo's, a pricey Italian restaurant a few blocks from the Capitol, or at Hunan Dynasty just down the street. Sometimes they ate catered food at Pelosi's apartment. Word quickly spread that Pelosi was campaigning for the whip job.

"My colleagues were saying, 'Oh my God, she's campaigning, she's campaigning,'" Pelosi said. The attention prompted dozens of phone calls from members telling her that if she were a candidate, they'd support her.

Pelosi's public posture was that this was about winning the House, not the whip's job. She had her eyes on four California districts where she thought Democrats could take seats from Republicans. It would take only seven Democratic pickups nationwide to win back the majority. She was optimistic. Yet no one doubted that the subtext was Pelosi's plan to run for whip.

"I was testing the waters, and the waters were warm," she said.

By August, Pelosi was off and running.

"I hope this letter finds you enjoying your family, your community and other sources of renewal before our return to Congress after Labor Day," Pelosi said in a note to fellow California Democrats in the first week of the August recess.

"During the August fund-raising doldrums, I have benefited from conversation with members on their expectations on *how we can achieve victory* in November 2000 for our Party and on *how we should proceed* after we achieve a House majority," she wrote.

"The response to my interest in becoming a candidate for Majority Whip in the Democratic-led House has been excellent and my endeavor to unseat Tom DeLay is going exceedingly well," she wrote.

Pelosi spent hours on the phone. By her count she talked to almost 150 members.

"I've spoken to everyone who wants to be spoken to."

Pelosi was as aggressive as she could be within the boundaries of House protocol. She said she was careful not to intrude on members' "legislative zone," saying she didn't want her colleagues to feel that they had to avoid her.

"What I have said is when you are ready to talk about this, I'm here."

Her rivals complained that it was too early to start such internal politicking. Representative John Lewis, who had said he was running, sent a letter to his colleagues quoting scripture: "The Book of Ecclesiastes reminds us that for everything there is a season." And 15 months before an election that Democrats had not yet won was not it. Hoyer also complained about the early start, saying that he would have to get active or be left behind.

Even veteran lawmaker Jack Murtha, whom Pelosi would enlist to run her whip campaign, grumbled, "I can't believe we're getting into this now. We don't have a goddamned vacancy for a whip. We don't even have a majority yet."[4]

But Pelosi had made a tactical decision to start early. She believed that Paul Kirk's early entry into the DNC race had cost her the chair's position in 1985. She believed that Hoyer had started too late in his bid against Bonior for whip almost a decade before.

Pelosi was not going to make the same mistake.

"In order to buck two hundred years of history, if I have to start earlier than someone else, so be it," she declared.[5]

PELOSI BEGAN THE RACE FOR WHIP with some strong advantages. She had a geographic edge by being from the largest state. When Phil Burton had lost his contest to become Democratic leader in 1976, California had 43 House members. By 1999 California had 52 members, 28 of them Democrats. Pelosi had spent hundreds of hours—and hundreds of thousands of dollars—getting her California colleagues elected and sitting with them on long flights between Washington Dulles and San Francisco International airports. She had strong support from the women of the House. And she was popular among liberals, with whom she voted consistently.

But that would not be enough. To win support from a majority of House Democrats, Pelosi needed help from conservative Democrats, who hardly recognized, let alone approved of, her district's politics. And she needed the support of the institutionalists, the old dogs who'd been around long before the notion of a woman leader was imaginable.

It is here that Pelosi distinguished herself from a previous generation of women leaders. Bella Abzug and Pat Schroeder had been popular and powerful legislators, but they had also worn their gender on their sleeves and at times gone to war with men who were far less accustomed to having women among them.

SCHROEDER RECALLED AN INCIDENT, predating Pelosi's arrival at the House, when her hallway neighbor Representative Charlie Rose of North Carolina couldn't use a pair of tickets to a black-tie sports banquet and kindly handed them off. Schroeder had no interest in the affair but thought her husband would kill her if she didn't take him, so they got a babysitter, dressed in formal attire, and arrived at the Washington hotel, where the event was taking place.

They walked in and suddenly Schroeder was surrounded.

"Do you want us to walk you out or should we carry you out?" she was asked.

"What do you mean?" she inquired.

"No women are allowed," came the response. Schroeder was beside herself.

"Really," she recalled telling the men. "The way I remember the Civil Rights Act of 1964, if you're a public hotel and you're selling tickets you can't . . ."

"Don't get smart with us," someone interrupted, as most of her colleagues stood around saying nothing.

"No one spoke up. It was, 'Oh, Pat, why do you do this? Why don't you just go home?'"

Such an incident would never have happened to Pelosi. She was an institutionalist. Her father had served. She understood the mannerisms and the tempo of the House. She had a way with the older members. She would chop her opponents off at the knee in a policy dispute. In a social setting, however, she would never come across as menacing.

HER FRIEND JACK MURTHA was a big help. Murtha was a crusty old Marine who'd been around for longer than almost anybody, holding court in the back row of the House chamber, known as the "Pennsylvania corner." He'd remind the old-timers of Thomas D'Alesandro and Pelosi's Baltimore roots.

She also needed the Blue Dogs, a coalition of several dozen fiscally conservative members who represented districts where the term "San Francisco Democrat" was not a term of endearment.

She enlisted Gary Condit of Modesto, one of the Blue Dogs' founding members, and Mike Thompson, whom she'd just helped win election.

Thompson, who'd received a Purple Heart in Vietnam, represented a district that stretched from Napa Valley, where Pelosi owned a small vineyard and vacation home, to the Oregon border. He had served in the California Senate for eight years and credited Pelosi with having cleared his path to Washington. In his run for Congress, he had faced a stiff primary challenge from Michaela Alioto, the granddaughter of former San Francisco Mayor Joe Alioto, Pelosi's old neighbor on Presidio Terrace. Alioto had run in 1996 and lost by less than 7 percentage points, leading many strategists to believe she had a shot the next time. Thompson, a budget hawk and self-styled moderate Democrat, didn't see it that way. Other local Democrats had won their races by 10 to 15 points in that same year. Alioto lost because she was too liberal for the district, whose politics Thompson figured were closer to his own.

He made the case to Pelosi, who then had a blunt conversation with Alioto and told her she'd support Thompson.

"Nancy got that, right away," Thompson said. "She told her, 'If Mike runs, he not only wins running away, but he can hold the seat.'"

Alioto backed off. Thompson was forever indebted.

It was a story that he'd tell countless Blue Dogs in Washington: You think Pelosi is a liberal ideologue? Then why did she support me? The answer is that Pelosi is committed to Democrats winning.

Pelosi had lived roughly half her life on the West Coast and half her life in the East. Her tactics recalled her Baltimore upbringing. But her outlook, she asserted in countless conversations, was rooted in San Francisco, which was in the midst of a technology-driven explosion.

Newt Gingrich had railed against big government, the institution of Congress, and Washington itself when he was a member of the minority trying to win power. That was not Pelosi's style. But Pelosi did fault the Republican majority for standing in the way of innovation and change, often comparing the mind-set of her two homes.

She was taken by journalist Michael Lewis's description of the creative genius behind the rise of Silicon Valley in his book *The New New Thing* and distributed scores of copies to her fellow Democrats.

"We are the source of so many ideas," Pelosi said in a lengthy interview. "I go home every week. I come back here and it's like going into a time warp. People come from all over the world to see what's happening in our area, to see the speed with which our technology is changing and what that means in terms of the economy and education, and that whole entrepreneurial spirit carries over to protecting the environment and dealing with education and other issues—just solving problems.

"Then you come back here and you're engaged in debates based on old, stale assumptions. It's practically irrelevant to what is going on in the state. It's not only about the state of California. It's a state of mind that exists in our area that has to be represented at the table."

Pelosi said she was not drawn by the publicity or ceremonial aspect of leadership. But she thought her western outlook could help Democrats win.

Pelosi reflected in the interview on what it meant to be a woman seeking such a position. She began, as she did each time she addressed the issue in dozens of subsequent conversations, speeches, and interviews, by asserting her credentials: "I did not run on that basis. I know the issues, politics, money. I think I score high in all those categories."

At the same time, Pelosi was well aware of how historic and appealing a woman's rise would be in what had always been a man's institution. If the party wanted to prove that it was committed to change, there was no more eloquent way to do so than to put a woman—for the first time in history—in the upper echelons of leadership.

"The fact that I happen to be a woman I think is a real asset; to say to people in our country, whether they are men or women, that when the Democratic Party wins, a woman will be one of the top leaders of the party.

"It says to women out there, we're going into a new millennium and guess what, we may have a woman for the first time in the history of our country in the top leadership and on the ladder. Where the ladder goes? Who knows? Eleven years I've been here, people have come and gone that we all thought were going to be Speaker one day. But I would be very happy to be at that table.

"I'm ready. I really am ready for this. I have been a slugger and a fighter and an advocate. It's a very big deal. You don't know what it could lead to, but understand, it's a very big deal."

Asked if she wanted to someday become Speaker, she diplomatically noted that she supported Gephardt. But she added: "I wouldn't rule it out."

"If the whip position were not a stepping-stone to Speaker," she noted candidly, "it wouldn't be as competitive."

THE WHIP CAMPAIGN PUT a great strain on Pelosi and Hoyer's long relationship. They had worked together for many years and even danced a salsa at a Democratic gathering as the year opened. But each was an obstacle to the other's ambitions. Animosity was building between their staffs. The media looked for conflicts between the two as a vehicle to keep telling the story. Pelosi was convinced that Hoyer's camp was feeding bad reports about her to the press. The race would not be over for another year, but it had already gone on for too long. It consumed Capitol Hill political conversations and defined nearly every extracurricular activity.

Most of the nation was paying little attention. Vice President Gore was battling Bill Bradley for the Democratic presidential nomination; Texas governor George W. Bush was fending off a challenge by Arizona senator John McCain on the Republican side.

Hoyer's campaign manager was Ben Cardin, a Maryland lawmaker who, coincidentally, held Pelosi's father's old congressional seat. Cardin claimed his candidate had the support of 70 members and at least 90 if the voting went to a second ballot.

"It is now clear [Hoyer] has the support of the largest number of members of our Caucus of any candidate," Cardin asserted in a letter to Democrats.[6]

It was a claim that the Pelosi camp didn't believe. Bonior, who'd run against Hoyer in 1991, told Pelosi not to trust Hoyer's numbers. Count your own votes, he advised, but don't trust Hoyer's totals.

"If the election were today, there's no question I would win. The only question is the margin," Pelosi said confidently.[7]

Pelosi remembered the lessons she had learned in her failed bid to become DNC chair in 1985 and was relentless in her persistent appeals.

Pelosi was raising prodigious amounts of money, distributing nearly $500,000 to fellow House candidates as the election year began. Hoyer had donated just over $100,000.

"If money is the arbiter of who's going to win this race, I don't expect to win it," Hoyer said.[8]

Republicans held a 13-seat advantage going into the election, their smallest margin since they had taken control in 1994. That meant Democrats needed to win seven seats in order to win back control. If Pelosi could help the party pick up four seats in California and Democrats across the rest of the nation could pick up three more, they'd be back in the majority.

Lewis dropped out in July 2000 after sensing he would never get enough votes to prevail. He backed Hoyer after receiving assurances that Hoyer would appoint minorities to key posts if he won. Pelosi contended that while Hoyer got Lewis's endorsement, she got most of his supporters.

Pelosi came through as promised on election night. Democrats made a clean sweep in California. Every House Democrat running for reelection won. Meanwhile, Democrats Mike Honda, Jane Harman, Susan Davis, and Adam Schiff all knocked off Republican incumbents. In addition, Democrats technically picked up a fifth California seat when Democrat Hilda Solis beat Republican Matt Martinez, who had switched his party affiliation after losing his primary. The news was not as good in the rest of the country. Outside California, Democrats lost three seats, which meant a net Democratic gain of just two. It would be another two years in the minority for House Democrats.

OF COURSE, ANOTHER POLITICAL story was making bigger news. Preliminary counts showed that Texas governor George Bush led Vice President Gore in Florida by just several hundred votes. Gore had 500,000 more votes nationwide, but neither side could win without Florida's 25 electoral votes. The news media had first called the state for Gore and then Bush. Now it was said to be too close to call.

Pelosi was dining with Leo McCarthy at the Globe Restaurant, a trendy establishment in downtown San Francisco, and checking in regularly with her daughter Alexandra, who was working for ABC News covering the Bush campaign in Austin. Shortly before midnight, she got a call from her friend Roz Wyman, who told her that Bush had just been declared the winner.

"It was like I had been hit in the head by a sledgehammer and kicked in the stomach by a mule," Pelosi said.

By 6:30 the next morning she was on a conference call with party leaders. Pelosi figured that if all the unsettled House races went the Democrats' way, they could get up to 216 seats, but she recognized that they couldn't get the 218 needed for a majority.

"We'll be ready to fight in any special election," Pelosi vowed that afternoon. "Today is the beginning of the election for 2002."

Without a majority there was no immediate opening in leadership. Gephardt would remain leader and Bonior the whip. Pelosi said it was just a matter of time.

"I am more confident than ever that I will be in the leadership. It's just a matter of when," she said.

The turn of events in Florida made it difficult for even a political pro like Pelosi to make a clear assessment of the future.

"I think that right now, today, everyone's judgment is impaired. *Surreal* is the word that comes to mind. It seems so unlike anything we have known before in politics," she said.

"It is clear to me from the election that the country is evenly divided on the issues. It's reminiscent of 1960 with Kennedy and Nixon. With the Republicans in Congress and 'we-don't-know-who' the president, it behooves the Democrats to be clearer with our message."

She immediately—and rightly—predicted that whether the election was resolved in Bush's or Gore's favor, the winner would claim a mandate.

"Bill Clinton never had a majority of the vote in either [of his two elections], and he proceeded with the idea that he had a mandate," Pelosi noted. "Once the president wins, the American people are willing to give him a chance to implement his own initiatives—and that is a mandate separate and aside from the size of his margin. Whoever wins this will claim a mandate.

"This is a conversation better had on Friday," she said of the overall political outlook, "when we know who is the president of the United States."

IT WOULD BE ANOTHER SIX WEEKS until the Supreme Court declared Bush the winner. Pelosi, like many Democrats, became increasingly strident about Gore's case and pessimistic over the prospects of a Bush presidency.

On the Sunday after Thanksgiving, when Florida Secretary of State Kathleen Harris—a cochair of Bush's election campaign—declared Bush the victor, Bush called upon Gore to drop his challenge, prompting Pelosi to compare Bush to Napoleon trying to seize the crown.

"I've told them from the start, Republicans will take this to the last grain of sand. This is a *tactic* to declare victory. Just because the cochair of the George Bush campaign is secretary of state of Florida does not mean George Bush is the president of the United States.

"I think it is absolutely essential for the Gore campaign to exhaust every remedy," she said as the election rolled into December. "Democrats are with Al Gore every step of the way.

"Any sense that George Bush is going into this as a unifier or reaching out in a bipartisan way is completely destroyed by the actions taken by his legal team," she declared.

Meanwhile, on Capitol Hill, Democrats were trying to figure out how they would retake the majority in 2002. Pelosi was again approached by Gephardt about running the DCCC. She had no interest. She was aiming higher.

THE SAME ELECTION THAT ultimately installed George W. Bush as president gave Republicans control of the Michigan legislature, and Pelosi knew that Bonior—faced with tough redistricting and likely a strong GOP challenge—was considering a long-shot bid for governor. To do so, he would need to leave his House seat.

"He can take all the time in the world to decide," Pelosi said. "He's a great whip, a great resource. I hope he stays here."

But even as she said it, Pelosi knew that Bonior's time was limited.

As the 107th Congress convened, Pelosi was named the ranking member on the Intelligence Committee, putting her in line to become chair if the Democrats took control. It also put her among an elite group who received more extensive intelligence information than their committee counterparts. The committee was already far more secretive than most. To reach the committee's offices, members needed to go to a private stairwell in the Capitol's basement, known as the Crypt, and ride an elevator to the fourth floor at the base of the dome. It was there, in specially encased, windowless rooms, that the nation's top secrets could be discussed.

The year 2001 would turn out to be a very important year for intelligence.

BONIOR MADE IT OFFICIAL IN MAY. He would run for governor rather than stand for reelection. The whip race, now well into its third year, took on a new urgency. Many members had already taken sides. But there were enough new or undecided members to keep either side from relaxing. When a congressman representing Virginia's tobacco country died, Pelosi and Hoyer each rushed $10,000 to the candidate they hoped would replace him.

Pelosi's team met weekly in her office. Lots of chocolate was consumed. Murtha, who was the campaign manager, recalled there being lots of women at the meetings who were thrilled by the prospect of Pelosi advancing ideas that would be popular to women and attract even more women to Congress.

"I'd say, 'Look'—with mostly women in the room—I'd say, 'Let me just make something clear. There are a hell of a lot more men in this goddamn Congress than women, so let's be a little careful about what you're pushing here.'

"And they'd quiet down for a while, and I'm sure as soon as I left they'd go right back to where they were," Murtha said.

Behind the scenes Murtha was playing a critical role. There remained a sizeable number of influential members who were concerned about a San Francisco liberal—an outspoken and partisan woman, no less—taking a job that might someday take her to the speakership. For many members this had less to do with sexism than winning. Based on past experience, many could picture a backslapping consensus builder like Hoyer leading them to victory. They had never seen a woman do that. Murtha told them that Pelosi was the one.

"I told them this woman had vision and political skills that nobody else in the Congress had," Murtha said. "Don't think she's from San Francisco. She's from Baltimore."[9]

Murtha also had frank conversations with Gephardt, who many thought was inclined to help Hoyer. Gephardt never interceded, which many believe was the result of Murtha's appeal to stay neutral.

On the flip side, Hoyer's camp was dismayed by the number of male members who told him they needed to vote for Pelosi for their own political well-being. They wanted to tell their constituents that they were making history.

By MIDSUMMER DEMOCRATS WERE obsessed with a counting game. With 215 eligible Democrats—including nonvoting House members such as Eleanor Holmes Norton of Washington, DC, and the representatives from American Samoa—it would take 108 votes to win. Pelosi released the names for 90 public endorsements and claimed to have another dozen who wished to remain anonymous.

The voting in a leadership race is conducted by secret ballot, which makes vote counts highly unreliable. When Phil Burton ran in 1976, he had assurances from a majority of his colleagues that they'd vote for him. And he lost. The same had happened with a succession of women candidates through the '70s and '80s. Their male colleagues would promise them their support, but when the votes were tallied, they'd lost. It was said that the only vote to count on was from a member who looked you in the eye and told you he or she was going to vote for your opponent. All others were suspect.

The public remained focused on other matters. Chandra Levy, a 24-year-old intern at the Bureau of Prison Affairs, disappeared in April, and her body was discovered in Washington's Rock Creek Park more than a year later. The tragic story was complicated by Levy's relationship with Representative Gary Condit of Modesto, which propelled the lurid tale into Washington's number one story for most of the summer.

Condit was a veteran of California politics and a vital link for Pelosi to the conservative Blue Dogs. As other members of Congress stayed clear of the scandal, Pelosi stood beside Condit, insisting that the firestorm had not affected his ability to serve as a member of Congress.

"I know one thing for sure, and that is Gary Condit had nothing to do with her disappearance," Pelosi said in a mid-July interview. "I know the person. I've known him for years. I know the state, I know the people in the district, I know the Democrats, the donor base as well. I don't think there's one person who thinks any differently than that."

Without taking away from the tragedy of Levy's disappearance, Pelosi was appalled by the amount of media attention, telling Condit, "What you can't do is let the press have that victory."[10]

THE BANNER HEADLINE OF the Capitol Hill newspaper *Roll Call* jarred the Pelosi forces during the first week of August, as members were embarking on their summer recess: "Pelosi Denies Whip Threats: Tauscher Charges Intimidation."

The article detailed accusations by Ellen Tauscher, who was the only California Democrat to publicly support Hoyer, that Pelosi was trying to punish her by using California's redistricting plan to redraw her congressional district boundaries.

"I frankly can't believe that [Pelosi] would risk the [House] majority to get a leadership post," Tauscher said in the article.

Tauscher said she supported Hoyer because, coming from a more conservative district, she thought his was the face the party needed to put forward.

It was hard to tell what angered Pelosi more: the accusation that she would tinker with a member's district as retribution, the idea that a fellow Bay Area Democrat whom Pelosi had helped win election would support her opponent, or the idea that an ideological divide separated her and Hoyer.

"It's not even worth my time to talk about," she barked at a reporter who quizzed her about the redistricting matter.

Pressed about the perception that Hoyer appealed to moderates while she appealed to liberals, Pelosi grew testy.

"Here I am on the brink of making history. Here I am on the brink of changing the way people think about these issues . . . and you are stuck on a record that has no real significance.

"You're talking new-old. You've got to reject that because that's holding you back. There's no real difference in our voting record. This is about how you do things. You're stuck in tired old assumptions of the past. You're being spun."

Pelosi did possess a more liberal voting record. In 1999, the *National Journal* ranked Pelosi as the 15th most liberal member of the House, while Hoyer ranked 109th. However, the year before, Pelosi had ranked 80th while Hoyer ranked 94th. While Pelosi consistently leaned further to the left, on the most consequential issues their votes were nearly identical.

Pelosi was frustrated by descriptions of the race as a contest between the left and right. She believed the difference between her and Hoyer was her western, "entrepreneurial" outlook and her ability to win elections.

"We have lost four times in a row. We have won in the West. I know how to win elections," she said.

"We get on the plane every week and come back, not to be wedded to the old way of doing things, or stale assumptions," Pelosi said in another interview. "We can find a way to get it done. It's in the water we drink, the air we breathe; you go back to Washington and it's like you hit a wall of . . . resistance."

Meanwhile, Pelosi had raised nearly $5 million for the party. Only Democratic leader Gephardt and Representatives Patrick Kennedy of Rhode Island and Charlie Rangel of New York, the senior Democrat on the Ways and Means Committee, had raised more.

She believed she had the votes, but it was close. Her staff sent out 18 letters from different combinations of lawmakers—Blue Dogs, Hispanics, blacks, New Democrats, women—pledging their support. The letters contained signatures but no printed names, making it hard to keep track of exactly who was committed. She was creating a sense of inevitability.

On the afternoon of September 10, 2001, Pelosi sat down for a lengthy discussion about her political education and her future in the House.

"I have become, I think, a very skilled legislator and appropriator. I just know how it works. I also know the people, and I respect them."

Pelosi recalled how her "junkyard dog" role as state party chair had evolved into a more diplomatic posture as a member of Congress. That evolution would need to continue if she were to climb the leadership ladder.

"I have gotten to a place where you have to sort of decide that you're going to smooth out your elbows and go to another place. To be a leader is a little different responsibility. It doesn't mean you abandon all that you believe in and what you're going to work for. It means you have additional responsibilities that you have to be ready for.

"Some people just don't want to make the transition," Pelosi said. "It's more work. You're doing a different kind of thing. For a long time, a woman in any arena has to always kind of say, 'Listen to me, hear me.' Now I'll be in a place where, ipso facto, just by virtue of the office, just by dint of what I'm doing and the position I hold . . . people will listen.

"I have to understand that when I say something, it's different from Nancy Pelosi, D-San Francisco, saying it."

Pelosi knew she was at a crossroads. She told friends that if she didn't win the whip's race, she'd sharpen her elbows and become even more outspoken. But she felt she could accomplish far more as a leader. Publicly, she never hinted at the possibility that she might lose.

When she was asked during the interview about Burton, she resisted the suggestion that the powerful lawmaker, whose statue she still kept in her office, was her mentor.

"Not to diminish in any way the enormous respect that I have for Phillip, but I was my own person in politics.

"I certainly will be faithful to the ideal that Phillip and my parents believed in," she volunteered. "But I have my own approach. I would hope that they would be proud of my success and what I know—that what I would do would be consistent with what he believed.

"But I am not—this is not about Phillip, and it's not about my father. It's about something that has happened in terms of how I have been shaped. I bring a woman to the table. I bring the changing nature of my district as part of it, the regional thinking that we have in California."

That same afternoon, Bonior drew up a press release to formally announce that he would step down as whip on January 15. His staff prepared to release it the following day.

And then the world changed.

On the morning of September 11, 2001, Nancy Pelosi could be heard by some early risers discussing the prospect of becoming the first woman whip on National Public Radio.

"It's not about left or right; it's about new or old in terms of our thinking," Pelosi told NPR's Steve Inskeep.[11]

The taped interview did not replay. Pelosi was at a meeting outside the Capitol when the planes struck the World Trade Center. Within minutes she called her longtime aide Carolyn Bartholomew, who was sitting in the Intelligence Committee offices on the fourth floor of the Capitol.

"Get out of the Capitol. The building you are in is not safe," Pelosi told her in a calm but firm voice. Bartholomew, who was watching the horror unfold on television, was not feeling the same urgency. Pelosi repeated herself. "The building you are in is not safe. You need to get out of there."[12]

Two minutes later, Capitol police came rushing into the committee's office with a sterner tone.

"Out!" they ordered.

Pelosi made a similar call to her district director, Catherine Dodd, who was already on her way to San Francisco's federal building shortly before 7:00 a.m. on the West Coast. Her cell phone rang.

"Catherine, this is Nancy."

"Are you okay?" she asked the boss.

"I'm okay. Where are you?"

Dodd told her she was just pulling up to the office.

"I want you to be out of that building within five minutes of the time you enter," Pelosi said calmly. "Call the staff and tell them not to come in until I say it's safe."[13]

No one knew what was happening, but Pelosi was not going to take any chances with her staff. She also told Dodd that she was trying to contact her daughter, Alexandra, who was living in Manhattan.

"If she calls, please put her through."

Pelosi ended up, along with more than 100 other members, at the Capitol Police's headquarters between the Senate office buildings and Union Station. They spent much of the day trying to get information and found their best source was the TV. As the senior Democrat on the Intelligence Committee, Pelosi kept pushing for a briefing, but it took until the end of the day for the administration to comply.

"It's terrifying," Pelosi said on the phone that afternoon. "It's worse than Pearl Harbor. There are more civilians. It's right in the heart of our country.

"Obviously members are very eager to return to the Capitol. They are telling us for now that is not possible from a security standpoint," she said.

"We know it has all the earmarks and finger marks of Osama bin Laden," she added. "We want to have our facts in a row. When we strike back, it will be fierce."[14]

The following morning, Pelosi took to the House floor and declared that September 11, 2001, was a "day from hell." She stood inside the Capitol's Statuary Hall with Speaker Hastert, Democratic leader Gephardt, and Intelligence Committee chairman Porter Goss at a news conference to let the world know that Congress was back in business.

Pelosi offered two messages. The first was to stay calm. The second was to insist that civil liberties not be a casualty of the attacks.

While the entire nation mourned, emotions were very different in Washington than in California, which was 2,500 miles and three time zones away from the attacks. The gulf was apparent at a huge San Francisco memorial service held a few days later and attended by many politicians. The Reverend Amos Brown of the Third Baptist Church, a former city supervisor, drew loud cheers when he asked, "America, is there anything you did to set up this climate?

"America, America, what did you do—either intentionally or unintentionally—in the world order, in Central America, in Africa where bombs are still blasting? Oh, America."

Paul Holm, former partner of Mark Bingham—one of the heroes of United Airlines Flight 93, which was headed toward Washington before passengers fought the hijackers and crashed the plane into the Pennsylvania countryside—

got out of his chair and approached Senator Barbara Boxer, telling her, "This was supposed to be a memorial service."

Senator Dianne Feinstein and Governor Gray Davis both walked out as Brown was speaking. But Pelosi was the one who took it on as she strayed from her prepared remarks.

"With all due respect to some of the sentiments that were earlier expressed— some of which I agree with—make no mistake . . . the act of terrorism on September 11 put those people outside the order of civilized behavior, and we will not take responsibility for that."[15]

Pelosi later approached Holm and, fighting back tears, told him how sorry she was for Brown's comments.

The whip's race seemed trivial by comparison. But the business of the House marched on. Two weeks after the terrorist attacks, Democratic leader Dick Gephardt scheduled a caucus vote for October 10 to choose a new whip. After three years of jockeying, the election was set.

As THE VOTE APPROACHED, one thing was certain. Somebody was lying. Pelosi claimed 120 commitments, and Hoyer claimed 102. That's a total of 222 votes. Yet there were only 215 eligible voters.

That meant that either Pelosi or Hoyer was inflating their number, or more likely that several members were promising their support to both. The same had happened to Burton, who had seemed destined to become majority leader in 1976. Burton had appeared on NBC's *Meet the Press* the Sunday before the vote and shrugged off the possibility that someone wasn't being straight, noting that his colleagues were "noted for their candor and directness."

"I don't think my colleagues lie to any of us who are candidates," Burton had said out of either false hope or naïveté. "I do believe I am ahead. I don't think there is any dispute about that."[16]

The final tally had been Wright, 148 votes; Burton, 147 votes.

At Hoyer's request, the vote on October 10 was set up so that members who did not want anyone peeking over their shoulders could vote in private. Those who wanted to publicly display their ballots—in a show of loyalty—were free to do so. Those who wanted to cast them behind dividers could remain anonymous.

"There are members who publicly said they are voting for Nancy Pelosi that have indicated privately that they are voting for Mr. Hoyer," said Hoyer's spokeswoman, Stacey Farnen.

A week out, Pelosi expressed great confidence.

"We've all put it on the back burner for the past three weeks," Pelosi said. "Fortunately for me, I had my votes lined up before. I can ignore the race for three weeks.

"I wish the election were right now. I'm in excellent shape."

ON THE MORNING OF OCTOBER 10, both sides gathered inside the grand caucus room in the Cannon Office Building, with its gold-trim ceilings and crystal chandeliers. This was a day when futures would be determined. Each side had an elaborate system for making sure their supporters came through. Aides with special passes hanging around their necks hurried in and out of the caucus room with clipboards and nervous looks on their faces. Every vote was critical, as the Burton-Wright race had established 25 years before.

"We're confident we have the votes to win," Pelosi deputy Jon Stivers said as he nervously checked off members' names on a list when they entered the room. "We just have to make sure they all show up to vote."

The Pelosi team was taking no chances. Seven-thirty a.m. wakeup calls were made to each of her 100-plus supporters. A breakfast was served so members could check in before the vote. Cars were available in case anyone had trouble getting to the Capitol.

Robert Underwood, a nonvoting House member from Guam who was eligible to vote in the whip race, had been at a funeral across the international date line. He took four flights—including a charter plane to Tokyo at his own expense—to make it back in time to cast a ballot for Pelosi. As the votes were being cast, no one could find Representative John Conyers, the veteran Detroit-area congress-man and a Pelosi backer. Cheers went up when Tom LaFaille, an aide to Repre-sentative Mike Thompson, finally tracked Conyers down in his office and personally escorted him into the Cannon caucus room.

Leo McCarthy paced the hallway outside the room. So did daughters Alexandra and Christine. Speeches were made behind the closed doors, where only members and selected staff were allowed. John Dingell, the dean of the House, nominated Hoyer. Murtha nominated Pelosi.

Pelosi told her colleagues that her service on the Intelligence Committee and the Foreign Operations panel would serve the caucus well "at this particularly difficult time." She said she'd make the economy the "central issue of the whip operation" and pledged to showcase "the galaxy of talent and expertise that House members possess."

"With my election as whip we will make history, we will make progress, and, working together, we will win back the House."

IT WAS NOT UNTIL the last of four ballot boxes was opened that the race was settled. The final vote was 118 to 95. Anna Eshoo (D-CA) came out at 10:19 and announced to the gathered crowd, "It's Pelosi."

Pelosi emerged a few minutes later with an enormous grin on her face. Her supporters let out a loud cheer as reporters pushed to get in position to hear her words. Bonior presented Pelosi with a large black leather whip and told her she had already served with "grace and guts."

Pelosi smiled as she took the whip and held it aloft before a bank of television cameras. Asked by a reporter whether her election might add to the perception that House Democrats were too liberal, Pelosi brandished her new whip with a menacing smile.

"I don't know why you say that," she laughed, before returning to her formulation that the liberal-conservative divide was an old formula that overlooked her home's entrepreneurial spirit.

"It's in the air we breathe. It's in the water we drink," Pelosi said.

"This is difficult turf to win on for anyone. But for a woman breaking ground here, it was a tough battle," Pelosi continued. "We made history, now we need to make progress."

It was 90 years to the day after California women had been guaranteed the right to vote.

When word reached a group of Republicans meeting in the basement of the Capitol, they reportedly cheered.[17] Many Republicans viewed Pelosi as too much of a liberal ideologue to lead the Democrats and figured their majority was that much safer.

"Republicans in general view Steny Hoyer as a much more formidable adversary," said Republican campaign committee spokesman Steve Schmidt. "If Republicans could vote in this whip race, Pelosi would win unanimously."

Hoyer licked his wounds and moved on. "If she hadn't been a woman or from California, I think we would have been okay. Gender and geography in this case were overwhelming. *C'est la guerre.*"[18]

Pelosi had stepped into history.

It was fitting that the official duty of the whip—taken from the British hunting term for the "whipper-in," the rider who keeps the dogs in line—was to keep Democrats together and count votes.

As Pelosi boasted afterward, "My votes were so right on the money."[19]

CHAPTER TWELVE

Woman with a Whip

"I intend to win whatever I run for. Whether it's by more votes or fewer votes,
I intend to win. I don't have any thoughts of anything other than winning."
—NANCY PELOSI, 2002

"She's tough as all get-out. The Republicans don't
like her and that tells you something good."
—REPRESENTATIVE JOHN DINGELL (D-MI), 2006

PELOSI WAS SEATED AT the long mahogany table in the Cabinet Room, just next to the Oval Office, when it happened.

It was her first visit to the White House in her capacity as whip, and Pelosi was among the senior congressional leaders meeting with the president. Seated on Pelosi's side of the table were House Democratic leader Dick Gephardt, Senate Democratic leader Tom Daschle, and Senate whip Harry Reid. On the other side were House Speaker Dennis Hastert, majority leader Dick Armey, whip Tom DeLay, and Senate Republican whip Don Nickels. Vice President Cheney was there.

The door closed and Bush started speaking. It was then that Pelosi realized that she was sitting where no woman had been before. Plenty of women had *been* to the White House. Pelosi herself had been there dozens of times, dating back to President Kennedy's appointment of her father to a federal panel. But in the two centuries of the republic, no woman had ever participated in a session between the president and the top leaders of Congress.

"I'm looking at them and I'm thinking, *Do they know what's happening to me here?* I'm getting squeezed in my chair. And all of a sudden I feel the presence of all the women who had worked so hard to get women the right to vote—Susan B. Anthony, Elizabeth Cady Stanton—and the women who had worked to advance women in politics. We were all women on that chair. They were almost there to say, 'At last we have a seat at the table!'

"And then they were gone."

Pelosi told the story over and over. Sometimes she'd add abolitionist Sojourner Truth to the women crowding her on the chair and sometimes Emily's List founder Ellen Malcolm.

"It really did happen. It was quite a remarkable phenomenon," Pelosi insisted.

The story always ended with the same line. Pelosi said that as the women cheered their place at the table, "my first thought was: We want more!"

In 2002, there were still six states that had never elected a woman to Congress. In the history of the institution, only 10 women had ever chaired a committee, and never a committee as muscular as Appropriations or Ways and Means. Among the panels presided over by women were the House Post Office Committee and the Select Committee on the House Beauty Shop. Eleven women had served as caucus secretaries, and six as vice chair. None, besides Pelosi, had risen higher.

Pelosi made it plain from the outset that she was willing to mix it up with the men. The Michigan redistricting plan that drove Bonior from his seat had squeezed incumbents John Dingell and Lynn Rivers into the same district, and Pelosi did something that stunned Capitol insiders. She took sides.

Pelosi donated $12,000 from her campaign funds to Rivers, a third-term lawmaker from Ann Arbor. The conventional wisdom among insiders was that Pelosi had goofed. It was bad enough to take sides between incumbents. But it was a sign of Pelosi's naïveté to put money against Dingell, the senior Democrat on the House Energy Committee who'd served in Congress since Pelosi was a teenager.

Dingell was furious. Rivers lost the primary. The chattering class dismissed it as a rookie mistake

It was no mistake. Rivers had been with Pelosi in the whip's race. Dingell had been with Hoyer. Such tactics had earned Republican whip Tom DeLay the nickname "The Hammer." For the first woman in leadership, it was cast off as a "rookie mistake."

"Understand: Mother-loyal. Turn the world upside down, I will be there for my friends," Pelosi explained a few years later, scoffing at the suggestion that she hadn't considered the consequences. "I knew exactly what I was doing. She was for me. He was not."[1]

Pelosi and Dingell—whose fathers had served in the House together in the 1930s—would have more disagreements down the road. But they understood each other. They were both creatures of the House. And they spoke admiringly of one another.

"He's a politician. He understands about loyalty," Pelosi said.

"She's tough as all get-out," Dingell said of Pelosi. "The Republicans don't like her and that tells you something good."

The installation of a new whip is typically an insider affair, but Pelosi was sworn in amid much fanfare. Guitarist Bob Weir and drummer Mickey Hart of the Grateful Dead and guitarist Steve Miller played to a crowded celebration at the Post Office Museum a few blocks from the Capitol.

Scores of Californians were among those feasting from the huge tables filled with chocolate, including John Burton, now president of the California Senate; Jerry Brown, now mayor of Oakland; and Leo McCarthy, now treasurer of Pelosi's political action committee.

The sight of House members dancing to the pounding rhythm of "Iko Iko," the Dead's "Friend of the Devil," and Bob Dylan's "She Belongs to Me" made it plain that elevating a San Francisco woman to the upper echelon of congressional power would change the tempo on Capitol Hill.

Mezzo-soprano Denyce Graves had sung "America the Beautiful" at a more traditional swearing-in ceremony earlier in the day. The lines "Thine alabaster cities gleam / Undimmed by human tears" had always reminded Pelosi of San Francisco.

"Much has been said about my being the first woman to rise this high in the Congress. One only need look to my family to see the reasons why," Pelosi said as Paul, her five children, and her grandchildren looked on. "Our love of each other, our love of our country, and an understanding of why we must all take responsibility for the next generation.

"I was raised in a tradition that believed that public service was a noble calling and a sacred trust. My mother and father imbued us with a pride of country, a spirit of patriotism," Pelosi said.

Every living woman who had served in Congress was invited to a lunch at the Library of Congress. Of the 11,644 Americans who had served in Congress, 11,435 had been men. Two hundred and nine had been women. Hawaii representative Patsy Mink, the first minority woman elected to Congress, said, "I look at Nancy Pelosi as not just a whip, not just a leader, but the next Speaker of the House."

Pelosi, displaying her ambition while gracefully avoiding the awkwardness of being seen as trying to jump over Gephardt, interjected with a smile, "Well, maybe not *next*."

On the eve of her swearing-in, Pelosi had sat down for a lengthy interview in which the topic of her pioneering role never came up. Instead, Pelosi was focused on her party's plan to counter Bush's tax cuts, push new spending on health care and schools, and win back control of the House.

"If the Democrats make a clear presentation of the differences, the contrast between us and the Republicans, I think the public will favor the positions we are taking," she said.

"I don't consider myself confrontational," she said, rejecting a comparison between herself and DeLay, her GOP counterpart. "I can be confrontational, but that's not where I start. You start with a feather, and you work your way down the line. I'd rather start with a handshake than a fist shake."

"I don't intend to go into the whip's office as the junkyard dog of Democrats," she added. It was a role she said she'd found distasteful as party chair two decades earlier.

At the same time, she complained that "the other side always had as its priority protecting the assets of the wealthy. We have been a party of working people."

Four months after the September 11 attacks, she praised Bush on his handling of terrorism.

"I think the president has done a good job in that regard. It remains to be seen how he will deal with the economy, if he will keep two balls in the air at the same time."

In addition to her new responsibilities, Pelosi said she would keep her committee assignments for another year and revisit the plan if Democrats didn't win a majority. She quickly caught herself: "I don't think in terms of not winning."

Pelosi didn't hang pictures on the walls of her new, roomy office inside the Capitol. She said she didn't plan to stay long. Pelosi expected Democrats to win back control of Congress later that year, and then she would move into the more spacious office of the majority leader.

Pelosi beefed up her staff with the addition of Capitol Hill veteran George

Crawford as her top aide, Brendan Daly as communications director, community organizer Cecile Richards—the daughter of former Texas governor Ann Richards—as deputy chief of staff, and Lorraine Miller, who had worked for Speakers Jim Wright and Tom Foley as well as in the Clinton White House.

When Pelosi became Speaker five years later, she would name Miller clerk of the House, making her the first African American to hold the body's top administrative post.

House Democrats had few opportunities and even fewer victories under Republican rule. Pelosi won what was described as her first "mano a mano" with Republican whip Tom DeLay after the landmark Shays-Meehan campaign finance bill came to the floor over Republican objections and Pelosi ensured its passage by getting all but 12 Democrats to vote for it, while DeLay lost the votes of 41 Republicans.

Pelosi had a good personal relationship with DeLay, though their politics were worlds apart. DeLay had taken Pelosi up on an offer to view AIDS treatment centers in her city several years earlier and had stopped by her swearing-in ceremony as whip. She would be quick to condemn DeLay when he faced ethics troubles a few years later, demanding the appointment of a special prosecutor and labeling him the "ringleader" of the Republicans' culture of corruption. But she abided by what her father had taught her many years before: "Always keep the friendship in your voice."

She was more aggressive and visible than Bonior, her predecessor. She was perpetually receiving information from or imparting it to fellow members on the floor, in her office, or in the corridor in between. She added a weekly Tuesday whip meeting to a regularly scheduled Thursday meeting so her deputies would be on the same page as the legislative week began.

And she instilled a sense of optimism in her fellow Democrats. They would soon be the majority.

"When we returned from the spring recess, she told [members] that they need to think about themselves as Mr. Chairman or Madam Chairman," said Representative Jan Schakowsky, who served as a deputy whip.[2]

THE MOST CONSEQUENTIAL MATTER before the House in 2002 was an issue that was not "whipped," meaning that there was no party position.

On the one-year anniversary of the September 11 attacks, President Bush went to the United Nations and asserted: "Saddam Hussein's regime is a grave and gathering danger. To suggest otherwise is to hope against the evidence. To assume this regime's good faith is to bet the lives of millions and the peace of the world in a reckless gamble. And this is a risk we must not take."

The White House pushed the House and the Senate to pass a resolution authorizing the use of force against Iraq. They wanted it done before election day so wavering lawmakers would feel pressure from their constituents. Bush insisted that the legislation was not a declaration of war. But few doubted that the White House would use it as just that once it made a decision to attack.

Pelosi expressed her skepticism immediately.

"I have not yet seen evidence of imminent nuclear or other kinds of threats that demand immediate military action," Pelosi said after Bush's UN speech. "If the administration brings us the evidence and makes a compelling case to the American public that a threat is indeed imminent or that Saddam Hussein was actively involved in the tragedy of last September 11, we may very well come together in agreement. We are clearly not there yet."

However, most members of Congress, including many Democrats, were lining up behind Bush, whose approval ratings had been over 70 percent for more than a year. New terror alerts and fresh memories of the September 11 attacks, which the White House suggested were linked to Saddam Hussein, made standing against the president a politically risky proposition. Senate Democratic Leader Tom Daschle and prominent Democrats including John Kerry, Hillary Clinton, and John Edwards all supported Bush's resolution.

On October 2, Bush stood in the Rose Garden and introduced a measure negotiated with congressional leaders authorizing the use of force against Iraq. To his immediate left was House Democratic Leader Richard Gephardt, who said, "We must do what is right for the security of our nation and the safety of all Americans."

The following day Pelosi issued a statement breaking with her party's leader.

"Because I do not believe we have exhausted all diplomatic remedies, I cannot support the administration's resolution regarding the use of force in Iraq. I am also extremely concerned about the impact of such action on our war against terrorism," Pelosi said.

"As the ranking Democrat on the House Select Committee on Intelligence, I have seen no evidence or intelligence that suggests that Iraq indeed poses an imminent threat to our nation. If the administration has that information, they have not shared it with the Congress."

Gephardt and Pelosi agreed that they would not "whip" the vote. Members were free to vote their conscience. But that did not stop members from trying to influence one another. Pelosi had broken with the rest of the leadership, and the vote was widely seen as a test of her strength.

Pelosi took to the House floor on the day of the vote and told her colleagues that Bush's Iraq policy was misguided.

"The clear and present danger that our country faces is terrorism. I say flat out that unilateral use of force without first exhausting every diplomatic remedy and other remedies and making a case to the American people will be harmful to our war on terrorism," she said.

Pelosi suggested that the United States spend its resources chasing down Osama bin Laden and warned that a war in Iraq would diminish the nation's standing and cost hundreds of billions of dollars.

"If we go in, we can certainly show our power to Saddam Hussein. If we resolve this issue diplomatically, we can show our strength as a great country. Let us show our greatness. Vote 'no' on this resolution."

The Senate voted 77 to 23 in favor of the resolution, with 29 Democrats voting in favor and 21 Democrats voting against. The House voted 296 to 133 to support Bush. However, 125 Democrats, 61 percent of the caucus, joined Pelosi and voted "no." Pelosi had staked out the antiwar position. And most House Democrats were with her.

The next day Pelosi took off on a weekend-long campaign swing that would take her from the Gulf of Mexico to the Rocky Mountains to Pennsylvania's coal country. Over a 72-hour span, Pelosi would fly 3,678 miles, ride 14 hours in rented vans, shake more than 600 hands, visit three grandchildren, speak to two dozen reporters, and raise money for eight House candidates. It was not a particularly unusual weekend.

War was the number one topic. After delivering a stump speech in Boulder, Colorado, at the mountainside home of vacuum cleaner tycoon Bruce Oreck, a guest asked Pelosi, given her assignment to the Intelligence Committee, to discuss national security.

Pelosi delivered a 1,100-word answer that touched on the kilometer range of Saddam Hussein's launch capacity, the CIA director's latest risk assessment, and the split between Iraq's Sunnis, Shiites, and Kurds. In Denver that evening at a Democratic Party function, her Iraq argument had grown to 1,500 words and included a discussion of force protection, potential unrest on the Arab street, and Bush's doctrine of preemption.

Over and over Pelosi told audiences that as a member of the "group of four"— the select group of Intelligence Committee lawmakers who received enhanced information—she had seen no evidence to back the president's claim that Saddam Hussein had the capability or intention to strike at the United States or its allies. Such talk prompted concern from some party elders in Washington and raised eyebrows among pundits, who warned that it would hurt the party in the coming election. Democratic audiences loved it.

Pelosi squeezed all the campaigning she could into her weekends. During one three-day stretch she flew from Washington to San Francisco in time to attend a

Friday evening fund-raiser for candidate Mike Honda at Shanghai 1930, a trendy downtown restaurant. The next day she was on a 1:30 p.m. flight to Hawaii, which touched down at 5:30 p.m., in time to attend a dinner event for Representative Mink. She then boarded a 10:30 p.m. flight and returned to San Francisco by 6:00 a.m. Sunday morning, which gave her a full day in the district before returning to Washington.

As the 2002 midterm election approached, Pelosi campaigned with added intensity. If she had been busy before, she was busier now. There was an urgency to winning back control of the House. This is what she had been enlisted to do, and she intended to succeed.

"I can only think about winning, not about losing. If I thought about losing, I'd go home right now and go to a play-off game," she said during one weekend's travels, referring to her San Francisco Giants, who were in the process of beating the St. Louis Cardinals en route to the National League pennant.

The weekend trip following the Iraq vote was typical of her furious pace. Pelosi departed Washington in midafternoon aboard a commercial flight bound for Houston, seated in economy class, devouring a Hershey's chocolate bar with almonds and reading the newspaper. She was appalled by a report in the *New York Times* concerning a plan to install an American-led military government in Iraq if the United States toppled Saddam Hussein.[3]

"Can you imagine Tommy Franks in charge for a year?" she asked scornfully, referring to the commander of US forces in the region.

Upon arrival she was taken by her security team to an upscale neighborhood for a fund-raiser on behalf of House candidate Chris Bell, with an escort provided by a Houston Police Department detail that had just finished providing the same service to the queen of Thailand.

She immediately began punching numbers into her cell phone, calling her office, her husband, and then her daughter Jacqueline, who lived in Houston. Arriving at the event she shook hands, posed for pictures, and made small talk with as many people as possible before her grandchildren showed up. She quickly disappeared to wash her hands and then returned to play with the grandkids, whom she later joined for dinner.

Checkout from the Houstonian Hotel, Club & Spa, scheduled for 5:20 a.m., was delayed briefly when Pelosi couldn't find her credit card, requiring a trip back up to her room by her security detail. The card was found in her purse.

"Anything new on the sniper?" Pelosi asked, inquiring about the mysterious rash of random killings that was terrorizing the Washington area in the fall of 2002. "I want to know every detail on the sniper."

Seven hours later it was still morning in Colorado, where Pelosi, huddled in another SUV, went over poll numbers, money, and local candidates with Representative Mark Udall of Boulder. As Andrew Wittman, the Capitol Police officer in charge of Pelosi's security detail, went searching for a "tankard of caffeine," Pelosi bought herself a decaf Chocolate Brownie Frappucino at a Boulder Starbucks. Pelosi doesn't drink caffeine. She doesn't need it. As her van powered up the mountainside to her next event, Pelosi pulled out her compact and began to wonder out loud if they actually served her decaf.

"Whoa," she said. "I'll be bouncing off the walls."

Pelosi spent the next two hours shaking hands, answering questions, and raising more than $20,000 for Udall and another Colorado House candidate. As her black Ford Excursion driven by the security detail sped past Colorado's snow-capped Front Range en route to Denver, Pelosi discussed the "cold-blooded reptilian analysis" she applies to House races in her quest to win a majority.

The first priority is to protect incumbents, she explained. Then she analyzes open seats and those held by vulnerable Republicans. In addition to the House campaign committee in Washington, Pelosi had her own brain trust in San Francisco, headed by her friend Leo McCarthy and Democratic consultant Mary Hughes, who helped handicap races around the country to assess where Pelosi could have the biggest impact.

Pelosi said she made the trips to raise money and inspire the troops. But her physical presence in districts also allowed her to make a quick assessment of a campaign's viability.

"I could tell you in a second if someone is making something happen or not."

She acknowledged Republicans would use her liberal reputation against her in some districts the way Democrats used Newt Gingrich against moderate Republicans.

"There are some races that I don't think it is in the interest of the candidate for me to go there," she said. "I always say to people when they ask me, 'Do you really want me to come? If you want me to come because you want me to raise money, I can do that better from a distance.'

"Why should we give them something to say," she said of the Republicans. "We know how irresponsible they are."

Pelosi said her Democratic opponents had made a mistake in the long whip race by playing up her liberal reputation.

"They should not have internally painted me that way in the race—especially because I was going to win. It gives grist for the mill for the other side to say [that] even her own people describe her that way."

But Pelosi was confident that her support within the caucus was growing. Whether Democrats won a majority or Gephardt decided to leave to pursue the presidency, Pelosi was convinced she would soon be the Democratic leader.

"Let me say it this way. I intend to win whatever I run for. I intend to win whatever I run for. Whether it's by more votes or fewer votes, I intend to win. I don't have any thoughts of anything other than winning.

"I haven't asked one person—one person—to be with me. I have not. I don't have a campaign. I'm busy doing my job as whip. It took a lot to be whip.

"But I will tell you this. Every time my opponents, or their toadies, go around poisoning the well, more people come up to me and say, 'Put me down for you. I wasn't for you [in the whip race], but I'm going to be for you this time, and I want to make sure you know that early.' So if anything, my universe has expanded."

As the SUV pulled into Denver for another pair of fund-raisers, Pelosi was asked whether the long days and grueling weekends on the road were lonely—or perhaps boring.

"No. No, no, no, no. Last week I saw my grandchildren in Arizona. This week, I see them in Texas. We're always working. You grab a few hours of sleep and then you're up again going to the next thing. I enjoy it. . . . I don't feel 'Oh my God, two more hours and we'll be out.'

"I always say to the candidates, 'Enjoy it because it's an experience in itself.'"

Pelosi said she relaxed by doing crossword puzzles and reading, laughing that she had been trading off between the latest *Beowulf* translation and *Goodnight Moon.* But there was no evidence of such leisure on this weekend. Pelosi filled her time between campaign stops reading briefing books and newspapers and punching numbers into her cell phone, calling members of Congress to point out what she'd seen or read, calling her staff, or talking to her husband or her children.

"I don't know what we did before these things," she said as she punched another number into her cell phone.

The question about travel seemed to gnaw at her, and she returned to it twice.

"I love the interaction with people. I'm learning all the time. I don't understand how people can do it if they don't enjoy interacting with people, hearing their concerns, hearing their enthusiasm or lack thereof.

"I have learned long ago to listen to a speech and listen to people. You know how you listen to a speech and think: *When is this going to end?* Well, if you listen, you learn something. You learn what they are going to tell you, or you learn their shortcomings. The speech goes faster if you listen than if you don't."

The same is true on the House floor, Pelosi said, where most speeches are delivered to an empty chamber. Pelosi said she sometimes catches herself rushing off the floor to a meeting, "and then I think, no—just listen. Just listen.

"I happen to love people, and I don't know if you could do this if you didn't. You never know what you're going to hear. You never know what new idea or fresh approach."

Later she volunteered that she didn't like being away from Paul, her husband, whom she'd had a long-distance relationship with since 1987. And while she wished she could take her children into the rain and make them shrink back to toddlers, they were now grown and scattered around the country.

Sixteen hours after her day began, Pelosi sat at the head table in the grand ballroom of Denver's DoubleTree Hotel, patiently waiting to deliver the keynote address to the annual Denver County Democratic Dinner. A mariachi band from a wedding in the room next door could be heard as the master of ceremonies introduced more than half of the 400 assembled Democratic faithful by name.

When it was finally her turn, Pelosi spoke for more than 30 minutes without notes.

"Are Democrats going to take back the House?" she roared.

"Absolutely!" she answered her own question, telling the party faithful that it could not be done unless Democrats won in Colorado.

"The Republicans in the House—I hate to be the bearer of bad news—are not committed to making the future brighter. They're committed to the special interests, they're committed to the top 2 percent of wealthiest people in America.

"It has to be the Democrats. Think about that, and just do one more thing or make one more contribution," she told the crowd, which was literally feasting on meat and potatoes.

The following night she was in Lackawanna County, Pennsylvania, speaking on a charcoal dark night at a pasta feed hosted by Representative Paul Kanjorski outside Scranton.

At first blush it was hard to see where Paul Kanjorski fit in Pelosi's political universe. He opposed legal abortions, gun control, and permitting gays to be able to lead Boy Scout troops. He supported the death penalty, a Constitutional ban on flag burning, and the resolution authorizing the use of force in Iraq.

He introduced Pelosi to the group of about 100 locals eating sausage and spaghetti as "this pretty girl from California."

The coal country of Lackawanna County is 2,500 miles from the corner of Haight and Ashbury and several solar systems from Pelosi's Pacific Heights constituents. Pelosi appeared to be right at home as she spoke through the tinny sound system and told the crowd how she fondly remembered her father coming to Scranton in the 1950s to campaign for Democrats. She talked of Kanjorski's record creating jobs and his commitment to miners and to education.

"When the Democrats take back the Congress in three weeks and three days . . . he will become the chairman of the Capital Markets, Insurance, and Government Sponsored Enterprises Committee," Pelosi gushed, drawing blank stares from the sausage-eating crowd.

She skipped her explanation of her war vote but assured the crowd that "when people ask me what the three most important issues facing the Congress are, I always say the same thing: 'Our children, our children, our children.'"

The crowd was impressed.

When the weekend was through, Pelosi had raised $50,000 for Democrats and made at least 10 appearances with candidates. The travel, the people, and the races energized Pelosi, whose staff always returned from such sprints exhausted.

By election day, Pelosi had visited 90 congressional districts spanning 28 states. She took credit for raising more than $7 million for House candidates during the election cycle. She dispatched 12 members of her staff to work on competitive campaigns in eight states.

"There's nothing I want more than winning the House for Democrats. Make no mistake about that," she said.

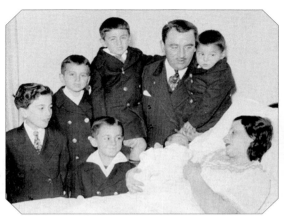

The future Speaker of the House in the arms of her mother. Her father and five brothers posed for the photo that ran in the next day's *Baltimore News Post* under the headline: "It's a Girl for the D'Alesandros."

Seven-year-old Nancy D'Alesandro holds a bible as her father is sworn in as mayor in front of Baltimore's city hall.

Nancy on her father's knee in the living room on Albemarle Street.
The family, from left to right: Hector (on floor), Joey, Annunciata, Young Tommy, Nancy, Big Tommy, Nick, and Roosey.

Mayor Thomas D'Alesandro Jr. waves to the crowd in the backseat of a car with his wife and daughter seated beside him.

Annunciata D'Alesandro had high expectations for her only daughter.

Politics was a D'Alesandro family affair. Here, 11-year-old Nancy (holding a white purse) and the rest of the family stand outside their home at 245 Albemarle Street, preparing to go to city hall for their father's second inauguration as mayor.

Nancy D'Alesandro, 16, and Senator John Kennedy of Massachusetts at Baltimore's Emerson Hotel during an event honoring his book *Profiles in Courage*.

PHOTO COURTESY
OF D'ALESANDRO FAMILY

Nancy (right) hoists a Kennedy for President poster at a student rally in 1960.
Holding the other end of the poster is classmate Cecelia Lynett Haggerty.

PHOTO COURTESY OF TRINITY (WASHINGTON) UNIVERSITY

Senior year portrait from the
1962 Trinity College yearbook.

Thomas D'Alesandro Jr. chats with President Kennedy
at the White House after winning appointment to the federal Renegotiation Board,
as Nancy and her mother look on.

A Pelosi 1987 campaign brochure.
COURTESY OF THE AUTHOR

Nancy Pelosi became
chair of the California
Democratic Party in 1981.
PHOTO BY VINCE MAGGIORA/
SAN FRANCISCO CHRONICLE

Pelosi celebrates her first election to the House with John Burton at the campaign's
Mission Street headquarters. Her husband Paul is in the background. Campaign
strategist Clint Reilly is on the left. PHOTO BY ERIC LUSE/SAN FRANCISCO CHRONICLE

Pelosi, a fan of the Irish
rock band U2, walks with
lead singer Bono to the
Rayburn Building after a press
conference on third world debt
relief at the US Capitol in 2000.

PHOTO COURTESY OF
© ROLL CALL PIX/NEWSCOM

Pelosi became the highest-ranking woman ever in Congress after winning election
as Democratic whip in 2001. Outgoing whip David Bonior of Michigan presents Pelosi
with a memento outside the Cannon Caucus room moments after her 118 to 95
vote victory over Steny Hoyer. PHOTO COURTESY OF AP PHOTO/JOE MARQUETTE

The Pelosi family pictured in a 1987 campaign brochure. From left: Nancy Corinne, Alexandra, Paul Jr., Nancy, Jacqueline, Paul, and Christine. COURTESY OF THE AUTHOR

Pelosi celebrates the Democratic takeover of Congress on Capitol Hill, election night 2006. Standing behind Pelosi are incoming Senate Majority leader Harry Reid of Nevada and Representative James Clyburn of South Carolina. PHOTO BY MICHAEL MACOR/SAN FRANCISCO CHRONICLE

Two sights never before seen in the halls of Congress. Above, Pelosi invites children
to join her at the podium moments after she is sworn in as Speaker of the House.
Below, Pelosi is the first woman to preside over a State of the Union address.

ANOTHER STEP UP THE LADDER

*"I would have hated to have gone through life as a
beautiful woman. They are all too often dismissed.
Nancy's got more ability than people give her credit for."*
—FORMER HOUSE MAJORITY LEADER DICK ARMEY, 2002

*"Whoever criticizes Nancy Pelosi for simply being
too liberal is going to have to eat their words."*
—FORMER VICE PRESIDENT AL GORE, 2002

VICTORY ELUDED HOUSE DEMOCRATS again in 2002. Republicans picked up
six additional seats to win a majority for their fifth consecutive election,

their longest grasp on congressional power since the Depression.

Gephardt phoned Pelosi in her San Francisco office the next afternoon. He was stepping down as Democratic leader to focus on running for president. Pelosi was ready for the call. For the past year Pelosi had patiently refrained from openly campaigning for Gephardt's job. She knew that either Democrats would win a majority and Gephardt would become Speaker or they would lose and Gephardt would likely move on. But she thought it unseemly to ask for support before he was gone. When members pledged their support, she thanked them but always added, "You understand I'm not asking?"

Now it was time to ask. Over the next 36 hours, with a phone affixed to her ear, an aide at her side, and a list of names and phone numbers and a sweeping view of San Francisco before her, Pelosi placed more than 100 calls to her Democratic colleagues. She started with calls to the eastern time zone and moved west as the hour grew late. She enlisted deputies from each region of the country and the entire spectrum of the party. Her friend Anna Eshoo made calls from her Palo Alto home in her bathrobe.

The pitch was straightforward: Congratulate members on their election. Inform them if they didn't already know that Gephardt would not be standing for election as leader. Ask for their support. Some calls lasted a minute. Others lasted an hour.

Before Democratic Caucus chair Martin Frost went before television cameras the next morning to announce his own candidacy, Pelosi already knew she had the race won.

"Everyone said, 'How come you're not on TV,'" Pelosi recalled a few days later. "I said, 'They're on TV, I'm on the telephone. That's where the votes are.'"

If there was any doubt that House Democrats had become Pelosi Democrats, the short contest to become leader would erase it. A vote of the Democratic Caucus was scheduled for the following week.

Pelosi was thriving as the Democratic whip. She quickly grasped how to count votes and precisely where to push and pull if the votes weren't there. She was the daughter of a former member and understood how to soothe egos in a mostly male institution. She knew when to flirt and when to play tough.

Pelosi still refused to accept that Republicans were winning because America supported their policies. It was Democrats who sought to protect children, the elderly, and the vulnerable. Pelosi insisted that Republicans had prevailed in the midterm election because they were masquerading as Democrats and her party had failed to make the distinctions clear.

"If Republicans won, it's because they stole our issues," Pelosi said on election night as votes were still being counted, dismissing the effect of the nation's post-9/11 jitters and President Bush's approval ratings, which were hovering around 65 percent.

"I think the issue is more that Republicans were successful in misrepresenting their positions on issues that were popular with the people. They ran on a Democratic platform that they have no intention of honoring.

"We can never again have an election where the Republicans hijack our issues," she vowed.

Frost offered an analysis of the election totally at odds with Pelosi's as he announced from Washington his intention to run for Democratic leader. Frost said the results showed that the country had grown more conservative, and Democrats would compound their problems if they nominated a liberal like Pelosi to lead.

"There are an awful lot of Democrats who are very uneasy about the party moving sharply to the left and who want a party that's in the middle," Frost said. "I believe our party must occupy the center if we are to be successful, if we're to come back to the majority and not move farther to the left. It's a clear choice."

Frost was a highly regarded inside player from Fort Worth who had run the House campaign committee in the 1990s. He was a prolific fund-raiser who had defeated Rosa DeLauro to become caucus chair after Fazio left in 1998. To outsider's, his frumpy appearance made him indistinguishable from hundreds of other middle-aged men who trudge in and out of the Capitol, yet many inside Washington believed he was the future of the party.

Frost took what he regarded as his best shot, warning fellow Democrats that embracing Pelosi could keep them in the minority for years.

"I think that her politics are to the left," Frost said of Pelosi. "I think that it will be . . . more difficult for the moderates and conservatives to have a strong voice in the party if she were leader."

While Pelosi had staked out a position opposing Bush on Iraq, Frost insisted that the issue should not be part of the Democratic platform and that Democrats would fail if they challenged Bush on foreign policy.

"If that is the position of the Democratic Party, the Democratic Party will not win the next election," Frost said.

He was right, and Democrats did not win the next election. But it was foreign policy, and Iraq in particular, that won them back the majority in the election after that.

Frost feigned a nonanswer when he was asked if it was the "kooky image of San Francisco" that would allow Republicans to use Pelosi to their advantage.

"Oh, I can't—I don't have an opinion on that. I will tell you that during the election, some candidates—some Republican candidates in swing districts did talk about the fact that their opponents—their Democratic opponent would be aligned with the liberal leadership of the Democratic Party, and in one or two cases actually mentioned her by name."

The Pelosi camp saw Frost's charges as an undignified "Hail Mary" pass, a desperate, last-ditch attempt to shake up the race by seeing if an attack on Pelosi's liberalism would work.

It didn't.

There was a widespread feeling among House Democrats that Gephardt had been too accommodating. Jarred by Bush's high standing after the September 11 attacks, the Democrats had virtually ceded all foreign policy issues to the GOP. It galled some Democrats to see Gephardt standing with Bush in the Rose

Garden as he presented his resolution to go to war with Iraq. Pelosi was marching the troops in another direction.

Frost dropped out of the race the next morning, telling fellow Democrats in a letter that "it is clear to me that Nancy Pelosi has the votes of the majority of the caucus." Frost released all those who had said they supported him from their commitments and announced that he would vote for Pelosi when Democrats chose their leader the following week.

Pelosi's well-oiled leadership operation had long prepared for this moment. Pelosi summoned reporters to her San Francisco office and released the names of 105 Democrats who had publicly committed to supporting her. The list contained more than enough names to secure her victory and was compiled even before Frost dropped out. Many of his supporters had called since to pledge their support. Pelosi had pledges from all 33 incoming California Democrats, nearly the entire membership of the Congressional Black Caucus and Progressive Caucus, and most of the women of the House. It didn't hurt that Pelosi had raised money for nearly half the House Democrats, including dozens of moderates.

"The race is over," Pelosi declared.

The challenge to Pelosi was not completely over. A new candidate, Representative Harold Ford Jr. of Tennessee, entered just as Frost was dropping out, declaring his intentions during a radio interview with Don Imus.

"The party elders are zero-and-4," said Ford, who had been elected to the House as a 26-year-old in 1996. "And in the political world or the business world, that's not a good record."

"Are you concerned about that?" Pelosi was asked about Ford's entry.

"No, I'm not concerned about it."

"He has implied that you're part of the past, he's part of the future."

"Well, I've been in office eight months, so I don't know," Pelosi laughed, referring to her tenure as whip. "I guess when you're very young, eight months seems like a long time."

Jon Stivers, the Pelosi aide who kept diligent track of the votes, was far more relaxed than he'd been a year before during the whip race.

"It took us three years to win the whip's race and 36 hours to win this," Stivers said.

MOST OF THE COUNTRY still had never heard of Pelosi. Walking through airports on her frequent campaign swings, Pelosi would occasionally be stopped by well-wishers but remained mostly unrecognized. Her security detail, which carried guns and communicated though earpieces and wrist microphones, attracted far more attention.

As the leader's race approached, the news media filled that void with dozens of articles and profiles about the rising Democrat.

Parade magazine put her picture on its cover, along with three other women, for a story speculating about who would become the first female president. She was honored as a "Woman of the Year" by both *Glamour* and *Ms.* magazines and featured in *Time, Newsweek, Women's Wear Daily,* and *Elle,* which gushed, "Nancy Pelosi is a babe."[1]

Her pioneering accomplishments on behalf of women were noted over and over. Her fashion sense and parenting instincts became standard fare in a way that had never been so for her male counterparts. But for the most part the stories devoted more column inches to geography than gender.

Gephardt and Bonior had been from the heartland. The idea that Democrats were preparing to install a San Francisco liberal as their leader prompted wide speculation about the direction of the party and outright ridicule from some opponents. Some suspected that her pragmatism and operational skills were overlooked because she was a woman. But most of the criticism focused less on her being a lady than a liberal.

"Are the Democrats about to go insane?" asked *Weekly Standard* columnist David Brooks in an article that bore the headline "The Pelosi Democrats: Are They Going to Become the Stupid Party?"

The conservative *National Review* tagged her a "latte liberal" who represented the Democrats' "most U.N. smitten instincts on matters of war and peace. Her rise would mark a shift to the left for House Democrats, a trend that is bad for Democrats and the country—but, quite possibly, good for Republicans."

The *Australian Financial Review* informed its readers halfway around the world that Pelosi was "about as San Francisco as you can get without digging up Jerry Garcia," a characterization that failed to appreciate the distance between Haight-Ashbury and Pacific Heights.

A columnist on the editorial page of the conservative *Washington Times* even suggested that Pelosi had ties to the Socialist International and compared her emergence to the *Manchurian Candidate,* a cold-war film classic about a brainwashed American programmed to carry out political assassinations for the Communists.

Some Republican House members fed the perception and professed great pleasure over Pelosi's selection.

"What's next, Barbra Streisand as DNC chairman?" smirked Florida representative Mark Foley. "Let the coronation of Congresswoman Pelosi begin—and the eventual fall of the Democratic Party follow."

Ironically, it was the fall of Representative Foley four years later over his soliciting sex from male former House pages that contributed to the GOP's loss and Pelosi's speakership.

The attacks from Republicans neither surprised nor particularly bothered Pelosi. Few in her camp believed the GOP joy was sincere.

"Gimme a break. If the Republicans weren't afraid of her and they thought it was a blessing to have the leader be from San Francisco, they would keep their fucking mouth shut and let her be elected by acclamation," said her friend John Burton. "They're afraid of her and hoping they can cause discord in the Democratic Caucus. . . . They're dealing with one tough Italian grandmother."

What bothered Pelosi was the hand-wringing among Democrats.

The Democratic-leaning *New Republic* lumped Pelosi in with Senator Ted

Kennedy of Massachusetts as a pair "who offer the country a message it will reject every time," warning that if the ideological vacuum atop the party were filled by the likes of Pelosi, "the United States will no longer be a 50-50 nation; it will be a 40-60 nation."

Al From, the founder of the centrist Democratic Leadership Council, compared the Democrats' position in 2002 to the GOP's position after the 1962 election, when Democrats won seats with Kennedy in the White House.

"The GOP had a choice. They could go back to their core, magnify their difference, or they could keep their eye on the vital center. They chose to go to the right, and the result was the Goldwater debacle. We can't go the same way."

Pelosi responded to such criticism by pointing to her record of winning House elections in the West and playing up the more traditional aspect of her profile.

"Liberal? Well, I guess you could describe an Italian grandmother that way," she said in an interview. "But I think you have to see me in my other perspective, which is someone who is in politics as an extension of my . . . role as a mother and a grandmother.

"I don't think they chose me as an outspoken liberal. . . . I think they chose me as a person who can lead the caucus to victory."

THE AFTERNOON BEFORE THE LEADERSHIP VOTE, Pelosi sat down for an interview and made it plain that she did not intend to impose her own liberal views on the rest of the country.

"It's not a matter of where you are on the spectrum. For other leaders it was never an issue of where they came from. It's an issue of how you can lead the troops."

Amid the flowers and congratulatory notes that had already begun to fill the whip's office she would soon leave behind, Pelosi said she appreciated the difference between trying to represent San Francisco and trying to lead Democrats coast-to-coast.

"To be a leader is not to say that everyone in Congress must vote along with the district. A leader has a different role. You must be bold enough to attract support . . . without being menacing. It's a different job."

The following day Democrats gathered in the Cannon caucus room, as they had the previous fall, to elect new leaders. The Pelosi team came equipped with clipboards but was visibly more relaxed. Marcy Kaptur of Ohio, the longest-serving woman in the House, had made a quixotic last-minute entry into the race 24 hours before the vote and then withdrew in the final minutes. Ford remained in the race and received 29 votes.

Pelosi received 177 votes—86 percent—and emerged from the room with the men who constituted the rest of the Democratic leadership.

"It's a staggering honor," Pelosi said to a mob of cameras and reporters squashed into the hallway.

One reporter tried to interrupt the new minority leader with a question.

"I'm not finished yet! I've been waiting over 200 years," Pelosi said to the cheers of supporters and other lawmakers.

"I didn't run as a woman," Pelosi continued. "I ran as a seasoned politician and an experienced legislator. It just so happens that I am a woman, and we have been waiting a long time for this moment."

Women made up roughly 54 percent of the nation's registered voters but only about 14 percent of the Congress. Pelosi was accustomed to being surrounded by men, and she had no trouble taking charge.

Pelosi pointed to Hoyer, who had been elected to fill Pelosi's spot as whip; Robert Menendez of New Jersey, the new caucus chair; and James Clyburn of South Carolina, the former head of the Congressional Black Caucus, who was elected vice chair.

"Isn't this a picture of America," Pelosi beamed.

CHAPTER FOURTEEN

WAR

*"I consider it one of the great disappointments of
my public life that I could not use my influence to stop this war."*
—NANCY PELOSI, MARCH 21, 2003

"She was right and I was wrong."
—REPRESENTATIVE RAHM EMANUEL (D-IL), APRIL 25, 2007

NO ISSUE DEFINED PELOSI'S TENURE as Democratic leader more than the war
in Iraq.

The conflict gnawed at her from many directions. She didn't believe war was
an effective way to rid Iraq of its weapons. She had a deep moral objection to

sending men and women to kill and die without exhausting diplomatic options. She didn't trust the president's judgment. The staggering cost shattered hopes of fulfilling domestic objectives.

And despite her intention to focus like a laser on the economy, there was no issue more important to the American people than war.

Twenty years earlier, before she was even a candidate, Pelosi had said, "I don't know what to do about the Middle East."[1] Such answers were no longer possible. She was now the number one Democrat in the House and the leader of the opposition party. A decade on the Intelligence Committee and even longer on the Appropriation Committee's foreign operations panel provided grounding for her position.

Pelosi was perplexed when the Bush administration first began building its case for war. She had seen the intelligence. She was the senior Democrat on the Intelligence Committee and was entitled to receive the best information the administration could share.

Either Bush was holding something back or he was overstating the danger.

Pelosi believed that Saddam Hussein possessed biological and chemical weapons. But she saw no evidence that he posed an imminent threat to the United States or its allies.

The louder the White House beat its war drums, the more concerned Pelosi grew. Either they knew something she didn't or they were rushing the nation into a dangerous conflict.

The administration sent its representatives to the Capitol's secure rooms to display aluminum tubes and documents purportedly showing the purchase of uranium "yellow cake" from Niger. There were satellite photographs showing activity around buildings where chemical and biological weapons were allegedly prepared. But they didn't prove anything. Bush kept talking about connecting the dots, but the lines seemed awfully faint.

Pelosi had seen enough intelligence reports to know that such information is typically ambiguous and subject to interpretation.

"I could show you a dining room table, with plates and forks and knives for 10, and I could say that's a beautiful setting. And you could say, 'There are 10 weapons,'" Pelosi said, explaining the different interpretations.[2]

But Bush's assumptions seemed to be built upon "worst-case scenario upon worst-case scenario upon worst-case scenario."

Weapons? Pelosi believed Iraq had them, but so did many other unfriendly countries. Ties to terrorists? No more than countries like Syria or Iran. Human rights atrocities? Yes, Saddam was a monster. But the United States wasn't in the habit of attacking countries over human rights.

"China kills monks," Pelosi pointed out incredulously.[3]

Pelosi was not unconcerned about biological and chemical weapons. In 1998, when President Clinton threatened Iraq with attack if the country did not allow in UN inspectors, Pelosi had said, "There is much more education that needs to be done for the American people on weapons of mass destruction."

In an interview five years before America went to war, Pelosi noted the dangerous intersection between such weapons and terrorism and said, "As a member of the House Intelligence Committee, concerns about biological and chemical weapons cannot be exaggerated."

Even then she insisted that all diplomatic options be exhausted before launching an attack, which she worried might only make the situation worse.

"Diplomatic solutions take a long time," she said. "I am closer to those who want no military action. Getting rid of Saddam Hussein, that is too broad a mission to be done without [Iraqi] civilian cooperation."

In the first months after the September 11 attacks, Pelosi stood with Bush, praising his global efforts to combat terrorism.

"There is no space, air, or oxygen between Democrats and Republicans on the war on terrorism," Pelosi said in January 2002.

She even voiced hope that Bush's aggressive threats might boost the chances of Saddam Hussein dismantling his weapons or allowing inspectors in. But sending US troops into Iraq to topple the Iraqi president was a policy she rejected from the start.

Bush traveled to Cincinnati in the fall for a prime-time address on the eve of a congressional debate on Iraq and warned of a gathering threat.

"Facing clear evidence of peril, we cannot wait for the final proof, the smoking gun that could come in the form of a mushroom cloud," Bush said. The public was with him, and so were many Democrats in Washington.

After the speech, Pelosi complained in an interview that the mushroom-cloud line was a "disservice to the debate," making it sound like war critics wanted to do nothing. She said it was curious that Bush had referred to President Kennedy's resolve in the 1962 Cuban missile crisis, when Kennedy had faced "a clear and present danger 90 miles away, and it was resolved without the use of force."

"I'm not denying anything he said. I'm just saying the threat is different than he presents it," she said of Bush. "No one has said they are not trying to develop weapons of mass destruction, it's a question of the immediacy of the threat. Many countries have capabilities. . . . If the president has any evidence for [Iraq's] plans or intentions . . . he has not shared those with the Congress."[4]

The safe political position was to support the president. Some Democrats warned Pelosi she would never advance from whip to Democratic leader—let alone lead the party to a majority—if she voted against authorizing the use of force in Iraq. Nevertheless, Pelosi led the opposition on the House floor later that week, taking 60 percent of her fellow Democrats with her.

"It is from the perspective of 10 years on the Intelligence Committee that I rise in opposition to this resolution on national security grounds. The clear and present danger that our country faces is terrorism. I say flat out that unilateral use of force without first exhausting every diplomatic remedy and other remedies and making a case to the American people will be harmful to our war on terrorism," she said.

It did not go unnoticed on Capitol Hill that more Democrats followed Pelosi than followed Richard Gephardt, the House Democratic leader who had stood with Bush.

Like many Americans, Pelosi listened to Secretary of State Colin Powell's presentation of evidence to the United Nations Security Council in early 2003 and said afterward that the case for "disarming Saddam Hussein is strong and well known." But she disputed the Bush administration's conclusion that the evidence warranted an attack.

"I am not in the category of people who say no war under any circumstances," Pelosi said. "I am just saying at this time, is this the best remedy to the problem that we have?"[5]

Weeks before the war began, Pelosi laid out her foreign policy approach in a speech to the Council on Foreign Relations in New York, saying that American foreign policy must rely on cultivating international alliances, promoting security, and advancing democratic values.

"The administration does not like to use the term *nation building*, but that is what we, working with the international community, must do. Rebuilding an Iraq that is a safer and better place will not be easy. It will be a long and difficult road."

She was adamantly opposed to going to war. She could also see it was inevitable. In early March Pelosi traveled with her friend Jack Murtha to Turkey to plead the US case for using their airstrips as staging areas. She also visited with troops in Kuwait and Qatar. She felt it was important to let them know that while she opposed the war, she would be fully behind them once it began.

"Sadly, we stand on the brink of war. If our troops are ordered into action, Americans will support and stand united behind our courageous men and women in uniform who will bear the burden of that action," Pelosi pledged.

Pelosi was not the only public figure speaking out against war. But in Washington, very few were so prominent. Senators John Kerry and John Edwards, who were both running for president, had each voted in favor of the war resolution in

November, as had Senator Hillary Clinton. Many Democratic-leaning opinion makers—from columnist Thomas Friedman of the *New York Times*, to Peter Beinert in the *New Republic*, to the editors of the *Washington Post* editorial page—supported the war.

"I'm not opposed to the use of force in the right conditions, in the right case. I just think they got it in their sights, and they won't be distracted," she warned.

ON THE THIRD MONDAY IN MARCH, Bush summoned Pelosi and other congressional leaders to the Oval Office, where he informed them he was giving Saddam Hussein 48 hours to get out of the country. He would go on television that evening to announce it to the world.

Pelosi had never seen Bush so solemn.

"He's usually quite amiable. He was quite somber," Pelosi recalled a few days later. "It spoke to the seriousness of the situation. It doesn't get any more serious than this. And *serious* doesn't seem to be strong enough."

Pelosi said she and the other members "expressed condolences to the president."

"He was convinced of his course of action. He appeared comfortable," she said.

That Friday, as the first wave of Shock and Awe began destroying central Baghdad, Pelosi spoke with sadness about the coming carnage and her inability to prevent it.

"I consider it one of the great disappointments of my public life that I could not use my influence to stop this war," Pelosi said in her office. "I know the limitations of my power. We're in the minority."

The start of combat put Pelosi in an awkward situation. She was the highest-ranking Democrat opposed to the war. She had no second thoughts or intention of acquiescing. She also didn't want to say anything that might be regarded as undermining the troops.

The walls of St. Leo's Church in Little Italy memorialized the names of hundreds of neighbors who had fought and died on behalf of their country. Pelosi revered the sacrifice even as she deplored the policy.

She worried that antiwar statements in the opening days of battle would be misconstrued. It was one thing for a member of Congress to speak his or her mind. It was quite another for the House Democratic leader to do so.

Pelosi did not attend antiwar rallies held in San Francisco the week the bombings began.

"I do not have any intention of second-guessing the strategy of the commander in chief and those who are waging this war," she said.

When House Republicans offered a motion that supported the troops and praised President Bush's leadership as commander in chief, Pelosi voted in favor.

"I disagree with the policy that took us to this war. I dispute some of the arguments used in favor of this resolution," Pelosi said on the House floor. "But even those objections cannot overcome the pride and appreciation that I have in our troops and the message that I want them to hear from us tonight.

"There is no heavier burden for a president and no more solemn choice for this nation than to send our young men and women into battle," Pelosi continued. "As commander in chief, President Bush has made that difficult choice."

Some antiwar activists, including some of her own constituents, accused her of playing politics by opposing the war so vehemently and then standing by the president once it began.

"That was then. This is now," Pelosi responded sharply in an interview. "Our young—our men and women are in harm's way."

At the same time, she jumped to the protesters' defense when administration confidante Richard Perle, a former member of a Pentagon advisory board, observed that "there are more demonstrators in the streets of San Francisco than there are people prepared to die for Saddam."

"It may give the Richard Perles of the world comfort to think that way," Pelosi said in the same interview, "but he's absolutely wrong. He's avoiding the truth, which is that there are legitimate reasons to oppose this policy. Those who would like to simplify their thinking by saying that there is any sympathy for Saddam Hussein in the world do a grave disservice to the debate."

Pelosi's daughter Christine reminded her that when Pelosi had protested the Gulf War in 1991, she had told Christine that she was "advocating for peaceful resolution to the conflict." That was what she should be doing now.

Pelosi's criticism of the war remained restrained as Baghdad fell and Bush declared the mission accomplished. But it did not take long for Pelosi's diplomatic posture to give way to more vocal criticism.

Appearing at the Pacific Exchange in San Francisco on the last day of May, Pelosi said the "fog of war" had shielded Bush from political attack and scrutiny, but as the war neared the end of its third month, she believed his policies were now "fair game."

"One of the reasons that he retains popularity is that he hasn't been adequately challenged," Pelosi said. "Now he will be."[6]

Pelosi was growing increasingly alarmed about what she viewed as the administration's failure to plan for Iraq's reconstruction. Once again, either the administration had no plan or they weren't sharing it with Capitol Hill.

When Bush came to Congress asking for $87 billion in war funds—the measure that Democrat John Kerry awkwardly boasted that he voted for before he voted against it—Pelosi was dead-set opposed to it.

"As long as the Republicans in Congress keep writing the president blank checks, the American people will lose," Pelosi said, warning that ultimately the war was going to be "a quarter of a trillion dollar expenditure."

Pelosi grew more vocal as the election year began.

Delivering the Democratic response to Bush's State of the Union Address, Pelosi accused the president of pursuing "a go-it-alone foreign policy that leaves us isolated abroad and that steals the resources we need for education and health care here at home. The president led us into the Iraq War on the basis of unproven assertions without evidence; he embraced a radical doctrine of preemptive war unprecedented in our history, and he failed to build true international coalitions."

She stepped it up in a speech to newspaper editors that spring, telling them that "the president's resolve may be firm, but his judgment is not sound. It is ironic that in a nation obsessed with reality television, we have a president who is increasingly divorced from reality."

But Pelosi didn't believe the criticism was getting through. After 14 months of fighting, nearly 1,000 Americans were dead and tens of thousands of Iraqis had been killed. Washington was being too timid in challenging an inept president and a war that had gone amok.

On the afternoon of May 19, Pelosi sat down for an interview with the *San Francisco Chronicle*, determined to let her criticism be heard.

Seated on the couch in her spacious office, the same office that Tip O'Neill had used as Speaker 20 years before, Pelosi unloaded on Bush, laying bare her utter lack of confidence in the commander in chief.

"The only way to improve the situation in Iraq is to elect a new president of the United States," Pelosi said at the outset. "The president has demonstrated very clearly that he does not have the capacity to present a plan to transition Iraq from combat and the fall of Baghdad. He didn't have a plan for the immediate fall of Baghdad, period.

"George Bush is in over his head. He either did not know or did not care to learn about what would happen after Saddam fell," she said.

Her words turned uncharacteristically personal, asserting, "It's hopeless for George Bush. He has made it hopeless. In the private sector he would have been long gone. . . . He simply doesn't have the capacity to lead us to a resolution in Iraq. We need a new commander in chief."

She kept coming back to the point for emphasis.

"Some people say the president has strong resolve. The president may have strong resolve, but he has no judgment and no plan. His resolve only comes through stubbornness. The only way out of Iraq is for us to have a new leader."

The talk of replacing Bush was not surprising in an election year. But Pelosi went far beyond what any other leader had said in criticizing the wartime president.

"He has on his shoulders the deaths of many more troops because he would not heed the advice of this own State Department of what to expect after . . . he declared that major combat was over. . . . The president has created a hotbed of terrorism in Iraq.

"They're still selling this bill of goods that they had this great coalition. They are so pathetic; they are so in denial about their own ineffectiveness. This administration refused to realize that we would be met by rocket-propelled grenades, not roses."

Pelosi worried that the president was "so irresponsible and knows that there is no way for him to succeed that he may rationalize some course of action to bring the troops home and just walk away from it and declare victory."

She was certain that the public's frustrations with his ineptitude had cost him his shot at reelection.

"He's gone. He's so gone."

Such views were not far from the mainstream by the time Pelosi became Speaker 2½ years later. In the spring of 2004, Pelosi was going far out on a limb. Her invective grew stronger as the 45-minute interview went on.

"Bush is an incompetent leader. In fact, he's not a leader. He's a person who has no judgment, no experience, and no knowledge on the subjects that he has to decide upon," she said.

"As far as we can tell, the shallowness that he has brought to the office has not changed since he got there. Not to get personal about it, but the president's capacity to lead has never been there. In order to lead you have to have judgment. In order to have judgment you have to have knowledge and experience. He has none."

When the interview was over, she turned to her communications director, Brendan Daly.

"I made news there, didn't I?"

Daly told her she had and asked why she didn't tell him she was going to do that in advance.

"I didn't want you to talk me out of it," she responded.

The comments had the intended effect. Bush's ability to wage war and the Democratic leader's lack of confidence in him were the talk of Washington. The debate was engaged.

At the White House, press secretary Scott McClellan told reporters that Pelosi's comments were not "worth dignifying with any response from this podium." However, across the Potomac at Bush-Cheney reelection headquarters, campaign chair Marc Racicot said the comments were a "reprehensible attempt to blame America for the action of terrorists and represent a fundamental misunderstanding of the war on terror."

House majority leader Tom DeLay said Pelosi was "apparently so caught up in the partisan hatred for President Bush that her words are putting American lives at risk." And Representative Tom Reynolds, chair of the House Republicans' campaign committee, suggested that if Pelosi had nothing more productive to "offer the troops . . . then she should go back to her pastel-colored condo in San Francisco and keep her views to herself."

By the following day, the Republican Party had gone into a full Pelosi spin cycle, distributing an 11-page critique of Pelosi's liberal record as a member of Congress entitled "Totally San Fran: 17 Years of San Francisco Liberalism."

At her weekly news briefing the next morning, every question was about Iraq.

"What is your evaluation of the president's competence as a leader, his judgment, his experience and knowledge, his depth that he has brought to the office?" was the first question.

Pelosi had no intention of backing down.

"I think the time has come to speak very frankly about the lack of leadership in the White House, the lack of judgment," she said. "So the emperor has no clothes. When are people going to face reality?"

Pelosi told reporters that it wasn't her words that were undermining his leadership, it was his decisions. "My statements are just a statement of fact."

The attack on Bush had been classic Pelosi. Her words were bold. Some viewed them as over the top, while others called them appropriately blunt. They were brusque and belligerent. They were also calculated. Pelosi was not prone to emotional outbursts. Many of the same Democrats who cringed at what they believed was too hostile an attack used some of the same words months later.

"The risk in many of us speaking out in the way I'm speaking out to you right now is that people will say, 'Oh, it's just political,'" Pelosi said in the initial interview. "I think people know this is a situation of [Bush's] own making."

As presidential candidate John Kerry danced carefully around his opposition to the war, telling reporters that if he had the chance he'd vote to authorize the war all over again, Pelosi was unequivocal in her disagreement.

"When I was elected House Democratic leader, I pledged: Never again will Democrats go into an election without telling the American people who we are, what we stand for, what our differences are with the Republicans, and what we are going to fight for as Democrats," she said to a rousing ovation before 2,000 activists at the Campaign for America's Future. "What does President Bush say? He says we must stay the course. In order to prevail in Iraq, we must change the course. And we can only change course by changing the commander in chief."

Pelosi was certain Kerry would win and was hoping he would carry some Democratic House candidates with him.

"I put my credibility on the line here—John Kerry will be the next president of the United States," Pelosi confidently predicted on national television the Sunday before the vote.[7]

To Pelosi's great surprise—and horror—Americans reelected their commander in chief. Both houses of Congress remained in Republican hands. The war continued to gnaw at her, and there appeared to be little she could do to stop it.

Pelosi fell back on her grassroots instincts. The more people she could bring to her position, the more difficult it would be to sustain the war.

Pelosi had regularly asked her friend Jack Murtha for his ideas on how the United States should change course in Iraq. She had relied on Murtha's military advice for years. As a 37-year veteran of the Marines and the senior Democrat on the appropriations panel that distributed money to the Pentagon, no Democrat understood the military better or had more friends at the Pentagon than Murtha.

Murtha had voted in favor of Bush's use-of-force resolution and was regarded as a hawk. But he privately began to doubt that vote just weeks after he cast it and had grown increasingly critical of Bush's operation of the military.

In early November 2005, Pelosi approached Murtha once again.

"Come up with a policy that Democrats can live with," she told him. Murtha was more prepared than she knew. He had come to the conclusion that the war as it was being fought was unwinnable. The next day he outlined to Pelosi a plan to quickly begin withdrawing troops. The withdrawal could be completed in roughly six months, depending on conditions on the ground, and then a small force could be kept "over the horizon" to provide security.

Pelosi was a bit surprised by how far Murtha was prepared to go, as well as by how quickly he responded. She was thrilled. She embraced it without hesitation and asked Murtha to introduce the plan to the entire Democratic Caucus. Murtha agreed and asked Pelosi to let him present it alone.

"I felt it would have more impact if she weren't standing with me," Murtha said.

It was partly a matter of honor. But it was also a matter of politics. A plan presented by the grizzled hawk with two Purple Hearts and a Bronze Star would be received differently than one embraced by a San Francisco Democrat. Pelosi gladly obliged.

The following day Murtha explained his plan, first to a closed-door meeting of Democratic members and then to reporters, fighting back tears as he recalled his hospital visits to wounded soldiers returning from Iraq. By chance, Pelosi had her weekly news conference scheduled for that morning and, not surprisingly, Murtha's plan was the focus of the questions. Pelosi, by design, wasn't talking.

"Mr. Murtha—this is his day," Pelosi said as reporters tried to gauge the level of support from the party's leader.

A reporter asked for clarification: "Do you agree with the call for immediate withdrawal?"

"As I said, that was Mr. Murtha's statement, and I will take it under consideration."

His statement? Take it under consideration? American troops were being killed at a rate of more than 75 a month, and the most prominent Democratic critic representing America's most antiwar city wouldn't speak out at her own news conference?

Nine times Pelosi was asked whether she supported Murtha's proposal. Nine times Pelosi found a way not to answer the question.

"When would we expect to hear from you on that front?" a reporter inquired.

"Today, I think we should all savor the very thought-provoking statement that Mr. Murtha made. He made it with great knowledge. He made it with great passion. He made it with great determination," she answered.

The silence angered many of her constituents in San Francisco. Some protested at her appearances. Others organized a mock trial.

Inside the Democratic Caucus it was clear that she supported Murtha. She had said as much at their closed-door meeting when he introduced his plan. But the calculation was that for Pelosi to speak up on the same day would change the headline from "Decorated Pennsylvania Hawk Speaks Out Against War" to "San Francisco Democratic Leader Calls for Withdrawal." And she had given Murtha her word.

Republicans attacked right on cue. Speaker Dennis Hastert said Murtha's plan would "wave the white flag of surrender," and Representative Jeanne Schmidt of Ohio took to the House floor and said she had just received a phone call from a Marine colonel who asked her "to send Congressman Murtha a message: that cowards cut and run, Marines never do."

The House's decorum broke down as Democratic members erupted in boos.

"You guys are pathetic. Pathetic," Democratic representative Marty Meehan of Massachusetts shouted across the aisle. Representative Harold Ford of Tennessee had to be restrained as he charged the Republican side of the room, demanding a retraction.

It would be one thing to attack the antiwar leader from San Francisco. Going after the vet from Pennsylvania with 37 years of Marine service made Republicans look brazen. Schmidt became the laughingstock of late-night comedians.

Asked a few months later if it had been difficult to stand in front of half a dozen news cameras and 50 reporters and provide implausible nonanswers to questions about a proposal she clearly had a strong opinion about, Pelosi acted as if it were a silly question.

"Noooo," she said dismissively. "There was a point to it. The point to it was whatever my position was going to be on it, yes or no, it was important for this man with 35 years of national security experience and leadership to go out there and say it from his perspective. . . . I thought it was really important that he be the messenger."

Just before the House adjourned for Thanksgiving, Republican leaders tried to drive a wedge through the Democratic Caucus by rushing to the floor a nonbinding resolution that would have called for an immediate withdrawal of all troops from Iraq. It was an oversimplification of Murtha's plan that they knew didn't have the support to pass, and they wanted to put Democrats on record as calling for surrender.

Pelosi wasn't going to give them the satisfaction. She rose to the House floor and excoriated Republicans for their tactics, at one point declaring, "Mr. Murtha has dealt the mighty blow of truth to the president's failed Iraq policy. The American people have rallied to Jack Murtha's message of truth.

"But you," she cried, turning to her Republican colleagues, "can't handle the truth!"

She then instructed Democrats to join Republicans in voting against the proposal, rendering the exercise moot.

However, divisions within the Democratic Party were evident when Pelosi publicly embraced Murtha's proposal at the end of the month.

At a noon news conference in the House Radio-TV Gallery, Pelosi announced, "We should follow the lead of Congressman John Murtha, who has put forth a plan to make America safer, to make our military stronger, and to make Iraq more stable."

Roughly 90 minutes later, Hoyer released a statement that read: "I believe that a precipitous withdrawal of American forces in Iraq could lead to disaster, spawning a civil war, fostering a haven for terrorists, and damaging our nation's security and credibility."

Pelosi was displeased. Murtha was incensed.

The tensions were apparent the following week at a closed-door meeting of the entire Democratic Caucus to discuss Iraq. An advisory to the press announced that Democrats would talk about their policy when the meeting concluded at 10:00 a.m. The question was, *which* policy?

Behind closed doors, members heard from Murtha, as well as from Representatives Ike Skelton, Neil Abercrombie, David Pryce, and Ellen Tauscher. Ideas ranged from sending in more troops to an immediate withdrawal. There was no consensus.

"So we're not a party that is in lockstep with each other on every subject," Pelosi explained when the meeting broke up. "And certainly, as I say, on the subject of war, everybody comes from their own place on it."

But their body language, as members emerged an hour late, made it clear that it had not been a unifying exercise.

That morning's *Washington Post* contained a front-page story quoting prominent Democrats under the headline: "Democrats Fear Backlash at Polls for Antiwar Remarks."[8]

The article quoted Democrats fearful that Pelosi's and Democratic Party chair Howard Dean's antiwar comments would reinforce the party's reputation for being soft on national security and cost the party any chance it had of winning the majority in 2006. The story cited Hoyer and Emanuel as warning colleagues that Pelosi's antics could backfire.

Asked after the caucus meeting about Hoyer's comments, Pelosi professed not to be familiar with the story. Pressed on whether she regretted endorsing Murtha's proposal, Pelosi was adamant.

"I'm so very proud of endorsing Mr. Murtha's proposal. I think that he has kicked open a door in our country to let in some fresh air and some sunlight into the debate on what's going on in Iraq. I'm very proud to have endorsed it, and today I will sign on as a cosponsor of his resolution."

By then Hoyer had already left the gathering.

Many pundits and strategists warned that Pelosi had seriously jeopardized her chances to become Speaker by embracing a far-out plan that would distract the public from its growing disenchantment with Bush.

They were mistaken. Murtha's proposal had changed the debate. More and more Democrats spoke out against the war. Antiwar activists said his plan had pushed the debate forward by six months. And the party's opposition was a critical reason that, one year later, Democrats won the majority, making Hoyer majority leader and Emanuel chair of the caucus.

Emanuel acknowledged the next year that Pelosi had seen it quicker than he had.

"She was right and I was wrong."[9]

CHAPTER FIFTEEN

Madam Leader

*"Bully me? No. I don't think so. I think they have been
disabused of that notion, should anybody have had it."*
—NANCY PELOSI, 2006

*"She's a pretty good politician. She really is. Her ability
to look somebody in the eye and be tough. She doesn't melt.
Republicans have come to the realization that she's not a foil."*
—FORMER SPEAKER DENNIS HASTERT (R-IL), 2007

HOUSE MAJORITY LEADER TOM DELAY phoned Pelosi on her second day as
Democratic leader. She didn't take the call.

Pelosi was in middle of her first steering committee meeting and had the delicate task of doling out committee assignments to her 202 Democratic colleagues.

DeLay phoned again. Pelosi told her staff she'd have to call him back. She had a meeting scheduled at the White House with DeLay later in the day, and she figured he wanted to discuss it in advance.

The steering committee's task of handing out assignments could make or break careers. A seat on the right committee allowed members to raise money, move legislation dear to their constituents, and determine the role they would play in Washington. The split on committees was supposed to reflect each party's relative strength in the Congress. The majority determines the precise number of slots each party gets, and then each party decides who fills them. Democrats had lost six seats in the 2002 election, but Speaker Hastert had told Pelosi that the committee numbers wouldn't change. Pelosi asked him to put it in writing, which he did.

Pelosi returned DeLay's call as soon as the meeting broke up.

"Hey, Tom, sorry I couldn't take your call. I was having our steering committee," Pelosi said.[1]

"Um, that's what I was calling about," DeLay said, as Pelosi recalled it. "I was calling to tell you that you have one less member on Ways and Means."

Pelosi was flabbergasted.

Ways and Means is no ordinary committee. It is the committee that writes the nation's tax laws and, along with the Appropriations and Energy and Commerce committees, it is among the most coveted assignments in Congress.

She had it in writing.

Pelosi told DeLay of her letter from Hastert. Democrats had already prepared press releases announcing the appointments. DeLay said he was aware of Hastert's pledge, but Republican members had a different view and had decided to cut back the committee's size. He suggested that she find someone to remove from the panel.

Pelosi remembered the exact words she used in response.

"Life on this planet as you know it will not be the same if you persist in this notion."

The Democrats had decided to fill two openings on Ways and Means with Max Sandlin of Texas and Stephanie Tubbs of Ohio, who would be the first African American woman ever named to the tax-writing committee.

"No way that I was backing down. He said, 'You can take someone else off the committee.' I said, 'You know that's not how it works.'"

The Congressional Black Caucus had a news conference on a different matter scheduled for later in the day. Pelosi told DeLay that if Republicans didn't back down, it could easily evolve into a news conference about the GOP going back on its word and depriving an African American woman of a seat on the committee.

The battle of wills wasn't through. Later in the day Pelosi's staff told her that Republicans had sent word that if she didn't back off, they were going to come after her personally.

"I'm shaking in my boots," Pelosi said sarcastically. "That is so pathetic. Tell them, C'mon. Come after me."

Hastert ordered the GOP to back off, and Tubbs got her seat.

"That was the first and the last time they ever tried that," Pelosi said. "They backed off because we made it too hot for them to handle."

Pelosi recounted the incident after being asked in an interview whether she thought anyone had tried to bully her because she was a woman.

"Bully me? No. I don't think so. I think they have been disabused of that notion, should anybody have had it—and I doubt that they did."

Republicans had a different version of the events. They said that Ways and Means chairman Bill Thomas found the committee too large—41 members—and had decided to remove a member from each party. Hastert had promised Pelosi that the balance wouldn't change, and by removing a member of each party, the Democrats' standing would have improved ever so slightly.

Hastert said he was fairly certain that Pelosi knew why DeLay was calling and figured she made a tactical decision not to respond.

"We tried to get her out to talk to her about it, and she wouldn't come out," he said.

Told of Pelosi's version of the events, he said, "I'm sure that's her story and she's sticking to it."

Hastert found working with Pelosi difficult. They were friendly at receptions, when greeting heads of state, and at other formal functions. Hastert tried to have chocolate on the table when Pelosi came to meetings, and she was always gracious.

But on policy, where they often had deep differences, he would receive stern phone calls in which it sounded to him like she was reading from a script.

"There's always this kind of stiffness there," Hastert said. "We wouldn't have a discussion. It would just go down the line of discussion. Couldn't get around it."

For her part, Pelosi said she got along just fine with Hastert and said much of their communication was through letters.

"The uncanny thing was on a face-to-face basis, we'd talk quite nicely," Hastert said. "But when we get back, we'd have a nasty letter, probably written by her [staff]. It happened time after time after time."

But Hastert said he always respected her.

"I give her credit. She's a pretty good politician. She really is. Her ability to look somebody in the eye and be tough. She doesn't melt. Republicans have come to the realization that she's not a foil. She's someone you have to deal with."

For most members of Congress, life in the Capitol is a constant struggle to stand above the pack. A member's annual salary—$165,200 when Pelosi was leader—travel budget, access to the White House, and other perks define America's image of influence and power. But the day-to-day reality is far less glamorous.

Members are assigned cramped workspaces, with as many as six aides sharing a single room. Constituents, lobbyists, interest groups, donors, reporters, and staff place enormous demands on their time, prompting hurried runs across Independence Avenue to cast votes. Behind the grand 19th-century House chamber, a cloakroom is furnished with worn brown leather sofas, a bank of phone booths, and a hot dog broiler resembling those in airport bars, where members can buy a hot dog for 50 cents.

Pelosi worked above the fray. Her suite of offices just steps off the House floor included four spacious rooms, a private kitchen, and a conference area with views of the Supreme Court. A mouse would occasionally startle the leader, but she was fiercely proud that this was the same suite occupied by Tip O'Neill during his 10-year term as Speaker.

On the walls she had paintings on loan from the San Francisco Museum of Modern Art; a photograph of her as a 16-year-old in a formal dress and white gloves, drawing an admiring grin from then senator John Kennedy; a picture of her father being sworn in as mayor of Baltimore in 1947 as she holds a Bible; a picture of her own swearing-in to Congress as her father watches from a wheelchair; and a picture of New Jersey congresswoman Mary T. Norton, who chaired three different committees in the 1930s and 1940s and famously remarked, "I am no lady, I'm a member of Congress."

There were bowls filled with Hershey's Kisses or Ghirardelli chocolates. She also had a bust of Phil Burton; a replica of the Goddess of Freedom statue that democracy protesters had erected in Tiananmen Square; a brick from Baltimore's Memorial Stadium, which her father had been influential in opening; baseballs autographed by Hank Aaron, Barry Bonds, Orlando Cepeda, and Bobby Thompson; and an encased Rawlings baseball bat that might have displeased some of her San Francisco constituents. The bat was inscribed: "Congresswoman Nancy Pelosi. M.V.P. Best Wishes, Frank & Jamie McCourt." The McCourts were big donors. They also owned the Los Angeles Dodgers, and the bat carried the team's insignia.

She not only appeared comfortable in her new office, she seemed comfortable in her new role as leader. She had been born to a member of Congress and surrounded by elected officials throughout her entire life. She understood the language, the rhythms, the egos, and, perhaps most important, the needs of her colleagues.

She now had five grandchildren and sometimes accompanied them to the House floor, joking to others that she'd raise them herself if not for her daughters' objections.

Her youngest daughter was drawing rave reviews for her campaign-trail documentary on candidate George W. Bush, and Pelosi hosted a Capitol Hill screening for members, proudly boasting of Alexandra's success.

When a reporter at her weekly news conference prefaced a question by calling it a "softball across the plate," she quickly interrupted: "I thought you were going to ask me, 'How many Emmy nominations did Alexandra Pelosi get this morning?' Six. Six Emmy nominations! Isn't that great? Isn't that a wonderful thing?"

Pelosi also tried to instill a sense of confidence in a party that had now lost five consecutive elections.

She brought in marketing and motivational experts to talk to the caucus, including University of California at Berkeley linguist George Lakoff, who believed Democrats could improve their standing by "reframing" the terms of debate. Twice she brought in Jack Trout, a marketing expert whose books included *The Power of Simplicity: A Management Guide to Cutting Through the Nonsense and Doing Things Right* and *Differentiate or Die: Survival in Our Era of Killer Competition.*

Pelosi was confident voters were on their side. Democrats just needed to find a better way to put their case before the American people.

"She sees us as the majority. We're already the majority, we just don't have the votes right now," said Michigan representative Bart Stupak.[2]

Pelosi was a coalition builder, and she quickly reached out to the conservative wing of her party. She named John Spratt, a budget hawk from South Carolina, as deputy leader and made him the face of the party's economic policies. She named at least half a dozen fiscally conservative Blue Dogs to open spots on prominent committees, including Jim Turner, a conservative from East Texas, to be the lead Democrat on the new homeland security panel.

Even before President Bush unveiled his economic stimulus plan, which featured the elimination of taxes on stock dividends, Pelosi and other House Democrats issued a counterproposal that called for tax rebates for the middle class. Though it stood no chance of passing in a Republican House, its reliance on tax cuts pleased conservatives in her party and started her tenure with a proposal that united Democrats.

Pelosi may have represented a congressional district that gave President Bush only 15½ percent of its votes, but she was keenly aware that she was now a leader of a national party. She had no intention of yanking her party to the left. Her goal was to win a majority.

Among her first tasks was to name someone to run the House Democrats' campaign committee, and she was under intense pressure from African Americans to name William Jefferson, who represented New Orleans.

Instead, Pelosi reached out to fellow Californian Bob Matsui of Sacramento, who wasn't particularly interested. Pelosi's choice turned out to be fateful.

Matsui died two years later of a rare blood ailment and was replaced on the campaign committee by Representative Rahm Emanuel of Illinois, a former aide to President Clinton. Jefferson was indicted on charges of bribery, racketeering, money laundering, and obstruction of justice after the FBI recovered $90,000 in marked bills wrapped in foil in his freezer.

Republicans used Jefferson with little success as evidence that both parties were touched by the corruption scandals enveloping the Capitol. Had Jefferson been head of the party's campaign committee, it would have deprived Democrats of one of their most potent issues in 2006 when they won back the House.

Pelosi said she had had no inkling of Jefferson's ethics troubles at the time. She was impressed by his achievements; Jefferson had grown up poor, graduated from Harvard Law School, and earned a master's degree in tax law at Georgetown while serving in Congress. Pelosi had enormous respect for him.

"I had to have someone there in whom I had total confidence," she explained of her choice in an interview. "I'd known Bob [Matsui] for 25 years. I'm not interested in surprises in politics."

Matsui took some persuading. He was the number three Democrat on Ways and Means and an expert on Social Security, and he looked forward to the coming debate over the program's future.

"Nancy kept calling him," recalled Doris Matsui, the congressman's widow, who was elected to replace him after he died unexpectedly on New Year's Day in 2005.

"She wanted him to think about the fact that we couldn't stay a minority party. She needed someone to take up the challenge."

IT IS A REALITY OF MODERN POLITICS that women who attain high positions must show toughness. Margaret Thatcher displayed nerves of steel as British prime minister. Jeanne Kirkpatrick was highly regarded for her unyielding stands as United Nations ambassador. Hillary Clinton projected an aura of resoluteness in her quest for the presidency.

For Pelosi, toughness was a quality that came naturally. It was also a necessary ingredient for winning back the majority.

Dick Gephardt had been leader since Democrats became the minority party following the 1994 election. He was a tireless advocate and money raiser. He kept peace among Democrats. He was beloved by his colleagues. He also had his eye on the presidency. Whether it was his Midwestern nature or his fear of alienating potential supporters, he couldn't say no.

Pelosi changed that.

She quickly established that the perks she controlled—committee assignments, fund-raising visits, assignment to high-profile legislation—would go to those who worked hardest for the Democratic team and be withheld from those who didn't. Just as she had rewarded Lynn Rivers over John Dingell in the Michigan primary race, Pelosi rewarded loyalty, and she demanded devotion to the Democratic Caucus.

When Brooklyn Democrat Edolphus Towns voted with Republicans on a trade bill and then missed a close budget vote, Pelosi made it known that his coveted seat on the Energy and Commerce Committee was in danger. Representative Albert Wynn of Maryland was told he would lose the use of the party's phones if he did not share more campaign dollars. When 15 Democrats joined Republicans to pass the Central American Free Trade Agreement, Pelosi erupted in a closed-door meeting, coming as close to screaming as many colleagues had ever heard her.

Had her father displayed such behavior during his House tenure, it would hardly have turned heads. A tough Italian American political operator from Baltimore fits a familiar stereotype. But the sight of a fashionable San Francisco liberal imposing discipline was something new.

Pelosi was not physically intimidating like former Speaker Jim Wright or Senate majority leader Lyndon Johnson, who towered over their colleagues in the corridors of the Capitol. Speaker Sam Rayburn, who stood only five feet seven inches tall, could exhibit a menacing "stare that would melt your collar," recalled Dingell, who served with Rayburn for three terms. Unlike her mentor Phil Burton, Pelosi was not prone to ranting or cursing. She was not a yeller. Even in the most heated political arguments, Pelosi remembered what her father had told her: "Keep the friendship in your voice."

But Pelosi let it be known when she was displeased. Her mouth tightened, her eyes grew wide, and she could speak with a pointed bluntness. She kept meticulous track of who had stood with her. She could invoke fear with the sternness of an angry parent. And like her mother, she had a long memory.

"People know she means business. If she asks you to do something and you say no, who knows what comes up in the future," said Representative Rosa DeLauro

255

of Connecticut, whom Pelosi chose to head the panel that determines committee assignments. "It will not be forgotten."[3]

Pelosi invited members to a "leaders' lunch" at the beginning of each week and let it be known that, barring extraordinary circumstances, she expected Democrats to hold together.

"She said, 'If you want out, come see me, because otherwise I'm assuming you're in,'" said George Miller, who represented a district across the Bay and was Pelosi's closest confidant in the Capitol. "'If you have no loyalty to us . . . then we have no loyalty to you.' She has made it clear that nothing is automatic anymore. We're all trying to win the House back, and you have to participate."[4]

When members disappointed, sometimes Miller would seek them out on the House floor, put his arm around them, and bluntly remind them of what the caucus needed. Other times they were summoned to Pelosi's office. Talks were private and brief and rarely included staff.

Very few punishments were ever meted out. But it had an effect.

"The worst part of it would be that *she knows*, and you're left wondering what will become," said Representative Anna Eshoo, a longtime friend who represented Silicon Valley. "It's a very strict state of mind. She sets very high standards for people. No one outstrips the standards she sets for herself. But she doesn't mess around. This is very, very serious business to her. This is not some game. This is deadly serious."

"It's like in the mafia—no one really gets their knees cut off. It's the threat," said Representative Pete Stark, who had represented the East Bay since shortly after Pelosi arrived in California.

Pelosi's children recalled how she would rarely discipline them by yelling. Instead, she'd tell them how disappointed their father would be. Similarly, Pelosi never told members they had let her down. It was the caucus that would be disappointed.

"We want to be as bold as we can be and as unified as we can be," Pelosi said of her tactics in an interview. "It's not a matter of the lowest common denominator. It's the boldest measure we can take. Once we arrive at that, there is an expectation that everyone is on board.

"Let me put it this way," Pelosi explained. "In my conversations with any of our members who abandoned—who were not part of our Democratic unity on key votes—my goal was to change behavior. And I think we've done that."

Democratic unity was not nearly so critical when Pelosi arrived in Congress in the late 1980s. With huge majorities, it didn't matter if 20 or 30 members peeled off to vote with Republicans. After Democrats lost their majority, Gephardt had done little to enforce party discipline, in part because he believed the party needed to protect its most vulnerable—typically its most conservative—members.

Pelosi took another tack. Her view was that Democratic unity forced Republicans to make sloppy votes. Pelosi figured that if Republicans received no help from moderate Democrats, it would force GOP leaders to ramp up their own efforts at achieving unity and force Republican centrists to cast politically uncomfortable votes. In essence, it would pressure Republicans to become more brazen in order to move their conservative agenda and, by doing so, make them more vulnerable in congressional elections.

THE CONTROVERSIAL TALE OF the 2003 Medicare reform bill provides a textbook example of how the strategy paid off. President Bush had proposed what he called a $400 billion expansion of Medicare—the cost turned out to be significantly higher—to provide prescription drug benefits to tens of millions of seniors. Heading into Bush's reelection campaign, it was the centerpiece of the White House's domestic agenda.

It was an iffy proposition before Congress. Most Democrats opposed the plan because they believed it did not go far enough and because it allowed private health plans to compete for Medicare patients, which they believed would undermine the program. Some Republicans objected to the plan's high price tag, which made its passage a close call.

An early version of the measure passed the House by a single vote. Nine Democrats voted in favor.

"I don't want that to happen again," Pelosi said during a closed-door Democratic Caucus meeting. "This can never happen again."[5]

It is hard to gauge the actual closeness of an issue by the final vote tally. It is not uncommon for members to tell leaders, "It will be easier on me back home if I vote one way, but if you absolutely need my vote I'll go the other way." Pelosi's point was that every Democrat that sided with the GOP let another Republican off the hook.

Pelosi called several defectors into her office to voice her displeasure. She also made it plain that Democrats would be campaigning hard against the bill, and they'd be on their own if they voted for it.

"It was not the happiest conversation I've had in politics," New York representative Steve Israel, one of the plan's initial supporters, told the *Washington Post.* "She was very clear and very firm in making sure I understood the caucus position on the bill and that unity was very important.

"I didn't leave the room with any questions about where she stood," he added, offering no complaint about her approach. "It's an extremely refreshing sign of leadership. There's no guesswork."[6]

The talk had an effect.

When the Medicare bill came before the House for final passage in November, Israel was with Pelosi and the rest of the Democrats. The unity wreaked havoc on the GOP, prompting one of the most embarrassing three hours of the Republican Congress.

Trying to jam the bill through before a recess, Republicans called for a 15-minute vote at 3:01 a.m. on the Saturday morning before Thanksgiving. By 3:48 a.m., 218 members had posted votes against it, which was enough to kill the measure. But Republicans refused to gavel the vote to a close. This was a top White House priority, and they would do what was necessary to get it done.

"After the vote was open about half an hour, I drove home," Stark told ABC's

Nightline. Stark was the senior Democrat on the House panel that oversees Medicare and a strong opponent of the bill.

"It takes me an hour to get home. And I was listening to C-SPAN radio. And listening, I said, 'We're winning.' And I got home, and I got in bed, and I looked at the television, on C-SPAN again. And we were winning. And then I said, *Wait a minute!*"

At 6:00 a.m., as the sun was about to rise, Republicans found just enough members to switch their votes—and the vote was gaveled to a close. The 15-minute vote had lasted three hours. In the process, Representative Nick Smith, a retiring Michigan Republican, said he was approached by his own party's leaders, who told him they'd pony up $100,000 for the campaign of his son, who was running to replace him, if he'd change his vote to "yes." When he told them to get lost, they warned him to change his vote or they'd make sure his son was defeated.

Smith later recanted the $100,000 charge, but House majority leader Tom DeLay was reprimanded for his arm-twisting conduct. The Medicare vote became the poster child for Republican abuse of authority and what Pelosi would later call a "culture of corruption."

"We had hoped the Republicans would want to win this vote fair and square. They didn't," Pelosi said after the vote. "We won it fair and square, so they stole it by hook or crook."

Democrats then set out to let Americans know how the Medicare bill was passed. In early December, just moments before the national Christmas tree was lit on the south side of the White House, Pelosi used her status as minority leader to offer a privileged resolution before the House.

The rare parliamentary procedure was used to offer a resolution that began: "Whereas the recurring practice of improperly holding votes open for the sole purpose of overturning the will of the majority, including bullying and threatening members to vote against their conscience, has occurred eight times since 2003, and three times in the 109th Congress alone . . ."

Six hundred words later it concluded: "that the House denounces the culture of corruption exhibited by the Republican leadership . . . and directs the Speaker to take such steps as necessary to prevent any further abuse."

The measure had no prayer of passing in a Republican House. But by demanding a vote, Pelosi was able to call on clerk Mary Kevin Niland to read the entire resolution aloud, which included a blow-by-blow account of the Medicare vote.

"I know you don't want to hear it, but you will," Pelosi said as she commanded the House be gaveled to order so each word could be heard in the chamber and by the nationwide C-SPAN audience.

Such tactics did not win Pelosi many friends among Republicans. When she was asked which Republicans she hangs out with, Pelosi responded, "I don't hang out."

However, Democrats under Pelosi's leadership achieved record levels of unity. *Congressional Quarterly* magazine examined 669 roll call votes in 2005 and found that Democrats voted unanimously against the GOP in 82 instances and against GOP measures 88 percent of the time. It was the highest measure of Democratic unity since the magazine began keeping track in 1956.

Democrats did not have enough votes to stop the GOP agenda, but their cohesion created major headaches for the opposition.

"It's not by alchemy that you get unity," DeLauro said. "It's by working on it. She's unrelenting in that regard. She's not afraid to tell people what the story is."

PELOSI REGARDED STOPPING PRESIDENT Bush's Social Security plan as her biggest triumph as Democratic leader.

Social Security was the heart of the New Deal legislation her father revered. It was critical to the well-being of many Little Italy neighbors. It was a compact between generations that spoke to what was good about America.

"It's fundamental to who we are as a country," Pelosi said.[7]

Pelosi had even grown emotional when Republicans tried to remove Roosevelt's face from the dime, calling it symbolic of their cold hearts.

"They want to undo all the social progress that has been made in this country in the last century—much of it springing from the Roosevelt years," Pelosi complained. "They are about the special interests and not the public interest. They are the government of the few, by the few, and for the few."[8]

So when Bush was reelected and announced he would spend his political capital trying to enact a program of private Social Security accounts, Pelosi took it as a battle for the generations.

"He's hitting us right in the core value of the Democratic Party . . . and for our country," Pelosi said.

She was annoyed that in a private meeting with congressional leaders at the White House, Bush had told them that while there was a problem with Social Security, there was no crisis. Then "he went right outside and said Social Security will be bankrupt in 20 years."

She also recognized that Democrats had a problem. Bush had just been reelected. Her party was in the minority. She recounted the Democrats' strategy during a conversation in her second year as party leader.

"He's up here," she said raising her arms, "and we're down here. We're kicking him in the shin, and he's socking us in the face.

"So we had to take him down."

Pelosi already knew that Democrats needed to take Bush's numbers down if they hoped to become the majority party. Going after him for threatening Americans' retirement security would do it.

"First, you have to have unity. It's absolutely essential. Otherwise you're building pillars on quicksand," Pelosi said.

She instructed members to return to their districts and hold town hall meetings on Social Security—lots of them—to advance the simple notion that Bush wanted to privatize it and Democrats wanted to preserve it.

Pelosi believed it was critical for Democrats to offer no alternative of their own. If they could pit Social Security as it existed against Bush's proposal, she was confident they would win. If they offered counterproposals and allowed the White House a chance to attack them point by point, she worried that the debate would become muddied.

"Our plan is to save Social Security, stop privatization, and stop raiding the trust fund," Pelosi told her troops. "It's going to be his privatization versus Social Security."

It was not easy to keep 200 members from publicly proposing their own ideas at more than 1,000 town hall meetings.

"Needless to say, there were those in the group who would say, 'We have to have a plan,'" Pelosi said. "All these people outside of Congress [were] saying, 'You can't beat something with nothing.'"

Pelosi told her colleagues to hold together. A plan would come when the time was right.

"I'm the leader. We'll decide the time," she said. "The timing will not be decided by pressure anyone feels at a town hall meeting. It's about how we defeat him. We must defeat him."

The time never came. From a political standpoint it was never needed. Pelosi and her troops went after what they called Bush's "risky privatization scheme," and it worked. Americans turned against the proposal. Bush's numbers kept falling. And Republicans in Congress never even brought it to the floor for a vote.

"We won. It's over," Pelosi said.

PELOSI WAS PULLED IN hundreds of directions and surprised by the demands of the office.

"I have absolutely no control of my time," she said at the end of her first year as leader. "You're scheduled from morning until night. There is no time that is not utilized. And I thought that there might be a little more time for reflection."[9]

Not that she had any regrets.

"It's so urgent. It's so urgent. What they are doing to this country," Pelosi said of the Republicans. "You know I've been involved in politics a long time, one way or another. And I was raised in a family with a great, fierce loyalty to the Democratic Party. But nothing in my experience would have prepared me for the lengths that [Republicans] will go to undermine opportunity in our country. It's amazing."

CHAPTER SIXTEEN

WINNING BACK THE HOUSE

Chris Matthews: *Miss Pelosi, the Bush administration is in turmoil, top Republican leaders are under indictment, and the vice president's top priority seems to be getting the go-ahead to attach a car battery to a man's nipples. Yet despite all this, the Democrats have stayed relatively quiet. What are the Democrats proposing to counteract all this corruption?*

Nancy Pelosi: *That's easy, Chris. We're going to do nothing.*

Chris Matthews: *You're going to do nothing?*

Nancy Pelosi: *That's right. And here's why. We've learned that whenever we do anything, people hate us. . . . It's not like we still don't have ideas, Chris, we do. It's just that when we have something to say, we record it on tape, put those tapes in a box, and we put that box in the garbage. It's really working well for us.*

—SATURDAY NIGHT LIVE SKIT, NOVEMBER 12, 2005

ON A SNOWY MORNING just before Christmas in 2005, when the talk in Washington was how Pelosi's support for a quick withdrawal from Iraq might cost Democrats the 2006 election, a reporter asked Pelosi whether she needed to gain seats in the coming election to return as Democratic leader.

"I fully intend to be standing here as Speaker of the House next year. Any other questions?" Pelosi responded.

Pelosi's confidence was not universally shared. Public opinion was beginning to turn against the war, the president, and Republicans in Congress. But House Democrats had lost six consecutive elections, and their greatest strengths seemed to be what they were not.

They were not the party that led the country to war in Iraq. They were not the party that tried to privatize Social Security, cut taxes for the rich, or add to the deficit. They were not the party responsible for the inept response to Hurricane Katrina or whose congressional leaders were under investigation. No one doubted that Republicans were in trouble. Yet many doubted that Democrats were in a position to take advantage.

House Democrats, in the minority and playing defense for more than a decade, found their status as the number two party deeply rooted.

"You see," comedian Jay Leno said as he marked the 33rd anniversary of the break-in at Democratic Party headquarters at the Watergate complex, "back in those days the Democrats actually had ideas worth stealing."

Pelosi had a sense of humor, even if she rarely displayed it before cameras. She was particularly a fan of political humor. She loved *The Daily Show with Jon Stewart.*

Saturday Night Live opened one show with a skit, featuring a heavily made-up Amy Poehler as Pelosi and a blow-dried Darrell Hammond as MSNBC host Chris Matthews, that skewered the party for not presenting a platform.

"We've learned that whenever we do anything, people hate us," Poehler said, mocking Pelosi's wide-eyed expression.

Pelosi was in Pennsylvania soaking in a hotel tub when Paul saw the show's opening and shouted for her to come see. The skit made Pelosi laugh. The notion that Democrats didn't stand for anything made her furious.

Pelosi felt Democrats had stood strongly for core values. They'd stopped Republicans from privatizing Social Security, drilling for oil, scaling back educational opportunities, and further cutting taxes for the rich. Republicans' priorities were *corrupt*. Their agenda was *immoral*. She had pledged to sharpen the distinctions between the parties and couldn't imagine why everyone didn't see the difference.

When the *San Francisco Chronicle* ran a story with the headline "As Republicans Stumble, Democrats Bumble: Strategists Say Dems Having Trouble Finding Identity, Offering Compelling Alternative," Pelosi felt maligned and rejected the writer's request for some behind-the-scenes access.

"She is very unhappy with your story on Sunday (and rightly so) and doesn't want to give you regular access, much less special access," a Pelosi staffer responded in an e-mail.

There was a strategic reason Democrats weren't putting forward their own agenda. It was part of a plan that Pelosi and Harry Reid—her counterpart in the Senate—had been working on for a year. Republicans had overreached. Their agenda was being driven by the far right. Pelosi was certain that Democrats could win the 2006 election.

In the last campaign, Pelosi had counted on John Kerry winning the presidency. The public and the political press had paid little attention to the congressional elections.

"We were like a lounge act in '04," Pelosi said. "It was all about the presidential. . . . We had hoped for a lift from the presidential. I honestly believed we would win the White House. I staked everything on that."

She was devastated when Kerry lost. Bush immediately began pushing his plan for private Social Security accounts, and some strategists suggested that the next good shot for Democrats would come in 2012, after the next redistricting.

"We were told we were the permanent minority. Give it up. Accept your fate," Pelosi recounted.

She and Reid sat down a month after the election and "decided we would have to create our own environment because that diagnosis was totally unacceptable."

Pelosi and Reid consulted experts from the corporate world, who advised them that they had to weaken their opponents before promoting their own agenda.

"They told us, 'You're number two and you want to be number one. You have to take down number one.'"

The experts told them that if they put their own agenda out too soon, opponents would attack it to save themselves. Better to keep the attention on Bush, "keep the spotlight on him. Keep the spotlight on him. Take his numbers down."

"If you go positive too soon, number one is too strong at the time and will crush your message. So that's what we did," Pelosi said in a candid conversation about the Democratic tactics.

"The president gave us the opportunity with Social Security to take his number down. We did."

Pelosi also began to talk persistently about the Republicans' "culture of corruption."

It was not just a matter of winning seats in districts where Republicans were charged with corruption. It was trying to convince voters around the country that the Republican majority wasn't looking out for their best interests. It didn't matter if your own representative was clean; if he or she was a Republican, he or she was not on your side.

Pelosi distilled the message to this: "They don't care about people like you because of their culture of corruption, cronyism, and incompetence—witness the prescription drug bill, witness the energy policy and the rest. It's all at *your* expense."

Pelosi labeled the GOP Congress "the most corrupt Congress in history." She said the Bush administration had "gotten off scot-free without any oversight from the Congress." She told a convention of the AFL-CIO that Republicans had launched a "relentless attack on working Americans."

The language and tone were hardly new for Pelosi. But when she said it as Democratic leader, it garnered far more attention.

Meanwhile, the unity of House Democrats forced Republicans, including moderates facing tough election challenges, to stand with the GOP's conservative leadership.

"We held together over and over again, making many Republicans walk the plank," Pelosi said proudly. "We created a new environment—and then along came Katrina and sealed the deal."

Most Democrats point to the hurricane that destroyed New Orleans in the summer of 2005 as a cataclysmic moment for President Bush and the Republican Party.

Searing images of impoverished inner city residents begging for water, shelter, and safety; corpses laying on flooded streets; and thousands of residents waiting in vain for the most powerful government in the world to come to their rescue raised widespread doubts about the administration's competence.

Pelosi went to the White House with congressional leaders the week after Katrina and called on Bush to fire Michael Brown, the much-maligned director of the Federal Emergency Management Agency (FEMA), whose previous job had been as commissioner of the International Arabian Horse Association.

"Why would I do that?" Bush responded to Pelosi, she recounted.

"Why would you do that? Because he's incompetent, he has no credentials for the job, because FEMA is the linchpin between the people and the government, and you have made it a weak link. He has to go because of everything that didn't go right last week," Pelosi responded, according to her account.

"Well, what didn't go right last week?" Bush asked.

"Can you imagine," Pelosi said in disgust as she retold the conversation several days later. "My attempts at bipartisanship really get tested when you have a president of the United States whose judgment is so faulty that he didn't even know by Wednesday of last week—now we're into day 10 of the storm—what went wrong!"

The White House said that Pelosi's account was out of context. Pelosi insisted it was not.

"Are you kidding me?" she said incredulously, insisting that Bush's query had been no rhetorical question. "He was saying it out of oblivion and denial. Oblivion and denial. This is not about Michael Brown. He becomes the scapegoat. This is about the judgment of the president of the United States."

Pelosi called Speaker Hastert and asked him to convene an emergency session of the House, which was on recess. She wanted the people of the Gulf region to know that this was the nation's top priority, "that everything else has stopped, that this moves to the front of the line."

She privately expressed concern that if Bush decided to shower the region with money, he'd have to do something else to shore up support among his conservative base.

"God knows what will be on the chopping block to save his butt—his hide," she quickly corrected herself, "with the radical right wing of his party."

Pelosi believed the GOP's response to Katrina was symbolic of their scornful attitude toward government. She didn't know exactly how the politics would play out, but she felt this was a situation in which most Americans' attitudes toward the role of government were far closer to the Democrats' than the GOP's.

"This is about the fabric of our country," Pelosi said. "People in politics, my colleagues who are here who are Democrats, they understand the role of government. The other side doesn't like government. They want to diminish government. They want to eliminate taxation—as far as I can see—for the high end.

"It's not just about Katrina. It's about where we go from here," Pelosi said.

Bush and his party's numbers steadily declined after Katrina, as even many conservatives began to voice grave doubts about his competence. Still, not many believed that Democrats could pick up the 15 new House seats they needed to win a majority and make Pelosi Speaker.

By historical standards, a 15-seat swing was well within reach. In the 10 previous congressional elections that had fallen in the sixth year of an administration, the president's party lost an average of 30 seats—twice what Democrats needed.

However, fewer and fewer seats were in play. Redrawing district lines with sophisticated computers, the enormous explosion of campaign cash, and the polarization of the parties in Washington contributed to an unprecedented advantage for incumbents. Over the previous 10 years, only 2 percent of House incumbents seeking reelection had lost. In the 2004 election, 98 percent had won election by more than a 5 percentage point margin.

Going into 2006, most strategists regarded only a fraction of the House's 435 seats—roughly one in 10—as even remotely competitive. Democrats would need to win nearly all of the competitive seats and might still be a few seats shy of a majority.

PELOSI HAD NAMED REPRESENTATIVE Rahm Emanuel of Chicago to run the House Democrats' campaign committee after her friend Matsui died.

On the surface, Pelosi and Emanuel were an odd mix. He was 19 years her junior and lacked Pelosi's social grace. He'd lost the top of his middle finger as a teenager slicing roast beef at Arby's, adding a certain shock factor when he'd give people the finger, which he did regularly. While Pelosi talked about people stepping in *doggie doo*, Emanuel said *fuck* almost as much as John Burton.

Yet they shared a boundless energy for the Democratic Party and a cold-blooded approach to winning. Several weeks after the 2004 election, Pelosi called Emanuel to enlist his help as he was spending Thanksgiving with his family in Union Pier, Michigan.

Emanuel told Pelosi she had to be prepared for a four-year campaign. It wasn't going to happen immediately. And he knew that his brusque demeanor had not made him nearly as popular as Pelosi among their colleagues.

"Do I have your confidence?" Emanuel asked her. He knew that he'd be making decisions that would cross some members, and he needed her support so the rest of the caucus would stay behind him.

"You do what it takes to win," Pelosi responded.

The call began an intense relationship that would sometimes involve several phone exchanges a day.

Emanuel was blunt and to the point and splattered his conversation with obscenities. Pelosi was also direct but always began the first conversation of the day the same way.

"How are the kids?" Emanuel recalled in an interview, imitating Pelosi's soft phone voice. "Remember to tell Amy [Emanuel's wife] thank you for letting me do this. Is tomorrow a swim or a bike day?"

Emanuel alternated swimming a mile and biking 10 miles every other day. Pelosi knew that Emanuel would phone her with thoughts that popped into his head during his workout and wanted to know if the next day's ideas would be aquatic or land bound.

When Emanuel was asked if he cleaned up his language when he spoke to Pelosi, he paused. "I would say yes, and she would say no," he answered.

The target list began with the districts of Republicans facing ethics charges, including DeLay's seat in the Houston suburbs. They looked at the 18 districts where Kerry had beaten Bush but a Republican House candidate had won. And they focused on GOP candidates who had won their previous election with less than 55 percent of the vote. That gave them roughly 50 target districts scattered throughout the country—each one considerably further to the right than Pelosi's San Francisco or Emanuel's Chicago.

Pelosi and Emanuel decided early on that they needed to recruit credible conservatives for the swing districts. House Republicans had moved so far to the right, they figured that if they embraced fiscally conservative Democrats, including those who opposed abortion rights and gun control and had supported the war, they could capture the center and build a Democratic majority.

They recruited Iraq war vets like Patrick Murphy in Pennsylvania, Tammy Duckworth in Illinois, and Tim Dunn in North Carolina. In rural Indiana the party challenged three GOP incumbents with antiabortion, pro-gun moderates. All three won.

Heath Shuler's conservative positions on social policy would have rendered him unelectable anywhere close to Pelosi's Pacific Heights home. But a more liberal candidate wouldn't have stood a chance in his North Carolina district, and the former NFL quarterback was given the party's blessing and dollars.

That Bush's approval rating was crashing and the GOP looked vulnerable for the first time in a decade only enhanced their ability to attract top-tier candidates. They embarked on an ambitious money-raising program that in the end would net $120 million, far more than the party had ever raised. Money was essential for the grassroots efforts that Pelosi had used so successfully in previous campaigns, including her own.

"I wouldn't give two cents to a campaign that didn't have that component in place," Pelosi said of grassroots mobilization. "I talk to my colleagues and the candidates about this all the time. If you do not have grassroots mobilization, you're not going to win the election. Period."[1]

Tip O'Neill had famously said that all politics were local, and Republicans insisted that would be the case in 2006. But Pelosi had been frustrated in previous elections by the Democrats' failure to present a unifying message. With public opinion turning against the GOP, she felt it was critical to nationalize the elections.

"In 2002 the decision was made not to have a Democratic message nationally. And I don't think you can do that. I don't think you have to go into great detail on it. I don't think you have to be menacing about it. But it has got to be about good jobs, better access to health care, best possible education for our children, clean environment, and a safe world," Pelosi said in a conversation about the 2006 election.

Each candidate could tailor the message to his or her district, "but can you imagine not having a message?" she said. "If you don't have one, Republicans will provide one for you free of charge."

Democrats originally had planned an event in November 2005 to present their national message. But between the war in Iraq, Hurricane Katrina, and rising gas prices, there was a growing belief among Democrats that anything they said would only get in the way of the GOP's implosion.

The challenge was to present an agenda bold enough to attract attention and bland enough to avoid dissension.

In May, the Democratic National Committee veered toward the bland, distributing hundreds of thousands of red, white, and blue door hangers that set out six elements of "The Democratic Vision," comprised of such focus-group-tested proposals as honest leadership, real security, and a health care system that works for everyone.

"I think that's a pretty good agenda, and I think that works from San Francisco to Selma, Alabama," Howard Dean, the DNC chair, said.

Pelosi was more specific a few weeks later when she addressed thousands of liberals at the "Take Back America 2006 Conference" and pledged that in the Democrats' first week in the majority, they would pass legislation to raise the minimum wage, cut by one-half the interest rate on student loans, roll back "multi-billion-dollar subsidies for big oil," cut the costs of prescription drugs, and adopt the recommendations of the independent 9/11 commission.

It was at the same gathering that Senator Hillary Clinton was booed when she said she did not think it smart to set a "date certain" for withdrawal from Iraq. Pelosi received a standing ovation during her speech when she called the war a "grotesque mistake" and noted that it had been two years since she had first called for the resignation of Defense Secretary Donald Rumsfeld.

Pelosi had vowed never again to blur the distinction between the parties. The 2006 election was to be no exception. Pelosi had been pushing for months for the rollout of a bold agenda. She needed to push Senator Harry Reid, who had been urging restraint.

In July Pelosi and Reid both presented the Democrats' "six for '06," which was essentially the five pledges Pelosi had made along with another to expand federal stem cell research. The list was noteworthy for what it did not include. There was no plan for Iraq, no call for universal health care, no plan to combat global warming. Those could come once Democrats won a majority. For now the list contained items that all Democrats—435 candidates in the House and 33 candidates in the Senate—could stand behind.

Pelosi had warned that if Democrats didn't put forward their own agenda, Republicans would do it for them. And they tried. Republicans portrayed Democrats as so driven by Bush hatred that they'd spend the next two years in the majority trying to impeach the president.

Disdain for Bush was a powerful emotion among the Democratic base. Pelosi represented a city where Bush received just 15½ percent of the vote. The San Francisco Board of Supervisors had voted to support articles of impeachment.

She was also a realist, and for Pelosi the calculation was a no-brainer. An impeachment battle would be incredibly divisive, as Washington had learned just eight years before.

If Democrats managed to put together the votes to impeach Bush, it would overshadow everything else the House did for probably a year. If convicted by the Senate, Bush would be forced from office perhaps one year before his term ended. And the new president would be Dick Cheney. It was ridiculous.

Challenged at a town hall meeting by her own constituents, Pelosi suggested that the energy of those who wanted to impeach Bush would be better spent trying to elect more Democrats.

Republicans and the news media wouldn't let the issue go away. When Representative John Conyers, the senior Democrat from Detroit, posted articles of impeachment on his Web site, NBC's Tim Russert asked Pelosi on *Meet the Press* if she supported the move.

"Democrats are not about impeachment. Democrats are about bringing the country together," Pelosi said.

"But that's the man who would be chairman of the Judiciary Committee," Russert interjected.

"Yes, but that is not where the decision would be made," Pelosi said curtly.[2]

To make sure there was no ambiguity, Pelosi told her caucus behind closed doors later that week that impeachment was "off the table."

The issue was so compelling to some liberals that Pelosi drew a challenge in the 2008 election from antiwar advocate Cindy Sheehan, who said Pelosi had abdicated her responsibility as Speaker by not introducing articles of impeachment.

Pelosi further alienated some members of her liberal base by calling on William Jefferson to step down from the Ways and Means Committee after he was videotaped receiving $100,000 in bribe money in a Virginia parking lot and then caught with most of the money stashed in his freezer.

The move was common sense to most everyone outside Washington. But Jefferson at the time had yet to be indicted, let alone convicted. The preemptive move angered some of Jefferson's allies, including Congressional Black Caucus chair Mel Watt of North Carolina, who ordered staff members out of one closed-door meeting and then raged at Pelosi, "We didn't elect you to be queen."

"You didn't elect me to be queen," Pelosi responded coolly. "You didn't elect me to be a fool, either."

The moves were hardly surprising to those who understood Pelosi's pragmatism. Pelosi had always said that the responsibilities of a party leader were different from those of a single representative. She was simply positioning the party, and herself, to be in the majority.

But they didn't fit the Pelosi caricature being drawn by Republicans, who used Pelosi in at least half a dozen ads hoping to tarnish Democrats running in moderate to conservative districts.

In Indiana, Republican incumbent John Hostettler warned in a radio ad that if his Democratic challenger, Brad Ellsworth, won, "Speaker Pelosi will then put in motion her radical plan to advance the homosexual agenda, led by Barney Frank, reprimanded by the House after paying for sex with a man who ran a gay brothel out of Congressman Frank's home."

In Illinois, Republicans ran ads against Melissa Bean that showed pictures of Pelosi and the Golden Gate Bridge as a narrator scolded: "Melissa Bean. Just another Nancy Pelosi wannabe."

House Republican whip Roy Blunt of Ohio distributed an e-mail that asked, "Can the American people trust liberal San Francisco values when it comes to our nation's priorities?"

Even President Bush made Pelosi a standard part of his stump speech in the closing days of the campaign.

"The top Democrat leader in the House made an interesting declaration. She said, 'We love tax cuts.' Given her record, she must be a secret admirer," Bush told a crowd in Macon, Georgia, several weeks before the election.

The attacks seemed to have no effect. In part, it was because most Americans still didn't know Pelosi. She had become one of the most recognizable faces in Washington, but until she became Speaker she could still walk through airports without turning heads.

"People know who the vice president is. They know who the president is. They don't know me," Pelosi noted at the end of another long campaign day thousands of miles from home.

There were other factors at work. Pelosi dressed conservatively, spoke moderately, and stayed away from districts where her presence would be a distraction. For all the ridicule of "San Francisco values," Pelosi had been married to the same man for 43 years and had five children, five grandchildren, and another grandchild on the way. When she appeared on the *Late Show with David Letterman*, she pointed all that out—and even got in a mention of her father and her Baltimore roots—in the first 55 seconds of the interview.

Just as Pelosi had impressed folks in San Francisco with her comfort level at house meetings in all parts of the city, she appeared at ease eating ahi tuna tartar in the Tonga Room atop Nob Hill or a pork chop on a stick in a muddy tent at Minnesota's Farmfest.

She traveled to rural Minnesota three months before the election to tell corn farmers of the Democrats' commitment to ethanol, and she talked soybeans and turkey manure as Congressman Collin Peterson, who would become chair of the Agriculture Committee in a Democratic majority, introduced her around.

Her clean camel blazer and pearly white earrings, as well as a film crew from *60 Minutes* that emerged from the Midwest cornfields like Shoeless Joe Jackson in *Field of Dreams*, attracted a few stares from the farm show crowd. Minnesota's Seventh Congressional District was the backdrop for Laura Ingalls Wilder's *Little House on the Prairie* and could not have been further—physically or culturally—from Pelosi's San Francisco or Washington homes.

Peterson acknowledged that he "probably couldn't get 10 percent of the vote in her district, and she couldn't get elected in mine." But he was thrilled to tell his constituents that he was turning a city slicker like Pelosi into "an aggie." Republican Michael Barrett, who was running against Peterson, made a point of telling local reporters what a mistake it was to bring Pelosi to the district. But he said he wouldn't spend any campaign dollars trying to link the pair. It had been tried in the last election and had failed.

"I'm not going to waste my money," Barrett said. "Nancy's not the issue."

Pelosi spoke inside a large white tent—where a breeze delivered the foul odor from a nearby portable toilet—as her comments were broadcast across the Corn Belt on the Linder Farm Network, "the voice of Minnesota Agriculture."

"When I return to Washington, I will tell them I have been to Minnesota and I have seen the future," Pelosi said to polite applause, steering clear of the "grotesque mistake" in Iraq and focusing on the promise of ethanol.

Later she told a crowd that while in Minnesota she'd picked up a present for her husband: "I got a recipe for pork chops on a stick."

As the sun set and Pelosi prepared for the 150-mile flight back to Minneapolis on a small plane, she reflected on what others might view as an unlikely campaign swing through the heartland for a San Francisco Democrat.

"It's the most natural thing in the world to me."

THE PHRASE "SAN FRANCISCO DEMOCRAT" was first used as a pejorative by United Nations ambassador Jeanne Kirkpatrick during the 1984 Republican convention in Dallas as a disparaging reference to the Democrats, who had met a few weeks earlier in San Francisco. The phrase was now being used regularly in reference to Pelosi on conservative talk radio shows, and Pelosi believed they meant something quite specific.

"Are they talking about protecting the environment, educating the American children, building economic success?" she said. "No, they are talking about gay people. Well, I was brought up to believe that all people are God's children. And the last time I checked, that included gay people."[3]

The attack on "San Francisco values" seemed even more of a reach when ABC News posted a series of sexually explicit Internet exchanges between Republican House member Mark Foley of Florida and young men who had worked as House pages.

The firestorm led to Foley's immediate resignation and admission into an alcohol rehab program and prompted questions about how much Republican leaders had known about Foley's indefensible behavior before the story broke.

Pelosi took to the House floor and offered another privileged resolution demanding an investigation. The House voted unanimously in favor. For many Democrats who were still skeptical about their party's ability to capture the House, the Foley incident convinced them that they would soon be in the majority.

Hastert recalled getting on the phone with Pelosi to discuss the possible composition of a panel to look into the matter. Pelosi, he recalls, was in no mood to negotiate. Returning Hastert's call from a small room at Georgetown University, where she'd just delivered a speech, Pelosi rejected Hastert's suggestion that former FBI director Louis Freeh head the investigation.

"It was very plain that she didn't want to do any of that," Hastert said. "Her attitude was: 'There's going to be a new sheriff in town, and we'll take care of it when I get there.'"

As election day drew near, Pelosi was keeping track of 60 to 65 races, flipping through an enormous binder that contained notes on every competitive race, and staying in regular phone contact with Emanuel and sources in the districts.

"It's the last thing she's doing when she goes to bed at night and the first thing she does in the morning," said Brian Wolff, Pelosi's political director. He was not the first to describe her hands-on tendencies by saying, "If she doesn't know about it, it's not being done."

Publicly, Republicans insisted to the very end that their polling showed they would keep control of Congress.

"I'm confident we're going to keep the Senate; I'm confident we're going to keep the House," White House political chief Karl Rove told the *Washington Times* in late October.

Pelosi knew otherwise. She saw close races breaking toward the Democrats and those that had favored Republicans turning into toss-ups.

"I've got more opportunity than I can afford," she said days before the election.[4]

In her daily phone conversations with Emanuel, she'd pepper him for his latest assessments. She was always more optimistic than he was. Emanuel told Pelosi of an old Jewish wise tale that frowned upon putting up a crib until a baby was born. He wasn't going to predict victory. He couldn't bring himself to do it.

Six days before the election, Pelosi brought former president Clinton to headline an event at San Francisco's Warfield Theater, where donors paid as much as $25,000 per couple to hear Jackson Browne, Graham Nash, and Bonnie Raitt.

"I could just see the Republicans licking their chops when Nancy got to be our leader. They love to make all those speeches about the San Francisco Democrats. It's part of their shtick, you know. It's part of their 'be very afraid' shtick," Clinton told the receptive crowd.

"They had forgotten that she's the nice Catholic girl from Baltimore with five kids, five grandkids. Her daddy was the mayor and she's tougher than all of them put together. And they are about to learn this."[5]

The event raised more than $2 million and was the House campaign committee's most lucrative event ever.

Afterward, Pelosi and Emanuel huddled at a table in the fifth-floor lounge of the Four Seasons Hotel on Market Street. Brian Wolff and Paul Pelosi looked on as the pair spent two hours going over a list of races. They huddled again at 9:00 a.m. the next morning to work their way through the rest of the list.

Democrats needed to win 15 seats to take over the House. Pelosi again asked Emanuel for his assessment. He told her that at worst Democrats would win 14, and at best they'd win 26.

"I told her, 'I'm going with the Jewish wise tale,'" Emanuel recalled, explaining his caution.

"I know you are," the far more optimistic Pelosi responded. "I'm ready to start setting up the crib."[6]

As the campaign entered its final hours, Pelosi's biggest concern was that Republicans would steal the election. Democrats readied a team of lawyers.

"They will try to steal it. I have no doubt about it," Pelosi said in an interview in her office the Friday before election day.

"I know where the numbers are in these races, and I know that they are there for the 15 or more. Today [it's] 22 to 26," Pelosi said.

"But the uncertainty I have today is that I have no confidence in the integrity of the election. I really don't. We're going to fight them tooth and nail if it comes to a place where we know that integrity has been violated. That's the only variable in this—will there be an honest count."

Pelosi hit the campaign trail the next day for one final swing. The trip would take her through Pennsylvania and Connecticut, where Democrats believed they had a shot at knocking off as many as six Republican incumbents.

Pelosi's youngest daughter, Alexandra, was expecting a baby and was already overdue. Pelosi had identified swing districts within a 100-mile radius of Alexandra's Manhattan apartment. If the baby came, she and Paul could be there within a few hours. Press secretary Jenn Crider e-mailed the busy schedule to reporters with a note at the top: "Reminder—if grandchild number 6 arrives, Pelosi will cancel her schedule."

The final day of the 30-hour campaign blitz included three pasta feeds, starting at the ballroom of the Generale Ameglio Civic Society in New Britain, Connecticut.

The floor-to-ceiling mirrors, pink venetian blinds, and elderly crowd serving themselves from large tin tubs seemed quite distant from Pelosi's own district. But it could have been a scene right out of Baltimore's Little Italy, and Pelosi looked right at home.

As she did at every stop, Pelosi went through each item on the Democrats' "six for '06" agenda. She talked about a new direction, the bankruptcy of Republican ideas, the GOP's devotion to the richest 1 percent, and the importance of their local Democratic candidate—in this case, Chris Murphy—to the party's chances to reclaim the House. The crowd ate it up along with their ziti and meatballs.

It was more pasta and sausage at the St. Joseph's Polish Society in Colchester ("Where tradition meets tomorrow") as Pelosi delivered the same speech on behalf of candidate Joe Courtney. Paul stood at the back of the room watching his wife and fretting over the possibility that Alexandra's baby might not come until he was back in California. At a certain point they'd have to induce labor, and he had to be back in San Francisco at the end of the week.

When it was mentioned that his daughter really didn't need for him to be there, he looked almost puzzled.

"Oh, *Alexandra* doesn't need me there," he explained. "Life is too short to miss these moments. I've been there for all five of my other grandkids. I'm not going to miss this one."

Like Paul, Pelosi was reveling in her Italian grandparent role. Her sound bites could be menacing, but her appearance never was. Pelosi may have favored Armani suits and pearls, but she had been raised in a working-class neighborhood and seemed particularly at home among the traditional crowd.

Pelosi was all lady, and she stuck to her script. At each stop she said that when she received the Speaker's gavel from the GOP, she'd be taking it "from the hands of special interests on behalf of America's children."

At an event outside Philadelphia, Pelosi was halfway through the line when she was interrupted.

"And when I take the gavel from Speaker Hastert, I'll take it on behalf of the children . . ."

"And you'll shove it up his ass!" a woman hollered out.

Pelosi kept going. She would never dignify such an outburst.

ON THE EVE OF THE ELECTION, Pelosi convened a conference call with her entire caucus. House Democrats had been in the minority for 12 years. Many felt oppressed. But she wanted no talk of revenge. This was not about getting even. Democrats would show from the outset that they were ready to govern.

Pelosi typically spent election night in San Francisco. This time she was in Washington, watching the returns and talking on the phone with candidates from the DCCC headquarters a few blocks from the Capitol.

At 9:19 Pelosi came out to address the volunteers. The polls had closed in the East, and the initial reports were that Democrats were going to do as well as expected. Perhaps better.

"I'm here to thank each and every one of you for bringing us to where we are now tonight, on the brink of a great Democratic victory," Pelosi said. It was as close as she was going to come to claiming victory. Polls were still open in much of the country, including her home in California, and she wasn't going to waste a chance to appeal to voters to cast ballots for a handful of western candidates, whom she dutifully rattled off by name.

Two hours later CNN officially declared that Democrats had won enough seats to guarantee their control of the House.

"We did it! I can't believe it," Pelosi said excitedly, hugging her husband and getting back to the phone. She called her brother Tommy in Baltimore. She called her friend Mark Buell in San Francisco, who had gathered a group of loyal supporters at Ben Swig's penthouse at the Fairmont Hotel. She called candidate after candidate to congratulate them on winning their districts.

She walked down the hall to Emanuel's office. "Fellas—Madam Speaker!" Emanuel roared as the two embraced.[7] She got in a car and rode with Paul to the Hyatt Regency, where Democrats had gathered.

"I can't believe it," she said over and over. "I can't believe it."

IT WAS MAYHEM AT the election party. Many of the young volunteers had never been to a Democratic victory party before. Shortly after midnight Pelosi strode out and claimed the victory she had felt was a certainty for the past several months.

"Today, the American people voted for change, and they voted for Democrats to take our country in a new direction. And that is exactly what we intend to do," Pelosi said. "The campaign is over. Democrats are ready to lead. We are prepared to govern. All across the country, in the north, in the south, in the east, in the west, my city of San Francisco to—from sea to shining sea, the American people voted for change."

As the crowd celebrated, Pelosi returned upstairs. There were more calls to be made. Two aides furiously punched numbers into cell phones and handed them to Pelosi when the calls went through. The calls went on until 1:45 a.m. before Pelosi finally departed for a few hours' sleep. She was now the Speaker-to-Be.

CHAPTER SEVENTEEN

MADAM SPEAKER

*"I want to demonstrate to the American people
that women can breathe the rarified air at this level."*
—NANCY PELOSI, JANUARY 5, 2007

*"In his day, the late congressman Thomas D'Alesandro Jr.
from Baltimore, Maryland, saw Presidents Roosevelt and Truman
at this rostrum. But nothing could compare with the sight
of his only daughter, Nancy, presiding tonight as Speaker of the
House of Representatives. Congratulations, Madam Speaker."*
—PRESIDENT GEORGE W. BUSH, JANUARY 23, 2007

AT PRECISELY 1:44 ON the afternoon of Thursday, January 4, Nancy Pelosi was cradling Paul Michael Vos, her seven-week old grandson, on the floor of the House of Representatives.

House clerk Karen Haas gaveled the House to order.

"The tellers agree the total number of votes cast is 435, of which the Honorable Nancy Pelosi of the State of California has received 233, the Honorable John Boehner of the state of Ohio has received 202," Haas said.

"Therefore, the Honorable Nancy Pelosi of the State of California is duly elected Speaker of the House of Representatives of the 110th Congress."

The chamber erupted in cheers. Pelosi calmly handed the baby from her left arm, embraced two more grandchildren standing beside her, and flashed an enormous grin to her Democratic colleagues.

"Thank you," she mouthed, the words completely swallowed by the roar.

"Thank you."

Her brother Tommy, her husband Paul, and her children applauded from the gallery. Representative George Miller snapped pictures with a digital camera.

Republican leader John Boehner was the first to cross the aisle and plant a congratulatory kiss on Pelosi's cheek. It was the first of hundreds. Never in the nation's history had a Speaker of the House received so many kisses.

Moments later Boehner and Pelosi stood together at the dais, and the Republican leader handed Pelosi a gavel to mark the passing of the majority to the Democratic Party.

"It is sometimes said that the Founding Fathers would not recognize the government that exists here in Washington today, that it has grown in size and scope far beyond anything they could ever have imagined, much less endorsed or advocated for our future," Boehner said, recognizing the historic nature of the moment.

"But today marks an occasion that I think the Founding Fathers would view approvingly. And my fellow Americans, whether you're a Republican, a Democrat, or an Independent, today is a cause for celebration."

The House erupted again in cheers. Democrats rose to their feet to voice their enthusiasm. Not all the Republicans shared Boehner's graciousness. Some stood and applauded politely during the repeated standing ovations. Others sat and read their newspapers. Speaker Hastert sat toward the back of the chamber and applauded slowly, as if on autopilot.

It was a special day in the Capitol. The opening day of the new Congress is typically a family affair. Many members bring children and spouses to watch them being sworn in, meet their colleagues, and experience the pomp and grandeur of the august chamber. On this day, it was particularly crowded. John Burton, Jerry Brown, and San Francisco mayor Gavin Newsom were seated in a visitors' gallery. Tony Bennett sat beside Tommy D'Alesandro. Carole King and Richard Gere looked on with Pelosi's family. Senator Barbara Mikulski, who had attended the same high school as Pelosi, and former transportation secretary Norman Mineta, who commuted with Pelosi on countless cross-country flights, were among the many former members who used their privileges to get onto the floor. Scores of aides wrangled passes to witness history in the making. The press gallery, directly behind the podium, was filled to capacity.

"For our daughters and our granddaughters, today we have broken the marble ceiling," Pelosi said. "For our daughters and our granddaughters now, the sky is the limit. Anything is possible for them."

The night before, Representative Eshoo had asked Pelosi if she had something of her mother's to carry with her into the chamber. Pelosi told her she didn't need it. "My mother's in here," she said, tapping her heart.[1]

"I was raised in a large family that was devoutly Catholic, deeply patriotic, very proud of our Italian American heritage, and staunchly Democratic," Pelosi said as she publicly thanked her family for "the confidence they gave me to go from the kitchen to the Congress."

As she neared the end of her remarks, Pelosi invited all the children in the chamber to come forward to touch the gavel. With her own grandchildren taking the lead, at least 50 kids were ushered up front, crowding Pelosi as she stood atop the dais.

The kids touched the gavel, the microphone, fidgeted with the papers on the podium, and waved to their parents in the chamber.

"For these children, and for all of America's children," Pelosi said resolutely as she pounded the gavel, "the House will come to order!"

Thousands of column inches and hundreds of hours would be spent that week attempting to explain the breadth of the changes in the Capitol.

Nothing would capture the new order better than the image—broadcast around the world—of Nancy Pelosi in a plum-colored suit, standing at the Speaker's podium, surrounded by 50 young children.

THE ROAD FROM ELECTION NIGHT to the speakership was not as smooth as Pelosi had hoped.

Five months before the election, her friend Jack Murtha had come to her office and told her that if Democrats won the election and she became Speaker, he would run for majority leader.

It was a surprising decision. Murtha was well liked, but he was a gruff social conservative with a rough edge. Liberals had recently embraced him because of his antiwar stance, but he was to the right of the Democratic mainstream. He had been implicated—though never charged—in the Abscam congressional bribery scandal 25 years before, and he seemed ill suited for such a high-profile post.

Steny Hoyer, who had assumed the role of whip when Pelosi became leader, had thought he'd be unchallenged for the majority leader's job, the second most powerful position in the House. Hoyer had pledged he would never challenge Pelosi for the speakership, yet Murtha felt he was stirring unrest.

"I really ran because I was irritated at Steny's harping at Nancy," Murtha said the following year.

Hoyer was on the House floor in June when he got word that Murtha was telling people he was running. Many members were stunned. Hoyer went to Pelosi's office later in the day to ask her what was going on.

Pelosi told Hoyer, "Jack has come to me and said he's going to run for majority leader."

She told Hoyer she'd asked Murtha, "Jack, why are you doing this? This is not your thing."

"Well, obviously he is running," Hoyer told Pelosi. "I think it's going to be divisive to the caucus."[2]

Pelosi made it clear to Hoyer that she had not encouraged Murtha to run. But her response made it equally plain that she had no intention of stopping him.

"Well, you know, I think competition is a good thing," Hoyer recalled Pelosi telling him.

The rivalry attracted headlines in Washington and was beginning to overshadow the cohesiveness that Pelosi had worked so hard to build. Pelosi asked Murtha to suspend his campaign until after the election. He agreed.

The day after the election, Pelosi faced reporters for the first time as Speaker-to-Be. Ed Epstein of the *San Francisco Chronicle* asked Pelosi if she was going to endorse anyone in the leadership races, publicly or privately.

"I haven't even gotten to that," she bristled, clearly not wanting to go public with her intentions. "We haven't even finished counting the votes from last night's election."

The next day Pelosi and Hoyer were at the White House for a meeting with President Bush. As they stood in the White House driveway waiting to get into their cars to take them back to the Capitol, Pelosi pulled Hoyer aside and told him she intended to endorse Murtha. There was no further discussion or explanation.

Hoyer felt he had been a dutiful deputy to Pelosi since she had beaten him in the whip's race. He said it had worked out best to have Pelosi on top, because she had more natural appeal to the liberal wing of the party, while he had an affinity with the moderates.

"The pecking order works out better this way. The other way around, I don't think it would work as well," he said.

So Hoyer was quite disappointed when Pelosi told him she was with Murtha, a decision made public in a letter Murtha released to the media a few days later.

"With respect to Iraq in particular, I salute your courageous leadership that changed the national debate and helped make Iraq the central issue of this historic election," Pelosi wrote. "Your presence in the leadership of our party would add a knowledgeable and respected voice to our Democratic team."

Despite Pelosi's endorsement of Murtha, few doubted that Hoyer would prevail. But it raised doubts about Pelosi's greatest attribute—her instinctive understanding of House Democrats. Murtha erroneously believed he had enough votes to win and had told her so. But Pelosi had made a career out of assessing votes and knowing when not to rely on other people's counts. Her leadership had been dedicated to unity, and this was creating division.

Words not typically associated with Pelosi—*hubris, pettiness, miscalculation*— were used to describe the first public decision of her speakership. Even members of her staff appeared confounded by the Murtha endorsement.

Of course, if not for Murtha, many believed Pelosi would not be Speaker. She had shown willingness in the past to take hits in public to make a point. Murtha accepted her endorsement as a sign of devotion.

"I think it was pure loyalty," Murtha said. "She's a friend."

It is the same explanation given by Hoyer.

"She was loyal to Jack. We never had a discussion about why she did it, the fact that she regretted doing it, or had to do it," Hoyer said. "I would have preferred that she didn't back Jack. I respect her loyalty. She took a huge risk and she lost, and I don't think she ever looked back. Nancy Pelosi is not one to second-guess herself. That's one of her great strengths."

A week after the election, Democrats unanimously named Pelosi as their choice for Speaker and elected Hoyer over Murtha by a vote of 149 to 86.

"We've had our disagreements in that room, and now that is over," Pelosi said after emerging from the closed-door meeting. "As I said to my colleagues, as we say in church, let there be peace on Earth, and let it begin with us. Let the healing begin."

"No regrets?" asked a reporter.

"No. I'm not a person who has regrets," Pelosi responded.

PELOSI RAN HER SPEAKERSHIP at the same frenetic pace as her first 20 years in Congress. She met with conservative Blue Dogs to hear their concerns. She met with the Progressive Caucus to remind them of their common roots. She sat down for chocolate doughnuts each Wednesday with House freshmen—the "majority makers"—to boost their chances of sticking around. She'd have so many consecutive meetings there was often no time for her staff to brief her on the day's developments. The quest for up-to-date information periodically prompted an interest in using a BlackBerry. But those close to her doubted she'd ever carry one. Pelosi was so old-fashioned that she hardly used e-mail.

Pelosi now occupied the finest suite of offices in the Capitol, spanning three floors directly under the Capitol dome. Twenty years ago her office overlooked the freeway. The new office looked out on the Capitol Mall—the red castle tower of the Smithsonian on the left, the National Gallery on the right, and the Washington Monument perfectly framed in the middle. A secure telephone with a connection to the White House sat in the corner. Capitol police officers paced the hallway outside.

A new level of confidence was apparent in television interviews, where Pelosi's answers were crisper and more focused. She softened her rhetoric and began to talk more openly about her private life and her Catholicism. She instituted regular news briefings, something her predecessor had not done. Like all politicians, she repeated the same sound bites over and over, but she no longer sounded like she was repeating herself. She conveyed a level of comfort in public that was not previously apparent.

She still paused occasionally to sneak glimpses of *Jeopardy!*, though she boycotted the show for many months to protest the wording of a "Final Jeopardy" answer that read "A group chaired by *her* produced a system that President Bush says now needs 'wise and effective reform.'"

The correct response was "Who is Frances Perkins?" a pioneering woman who helped create the Social Security system as President Franklin Roosevelt's secretary of labor. Pelosi disputed the characterization of Bush's privatization plans as "wise and effective" and was upset by the show's failure to mention that Perkins was the first woman to ever hold a cabinet post.

Several months into her speakership the show offered a "Final Jeopardy" answer more to her liking: "On January 4, 2007, she said, 'For our daughters and our granddaughters, today we have broken the marble ceiling.'"

All three contestants correctly guessed "Who is Nancy Pelosi?"

THERE WAS LITTLE TIME for such leisure.

The first two weeks of Pelosi's speakership were spent racing through the "six for '06" agenda that she had promised would be enacted within the first 100 legislative hours. The measures passed with an average of 62 Republicans joining Democrats on each vote, and with 58 hours to spare.

"We have delivered on change," Pelosi declared when it was done. "We have shown that the House is not a place where good ideas go to die."

The quick pace came at a price. The legislation moved quickly because it came to the floor without committee hearings and without giving Republicans a chance to offer amendments. Republicans accused Pelosi of violating one of her core promises—to open up House rules to give the minority more rights.

Pelosi chose accomplishments over accommodation. Democrats figured that for Republicans to argue that procedurally Democrats were behaving just as unfairly as they once had was unlikely to create much of a public stir.

"Whine me a river" was a common Democratic refrain.

The quick passage of legislation did not necessarily translate into law.

After vetoing just a single piece of legislation during his first six years in office, President Bush vetoed seven bills during Pelosi's first year as Speaker. In the Senate, Republicans held up more than 70 measures by threatening to filibuster.

Despite the tip of balance that brought her to power, Pelosi presided over a historically narrow majority. When she became Speaker, her party enjoyed a 31-seat edge over the Republicans. By contrast, when Tip O'Neill became Speaker 30 years earlier, Democrats had a 149-seat advantage.

The 110th Congress succeeded in raising the minimum wage for the first time in a decade; raised fuel efficiency requirements for automobiles for the first time in three decades; cut student loan rates in half; implemented security recommendations of the independent 9/11 Commission; and instituted stricter lobbying and ethics rules.

Yet they failed to change the course in Iraq. Efforts to expand health insurance for the poor failed. The partisan bickering that marked the 10 years of Republican rule showed no sign of improvement. And the public's confidence in Congress continued to fall.

THE WAR IN IRAQ overshadowed everything.

On her second day as Speaker, with a portrait of Abraham Lincoln hung by Dennis Hastert still on the wall of her new conference room, Pelosi declared getting US troops out of Iraq to be the most urgent issue before her.

"This war needs to come to an end. It is my highest priority as Speaker."

Pelosi believed the Democrats' victory in November was a clear rebuke of the White House's Iraq policy and that replacing Donald Rumsfeld as secretary of defense was just the beginning of an inevitable change of course.

Bush's Iraq, she declared, was "over."

"You cannot sustain a war of this kind with the division that we have in our country and the lack of support for this war," she said. "The president is going to have to step back."

The plan from the beginning was to grow the antiwar coalition. If Republicans joined the cry for a new direction, Pelosi believed the president would have no choice but to change course.

Pelosi was wrong. Bush was determined—*stubborn* according to his critics, *resolute* to his supporters—to keep a sizeable US presence in Iraq despite mounting public pressure to get out. The biggest challenge facing Pelosi in her first year as Speaker was to find a way for the legislative branch—still narrowly divided between Democrats and Republicans—to force an unyielding commander in chief to alter his strategy.

Bush could not have been more gracious when he came to the House floor to deliver the State of the Union Address. Prior to giving the speech, he met privately with Pelosi and wished her well on a coming secret trip to Iraq.

With Pelosi seated behind his left shoulder and Vice President Cheney behind his right, Bush opened his remarks by noting that he had the "high privilege and distinct honor" to be the first president in history to begin with the words "Madam Speaker."

"In his day, the late congressman Thomas D'Alesandro Jr. from Baltimore, Maryland, saw presidents Roosevelt and Truman at this rostrum. But nothing could compare with the sight of his only daughter, Nancy, presiding tonight as Speaker of the House of Representatives. Congratulations, Madam Speaker."

Pelosi knew the cordial words were coming, and she and Bush exchanged a warm handshake as members of the joint session of Congress delivered a rousing ovation. For many Americans watching on television, it was their first glimpse of a woman at the seat of such power.

Pelosi also knew that was as far as Bush would go to acknowledge the new political order. Bush spent the next 49 minutes speaking as if the November election had never happened. He made no mention of the "six for '06" legislation and made it plain that he had no intention of scaling back in Iraq.

Instead, Bush promoted his plan to send 20,000 to 30,000 more troops to Iraq, and he called on the Democratic Congress—which owed its existence to the public's frustration over the war—to "give it a chance." The postelection change of course amounted to sending more troops.

Pelosi opposed the plan, as did a majority of Congress and the American people. She had long ago lost confidence in Bush's ability to manage the war. The troop surge provided the perfect vehicle for displaying the nation's opposition to Bush's Iraq policy.

She and Senate leader Harry Reid agreed that while House Democrats were pushing their "six for '06" legislation, the Senate would pass a bipartisan resolution condemning the surge. The momentum would then carry it to an even bigger victory in the House. The plan fell apart, like many other Democratic ambitions, when Republicans prevented the Senate from even voting on the resolution.

Pelosi could not afford a similar stumble in the House. Antiwar liberals proposed a sweeping resolution calling for an immediate withdrawal. Conservative Blue Dogs wanted language demanding accountability for the billions of dollars being spent. Pelosi's calculation was that the resolution had to pass by as large a margin as possible. Democrats would stand united, as they had in their opposition to Bush's Social Security plan, and bring some Republicans with them. A bipartisan measure would be more difficult to ignore.

Pelosi embraced a simple, 94-word resolution praising the troops and opposing the surge. It was not nearly as strong as many had wanted, but it was something all Democrats, and even some Republicans, could support. This was about building a coalition. The measure passed with 63 votes to spare and was the strongest rebuke of a wartime president since the Vietnam War.

"This resolution today sets the stage for that new direction," Pelosi declared optimistically after the February vote.

But Bush showed no signs of relenting. The measure was nonbinding, and Bush had no intention of halting the surge. He returned to Congress in the spring, asking for $100 billion more to fight the war. Pelosi found herself once again seeking common ground between the liberals, who wanted to allocate only enough money for Bush to pull the troops out, and moderates, who wanted to confront Bush in a less restrictive manner. With nearly all the House Republicans siding with Bush, there was virtually no room for error.

In the spring she once again put forward a compromise measure that required all US combat forces to leave Iraq by September 2008, and she pleaded with her liberal allies to stay with her in a show of solidarity. It passed by a 218 to 212 vote.

"I stand here on this historic day for the Congress. This Congress voted to end the war in Iraq," Pelosi declared.

Bush vetoed the measure and the war went on.

A number of Pelosi's close allies on the left called for Congress to cut off the Pentagon's war budget. Since all money bills originate in the House, it wouldn't matter what the president or Senate said. The idea was to pass a war budget containing just enough money to bring the troops home.

Pelosi steadfastly rejected the tactic, expressing concern that without the president's cooperation, American troops could be left in Iraq without proper equipment or protection.

"You can't just say, 'Okay, let's cut it off—but I didn't mean to hurt the troops,'" she said. Even if she wanted to, she lacked the votes to pass such a confrontational approach.

That limited her options. Democrats could send more measures for Bush's veto, though they lacked the votes for an override. They could conduct oversight hearings to shine a light on the conduct of the war. They could demand that the president report back to them regularly on the war's progress. But short of cutting off the money, there was little they could do to force Bush to change course.

So Pelosi went back to her grassroots instincts. If the votes were not yet there to force Bush's hand, she would work to produce them. If enough Republicans told the White House that the war was no longer viable, Bush would need to adjust. And more and more Americans were turning against the war.

"Nothing is more eloquent to a member of Congress than the voice of his or her constituents," Pelosi said.

Pelosi would spend much of her first year as Speaker patiently trying to enlarge the coalition opposed to the war. The efforts frustrated her base, who believed she needed to stake out a more aggressive "out now" posture. Pelosi, whose opposition to the war had never wavered, saw her responsibilities differently. Repeated votes to end the war would not bring moderates and conservatives to their side. Pelosi had built majorities to combat AIDS, to stand up to China, even to create a national park in San Francisco's Presidio.

When activists, or even members of her staff, had pushed her many years before to promote AIDS programs that couldn't possibly pass, she'd asked them, "You want me to lose? You want me to show how little support we have?"

The argument here was the same. Behind closed doors, Pelosi assured members of the Out of Iraq Caucus that she was on their side. But the votes were not there. Not yet.

The strategy at times appeared to be working. Respected Republican foreign policy voices, including Senators Richard Lugar of Indiana and John Warner of Virginia, openly questioned Bush's policy. Yet by year's end there were more troops in Iraq than there had been at the time of the 2006 election.

"This president is just tone-deaf, has a tin ear, any way you want to say it, in terms of the wishes of the American people," Pelosi said as her first year as Speaker neared its end.

Pelosi found Republicans unwilling to break with the White House, and President Bush unwilling to negotiate.

"I don't like to use the word *surprised*, because you're supposed to be prepared for everything. But I thought that he would—at least when we extended some way to work together with him on this—would comply. But he hasn't."

Whether Pelosi had laid the groundwork for a change of direction in Iraq or simply been unable to find a way to challenge an inflexible president was a question that would consume the early months of her speakership. Antiwar protesters took up residence outside her Pacific Heights home, and the "netroots" began agitating about the party's lack of spine.

The give-and-take with the left was constant. She patched together a farm bill that some liberals said provided too many subsidies to agribusinesses. She supported a temporary measure that permitted warrantless surveillance of suspected terrorists and agreed to drop provisions pushing the development of renewable energy sources from an energy bill. She pushed the House to pass civil rights legislation protecting workers who were fired because they were gay, lesbian, or bisexual, but she was only able to get the measure passed by leaving out protections for those who regard themselves as transgender.

No one doubted Pelosi's own liberal credentials. In her 20 years in the House, the only major vote she cast that disappointed the left was her 1994 support of the North America Free Trade Agreement. Yet she now had different responsibilities. Pelosi had a deep affinity for liberals and the institution of the House, and she seemed caught in a constant tension between the two.

As her profile grew, so did attacks from Republicans. They complained when Pelosi flew home in a military jet that was larger than the one that Hastert had used, even though Hastert's plane did not have a fuel tank large enough to make the trip to San Francisco. They ridiculed her for wearing a scarf as headgear when she made a trip to Syria and for the timing of a resolution condemning Turkey for its slaughter of more than a million Armenians a century ago.

Yet Pelosi did not provide her critics with the ripe target they had hoped for. After the Murtha-Hoyer split, many Republicans—as well as many pundits— predicted that Democrats would be paralyzed by infighting. It was simply too hard to keep the representatives from Boonesborough, Kentucky, and Berkeley, California, on the same team. But a year into her speakership, Democrats had held together, and Pelosi governed with near unanimous support. Congress's approval rating was near historic lows, but Pelosi remained extremely popular among Democrats and reigned without any threat to her leadership.

The role of Speaker had evolved from that of a little-known presiding officer in the early 19th century to a near autocrat under Joe Cannon at the beginning of the 20th. The Speaker's influence had varied greatly, depending on the power of the president, the mix of the parties, and the size of the majority. Pelosi's first term came at a time of a narrow majority and a Republican president. She held out hope that if she did her job right, the majority would expand and a Democrat would hold the White House by 2009.

Such were typical concerns for a Speaker. And that, in many ways, was remarkable on its face. Within a year of her being sworn in, there were heated debates about Pelosi's tactics and priorities. But very few people thought twice about looking up at a woman presiding over the House of Representatives.

Pelosi had said on her second day on the job, "I want to demonstrate to the American people that women can breathe the rarified air at this level," and few would argue that she had succeeded.

THE SAME DAY SHE made that comment, Pelosi returned to her native home of Baltimore in a nine-car entourage that sped along I-95 with a police escort.

She stopped by a statue of her father that overlooked one of his prized urban renewal projects, remarking that "he had a love affair with the city of Baltimore."

Her old family friend Peter Angelos surprised Pelosi by pulling back a black rug to reveal, beside her father's statue, a plaque honoring her own election as Speaker. Pelosi seemed touched as she rearranged the flowers beside the image of her father.

"He was very particular about flowers," she said wistfully. "It is with great emotion I come to this spot."

Then it was off to the corner of Albemarle and Fawn streets, where 500 people were waiting outside her childhood home. On the sidewalk where she played as a girl stood a stage holding two US senators, half a dozen members of Congress, and the incoming governor of the State of Maryland.

"This is where it all started," Baltimore mayor Martin O'Malley, the govenor-elect, said as he pulled the bunting off a street sign that read "Via Nancy D'Alesandro Pelosi," the new name for the 200 block of Albemarle Street.

"So many hours of work," said her brother Tommy as he glanced at the family homestead, recalling how the doors had stayed open from 8:00 a.m. to 9:00 p.m. and how every family member pitched in to find people jobs, housing, "a way out of jail, in jail, or whatever the case may be."

Always the crowd-pleaser, he then sang a verse of "You Are My Sunshine." Over the crowd's groans, he then sang another.

"Take that, Tony Bennett," he crowed when he finished.

Looking toward the sky, D'Alesandro said his mother and his father "are in absolute ecstasy, to hear me introduce to this crowd, the Speaker of the House of Representatives—Nancy Pelosi!"

Pelosi, who had spoken at so many events, so many functions, in so many interviews that week, was almost subdued. She had never anticipated such a life when she left the neighborhood half a century before.

"My parents did not raise me to be Speaker of the House," Pelosi said. "Tommy was groomed to be mayor, and I was raised to be holy."

Her mother and father, she said, glancing at the house, "they were on the side of angels."

Pelosi looked down Albemarle Street, where her 101-year-old Aunt Jessie still lived, and up Fawn, where Mugs Confectionery still sold candy. She looked at the enormous crowd that filled the intersection, as it had on election night in her father's day.

"Every step I took to the speakership began in this neighborhood."

The Pelosi family gathered at Chiapparelli's Restaurant down the street. The politicians shook hands, and the neighbors greeted one another. Pelosi worked the rope line. She was no longer little Nancy. A throng of reporters pushed closer and closer, and cameramen jostled to get in position.

"The president's judgment has been impaired from the beginning," she told a cluster of journalists and neighbors who craned their necks to hear. "The president now knows he doesn't have a blank check from Congress."

Those out of earshot hollered for her attention.

"Madam Speaker! Madam Speaker!"

ENDNOTES

Note on sourcing: The information in this book is drawn from hundreds of interviews, news accounts, and first-hand observations. Each dialogue is a verbatim account as recalled by a participant or a source close to a participant.

INTRODUCTION

1 Nancy Pelosi. Interview with San Francisco reporters, November 8, 2006.
2 Ferrell, Jane. "Nancy Pelosi: Highly Conventional Democrat." *California Living Magazine* January 15, 1984.
3 Hastert, Dennis. *Speaker: Lessons from Forty Years in Coaching and Politics.* Washington, DC: Regnery Publishing, 2004. p. 169.

CHAPTER 1

1 "D'Alesandro Will Find New Boss in First Daughter, Prediction." *The Guide* March 28, 1941.
2 "Tommy D'Alesandro Announces Another Sure Vote—It's a Girl." *Baltimore Sun* March 21, 1940.
3 Sandler, Gilbert. *The Neighborhood: The Story of Baltimore's Little Italy.* Baltimore: Bodine & Associates, 1974. p. 23.
4 Ibid.
5 Tommy D'Alesandro III. Interview with author, May 17, 2007.
6 Thomas D'Alesandro Jr. Oral history. Maryland Historical Society. Interviewed by Francis Colletta, March 3, 1973.
7 Ibid.

CHAPTER 2

1 Nancy Pelosi. Interview with author, October 5, 1999.
2 "D'Alesandro Greeted as Tommy on Initial Visit to President." *Baltimore Sun* November 21, 1939.
3 "Congress Job Is a Tough One, D'Alesandro Wryly Concludes." *Baltimore Sun* June 18, 1939. p. 18.
4 Thomas D'Alesandro Jr. Oral history. Maryland Historical Society. Interviewed by Francis Colletta, March 3, 1973.
5 Ibid.
6 Ibid.
7 Thomas D'Alesandro Jr. Oral history. Maryland Historical Society. Interviewed by Francis Colletta, March 3, 1973.

8   Smith, Odell. "Mayor Gets a Big Hand after 6,234 Handshakes." *Baltimore Sun*, December 31, 1957.

9   Nancy Pelosi. Interview with author, January 25, 2006.

10 Liebert, Larry. "Demo Party Chief Raised on Politics." *San Francisco Chronicle* September 13, 1982.

11 "3-Term Mayor 'Tommy' D'Alesandro Jr. Dead at 84." *Baltimore Sun* August 24, 1987. p. 1A.

12 Liebert, Larry. "Demo Party Chief Raised on Politics." *San Francisco Chronicle* September 13, 1982.

13 D'Alesandro, Thomas Jr. Speech to Baltimore City-County Democratic Club, November 4, 1957. Special Collections Department, Langsdale Library, University of Baltimore.

14 D'Alesandro, Thomas Jr. Speech to Maryland Democratic State Convention, Emerson Hotel, Baltimore, May 28, 1956. Special Collections Department, Langsdale Library, University of Baltimore.

15 Connolly, J. P. "Another Side to 'Tommy.'" *Baltimore News-Post* October 31, 1958.

16 Thomas D'Alesandro Jr. Oral history. Maryland Historical Society. Interviewed by Francis Colletta, March 3, 1973.

17 Ibid..

18 "The Little World of Tommy." *Time Magazine* April 26, 1954.

19 Walter Sondheim Jr. "Reflections on *Brown*: A Conversation with Walter Sondheim, Jr." Maryland Humanities Council, Winter 2004.

20 Neuman, Johanna. "Hard Work, Political Roots Fuel Pelosi's Rise." *Los Angeles Times* November 10, 2002. p. A-1.

21 Wilson, Sara. "The Woman's Angle." *Baltimore Sun* 1940 [exact date unknown].

22 Olesker, Michael. "She Was a Power, a Democrat, and She Was Loyal." *Baltimore Sun* April 9, 1995. p. 1B.

23 Tommy D'Alesandro III. Interview with author, May 17, 2007.

24 "3-Term Mayor 'Tommy' D'Alesandro Jr. Dead at 84." *Baltimore Sun* August 24, 1987. p. 1A.

25 Peter Angelos. Interview with author, June 12, 2007.

26 Lewis, Peggy. "Profile: Nancy Pelosi '62: House Democratic Leader." Trinity University, 2002. http://www.trinitydc.edu/admissions/profiles/magazine_profile_pelosi.php.

27 Maraniss, David. *First in His Class: A Biography of Bill Clinton*. New York: Simon & Schuster, 1995. p. 58.

28 Ferrell, Jane. "Nancy Pelosi: Highly Conventional Democrat." *California Living Magazine* January 15, 1984.

29 Daniel Brewster. Interview with author, April 14, 2007.

CHAPTER 3

1   Ferrell, Jane. "Nancy Pelosi: Highly Conventional Democrat." *California Living Magazine* January 15, 1984.

2   Museum of the City of San Francisco. "A Great Civic Drama." The Virtual Museum of the City of San Francisco. http://www.sfmuseum.org/hist/timeline.html.

3   Liebert, Larry. "Demo Party Chief Raised on Politics" *San Francisco Chronicle* September 13, 1982.

4   Ferrell, Jane. "Nancy Pelosi: Highly Conventional Democrat." *California Living Magazine* January 15, 1984.

5   Ibid.

6   "San Francisco (Be Sure to Wear Flowers in Your Hair)," written by John Phillips, performed by Scott McKenzie. MCA Music Publishing, 1967.

7   Foster, Doug. Special Report, KQED-TV, San Francisco. April 1, 1987.

8   Art Agnos. Interview with author, March 22, 2007.

9   Nancy Pelosi. Interview with author, October 1, 2001.

10 "New Name on Library Commission." *San Francisco Chronicle* June 6, 1975.

11 Ferrell, Jane. "Nancy Pelosi: Highly Conventional Democrat." *California Living Magazine* January 15, 1984.

12 Shaw, G. "How Jerry Brown Did It in Maryland." *Los Angeles Times* May 24, 1976.

13 Nancy Pelosi. Interview with author, October 10, 2001.

14 Shaw, G. "How Jerry Brown Did It in Maryland." *Los Angeles Times* May 24, 1976.

15 Olesker, Michael. "Pelosi's Road to Success Started in Baltimore." *Baltimore Sun* January 13, 2002. p. 1B.

16 Hamilton, Mildred. "Plotting for a Democratic Victory Party in 1985." *San Francisco Examiner* January 28, 1981.

17 Leary, Kevin, and Stewart, Pearl. "All 3 Camps Think Their Man Won." *San Francisco Chronicle* September 22, 1980. p. 4.

18 Barnes, W. E. "Demos Plan Reforms to Give California More Election Clout." *San Francisco Examiner* November 16, 1980. p. 12.

CHAPTER 4

1   Kilduff, Marshall, and Tracy, Phil. "Inside Peoples Temple." *New West Magazine* August 1, 1977.

2   Shilts, Randy. *The Mayor of Castro Street: The Life and Times of Harvey Milk*. New York: St. Martins Press, 1982.

3   "Democrat Blasts GOP 'Crybabies.'" *San Francisco Chronicle* September 17, 1981.

4   Ferrell, Jane. "Nancy Pelosi: Highly Conventional Democrat." *California Living Magazine* January 15, 1984.

5   Hamilton, Mildred. "Plotting for a Democratic Victory Party in 1985." *San Francisco Examiner* January 28, 1981.

6   Hamilton, Mildred. "Plotting for a Democratic Victory Party in 1985." *San Francisco Examiner* January 28, 1981.

7   Art Agnos. Interview with author, March 22, 2007.

8   Jacobs, John. *A Rage for Justice: The Passion and Politics of Phillip Burton*. Berkeley, CA: University of California Press, 1995.

9   Ibid.

10 Bill Gardner. Interview with author, August 27, 2007.

11 Liebert, Larry. "Demos Like Bay Area for '84 Convention." *San Francisco Chronicle* June 28, 1982. p. 1.

12 Belva Davis. Interview with author, June 29, 2007.

13 Fosburgh, Lacey. "San Francisco." *New York Times* July 1, 1984.

14 Fogarty, John. "Pelosi Says She Leads for Demo Job." *San Francisco Chronicle* December 4, 1984.

15 Ibid.

16 Irving, Carl. "Can S.F.'s Pelosi Win Demo Post?" *San Francisco Examiner* December 23, 1984. p. A1.

17 Balz, D. "Pelosi Blasts Rival DNC Candidate, Decries Labor's Tactics." *Washington Post* January 29, 1985. p. 4.

18 Raines, H. "Unionist Accused of Sexism in a Race to Lead Democrats." *New York Times* January 29, 1984. p. B5.

19 Rothberg, Donald. "Is Government Still a 'Man's World'?" Associated Press February 4, 1985.

20 Johnston, David. "Party Picked Old Path, Pelosi Says." *San Francisco Examiner* February 3, 1985. p. A4.

21 Mellinkoff, A. "Nancy Pelosi and the Democratic Future." *San Francisco Chronicle* January 8, 1985. p. 34.

CHAPTER 5

1   Judy Lemons. Interview with author, August 16, 2007.

2   Caen, Herb. "Pocketful of Notes." *San Francisco Chronicle* November 5, 1986. p. 31.

3   Agar Jaicks. Interview with author, June 5, 2007.

4   Pelosi, Nancy. Speech to Women's Tea Honoring Speaker-Designate Nancy Pelosi, Mellon Auditorium, Washington, DC, January 3, 2007.

5   John Burton. Interview with author, June 7, 2007.

6   Agar Jaicks. Interview with author, June 5, 2007.

7   "Burton Isn't Quitting." *Newsday* January 25, 1987. p. 14.

8   Harry Britt. Interview with author, March 25, 2007.

9   Kilduff, Marshall, and Roberts, Jerry. "Pelosi Jumps into Race for Sala Burton's Seat." *San Francisco Chronicle* February 13, 1987. p. 5.

10 Eric Jaye. Interview with author, June 5, 2007.

11 "Send Pelosi to Washington." *San Francisco Examiner* March 15, 1987.

CHAPTER 6

1   Lowy, J. A. *Pat Schroeder: A Woman of the House*. Albuquerque, NM: University of New Mexico Press, 2003. p. 85.

2   Epstein, Ed. "Stronger than Ever after 20 years." *San Francisco Chronicle* June 10, 2007. p. A-17.

3   Liebert, Larry. "Rep. Pelosi's First Speech: College Commencement Talk." *San Francisco Chronicle* June 8, 1987. p. 8.

4   Fred Ross. Interview with author.

CHAPTER 7

1   Roberts, Jerry. "Pelosi Finishes No. 1 but Keeps on Running." *San Francisco Chronicle* April 9, 1987. p. 1.

2   Steve Morin. Interview with author, June 8, 2007.

3   Liebert, Larry. "Pelosi Learns the Ropes, DC Style." *San Francisco Chronicle* January 15, 1988. p. B3.
4   Abrams, Jim. "House Bars Needle-Exchange Funds." Associated Press, April 29, 1998.
5   Freedberg, Louis. "Pelosi Amendment Restores $36 Million in AIDS Funds." *San Francisco Chronicle* March 3, 1995. p. A2.
6   San Francisco AIDS Foundation. "HIV/AIDS Facts and Figures: A Quarterly Report, Third Quarter, 2006."

CHAPTER 8

1   Garcia, Dawn. "Presidio Data: Carlucci Accused of 'Stonewalling.'" *San Francisco Chronicle* January 10, 1989. p. A2.
2   Bruce Babbitt. Interview with author, January 31, 1994.
3   Lochhead, Carolyn. "House Passes Leasing Plan for Presidio: Bipartisan Support for Pelosi Proposal." *San Francisco Chronicle* September 20, 1995. p. A1.
4   Ibid.

CHAPTER 9

1   Viviano, Frank. "House Panel OKs Pelosi Bill Protecting Chinese Students in U.S." *San Francisco Chronicle* July 27, 1989. p. 11.
2   Viviano, Frank. "Bush Action Awaited: Chinese Students Rally for Bill Extending Visas." *San Francisco Chronicle* November 28, 1989. p. A20.
3   "Democrats Predict Defeat of Veto on China Students." Associated Press, December 13, 1989.
4   Liebert, Larry. "Chinese Students Bill Puts Pelosi Center Stage." *San Francisco Chronicle* January 24, 1990. p. A9.
5   Nancy Pelosi. Interview with Jim Lehrer, *MacNeil/Lehrer NewsHour,* January 23, 1990.
6   Liebert, Larry. "Chinese Students' Bill Puts Pelosi Center Stage." *San Francisco Chronicle* January 24, 1990. p. A9.
7   Mann, Jim. *About Face: A History of America's Curious Relationship with China from Nixon to Clinton.* New York: Alfred Knopf, 1999. p. 229.
8   Mann, James. "Compromise in Works on China Trade Foreign Policy: Congress Tackles Issue of Whether to Continue Favored-Nation Status." *Los Angeles Times* May 17, 1990. p. 16.
9   Viviano, Frank. "Pelosi Will Revive Her China Trade Bill: Favored Status Pegged to Human Rights." *San Francisco Chronicle* May 2, 1991. p. A16.
10 Liebert, Larry. "Pelosi's Pragmatic Approach on China Trade Issue." *San Francisco Chronicle* May 9, 1991. p. 31.
11 Sun, L. "U.S. Congress Group Honors Beijing Dead: Police Detain TV Crews Taping Ceremony." *Washington Post* September 5, 1991. p. 23.
12 Crothall, G. "Pelosi Takes Positive Line for Future." *South China Morning Post* August 20, 1993. p. 9.
13 Chugani, M. "Pelosi, Baker Clash on China Reform." *South China Morning Press* March 5, 1992. p. 16.
14 Nancy Pelosi. Interview with author, February 8, 1994.
15 Pelosi, Nancy. Speech to National Press Club, April 19, 1994.
16 Weinschenk, A. "Pelosi: Flogging the Anti-China Horse." *The Straits Times* August 21, 1994.
17 Nancy Pelosi. Interview with author, May 27, 1994.
18 Hentoff, Nat. "Dinner with Gen. Chi." *Washington Post* January 26, 1997. p. C07.
19 Nancy Pelosi. Interview with author, June 1996.
20 Nancy Pelosi. Interview with author, April 9, 1997.
21 Nancy Pelosi. Interview with author, October 27, 1997.

CHAPTER 10

1   Nancy Pelosi. Interview with author, June 1996.
2   Miller, Alan. "It's Trendy to Resent California: Analysts Say There's a Growing Backlash in Congress Against the Golden State." *Los Angeles Times* August 28, 1990. p. 1.
3   Lochhead, Carolyn. "Demo Platform Committee Post Gives Pelosi National Stature." *San Francisco Chronicle* April 29, 1992. p. 5.

4   Bunting, Glenn. "Pelosi's Prominence in Party on the Rise Lawmaker: The San Francisco Congresswoman Will Deliver a Speech and Preside Over Proceedings to Adopt the Platform." *Los Angeles Times* July 14, 1992. p. 6.

5   Nancy Pelosi. Interview with author, October 16, 2002.

6   Nancy Pelosi. Interview with author, June 1996.

CHAPTER 11

1   Wallison, Ethan. "Democrats Launch Quixotic Bids for Majority Whip but Some Wonder Whether Pelosi, Lewis and Hoyer Are Getting Ready for Eventual Gephardt Exit." *Roll Call* September 3, 1998.

2   Nancy Pelosi. Interview with author, November 9, 1998.

3   Nancy Pelosi. Interview with author, March 17, 1999.

4   Wallison, Ethan. "House Democrats Get Head Start on Whip Race: Pelosi's Activity Forces Hoyer, Lewis to Campaign." *Roll Call* August 2, 1999.

5   Clift, Eleanor. "Old Boys' Club: Will Nancy Pelosi Become the First Woman to Win a Top Dem Post?" *Newsweek* July 26, 2001.

6   Wallison, Ethan. "Hoyer Claims Plenty of Votes in Potential Majority Whip Battle." *Roll Call* November 22, 1999.

7   Wallison, Ethan. "Pelosi Claiming Victory in Whip Race." *Roll Call* July 27, 2000.

8   Holland, Judy. Hearst News Service, "Congresswoman raises cash to win House leadership post." January 9, 2000.

9   John Murtha. Interview with author, April 20, 2007.

10   Nancy Pelosi. Interview with author, July 5, 2001.

11   Pelosi, Nancy. Interview with Steve Inskeep, *Morning Edition*, National Public Radio, September 11, 2001.

12   Carolyn Bartholomew. Interview with author, July 25, 2007.

13   Catherine Dodd. Interview with author, June 6, 2007.

14   Nancy Pelosi. Interview with author, September 11, 2001.

15   Matier, Phil, and Ross, Andy. "Pelosi Lays Into Minister for Comments at Service." *San Francisco Chronicle* September 19, 2001. p. 15.

16   Jacobs, John. *A Rage for Justice: The Passion and Politics of Phillip Burton*. Berkeley, CA: University of California Press, 1995. p. 315.

17   Waller, Douglas. "Whipping Up a Fight: House Whips Pelosi and Delay, Battling Each Other for Control of Congress, Turn Out to Be Two of a Kind." *Time* May 13, 2002.

18   Hosler, Karen. "Calif.'s Pelosi Chosen as House Democratic Whip: She Defeats Hoyer, Will Be Highest-Ranking Woman Ever in Congress." *Baltimore Sun* October 11, 2001. p. 3A.

19   Clymer, Adam. "A New Vote Counter: Nancy Patricia Pelosi." *New York Times* October 11, 2001. p. 18.

CHAPTER 12

1   Nancy Pelosi. Interview with author, January 26, 2006.

2   Cohen, Richard. "After Gephardt." *National Journal* June 8, 2002.

3   Sanger, David, and Schmitt, Eric. "U.S. Has a Plan to Occupy Iraq, Officials Report." *New York Times* October 11, 2002.

CHAPTER 13

1   Wallace, A. "She Knows How to Use It." *Elle* November 2002.

CHAPTER 14

1   Ferrell, Jane. "Nancy Pelosi: Highly Conventional Democrat." *California Living Magazine* January 15, 1984.

2   Nancy Pelosi. Interview with author, June 13, 2003.

3   Nancy Pelosi. Interview with author, February 5, 2003.

4   Nancy Pelosi. Interview with author, October 7, 2002.

5   Nancy Pelosi. News conference, March 6, 2003.

6   Marinucci, Carla. "Pelosi Declares Bush 'Fair Game' for Criticism: His Handling of War, Security Put to the Test." *San Francisco Chronicle* May 31, 2003. p. 4.

7   Pelosi, Nancy. Interview by George Stephanopoulos. *This Week*, ABC, October 31, 2004.

8   VandHei, Jim, and Murray, Shailagh. "Democrats Fear Backlash at Polls for Antiwar Remarks." *Washington Post* December 7, 2005. p. 1.

9   Rahm Emanuel. Interview with author, April 25, 2007.

CHAPTER 15

1   Nancy Pelosi. Interview with author, January 26, 2006.

2   Bart Stupak. Interview with author, December 6, 2005.

3   Rosa DeLauro. Interview with author, December 9, 2005.

4   George Miller. Interview with author, October 15, 2005.

5   "Dem Leaders Upbraid Members for Supporting GOP Drug Bill." *CongressDaily* July 10, 2003.

6   Eilperin, Juliet. "Democrats Laud Pelosi's Style: House Minority Leader Commended for Focus on Party Unity." *Washington Post* November 30, 2003. p. 6.

7   Nancy Pelosi. Interview with author, January 13, 2005.

8   Nancy Pelosi. Interview with author, December 8, 2003.

9   Ibid.

CHAPTER 16

1   Nancy Pelosi. Interview with author, December 8, 2003.

2   Pelosi, Nancy. Interview with Tim Russert, *Meet the Press*, NBC, May 7, 2006.

3   Von Drehle, David, and Rosin, Hanna. "The Two Nancy Pelosis: New House Leader Stresses Her Political Skills." *Washington Post* November 14, 2002. p. 1.

4   Nancy Pelosi. Interview with author, November 3, 2006.

5   Gerstein, Josh. "Democrats Head Into Weekend in Buoyant Mood." *New York Sun* November 3, 2006.

6   Rahm Emanuel. Interview with author, April 25, 2007.

7   Bendavid, Naftali. *The Thumpin': How Rahm Emanuel and the Democrats Learned to Be Ruthless and Ended the Republican Revolution*. New York: Doubleday, 2007. p. 202.

CHAPTER 17

1   Anna Eshoo. Interview with author, May 22, 2007.

2   Steny Hoyer. Interview with author, May 22, 2007.

ACKNOWLEDGMENTS

THE WRITING OF THIS BOOK confirmed the wisdom of Philip Graham's observation that journalism is the first draft of history. This book would not have been possible without the reporting of many fine journalists, starting with my former colleagues in the *San Francisco Chronicle*'s Washington Bureau, Carolyn Lochhead, Ed Epstein, and Zachary Coile. Beyond the friendship and support they offered, their daily dispatches on the woman representing California's Eighth Congressional District provided the framework and the detail necessary to construct a history.

This book would also not have been possible without the support of the *San Francisco Chronicle,* my professional home for 21 years, which, in addition to allowing me to cover presidents, earthquakes, and World Series, provided me the opportunity to spend 14 years writing, interviewing, and observing the subject of the book. I am particularly indebted to Andy Pollack and Jim Brewer for their countless hours of editing, guidance, and patience. My first editor, Jerry Roberts, is a continuing source of inspiration as well as the author of many insightful pieces on Pelosi before she had ever won an election. The early reporting of *Chronicle* reporters Marshall Kilduff, Larry Liebert, John Fogarty, and Louis Freedberg was also instructive. Librarian Richard Geiger kindly steered me through the *Chronicle*'s archives. Dan Rosenheim had the good judgment to send me to Washington. Mike Wolgelenter, Tim Neagle, Carla Marinucci, and Allen Matthews each provided help at critical moments.

And special thanks to my old colleague Mark Barabak, who graciously shared years of his own work on Pelosi to greatly improve the quality of the book.

Unbeknownst to them, I also relied heavily on the work of journalists at the *Washington Post*, Juliet Eilperin in particular, as well as the staff at *Roll Call* and *The Hill*. Michael Barone's authoritative *Almanac of American Politics* was consulted habitually. The work of previous authors, in particular John Jacobs (*A Rage for Justice*), Randy Shilts (*The Mayor of Castro Street: The Life and Times of Harvey Milk*), Michael Olesker (*Journeys to the Heart of Baltimore*), and Kenneth Durr (*Behind the Backlash: White Working-Class Politics in Baltimore, 1940–1980*) added greatly to understanding Pelosi's background. *Women in Congress: 1917–2006* provided a fabulous guide to the evolution of women in the House.

More than 100 interviews were conducted for this book, most with subjects who had little to gain personally from speaking earnestly about a woman who still yields considerable influence in their lives. I greatly appreciate their trust in my writing and their commitment to providing an accurate history of the first woman Speaker.

Speaker Pelosi directed her aides not to cooperate in the writing of the book. However, for years I have worked with members of her staff—current and former—who have provided timely information and valuable insights. Special thanks to Brendan Daly, Jennifer Crider, Carolyn Bartholomew, Judy Lemons, Jon Stivers, Steve Morin, Perry Plumart, Michael Yaki, Catherine Dodd, George Papagiannis, and Eric Weiss for their help.

More than two dozens members of Congress, past and present, spoke to me about the Speaker. Special thanks to Anna Eshoo, Mike Thompson, Ellen Tauscher, John Burton, Vic Fazio, Pat Schroeder, Leon Panetta, John Dingell, Pete Stark, Tom Downey, Lynn Woolsey, Doris Matsui, Rahm Emanuel, Barbara Kennelly, Ben Jones, Jack Murtha, Steny Hoyer, Dennis Hastert, Barbara Boxer, and the late Daniel Brewster.

In California, those particularly helpful with their time and memories included Art Agnos, Harry Britt, Willie Brown, Agar Jaicks, Fred Ross, Clint Reilly, Rose King, David Binder, Kevin Shelley, Gavin Newsom, Eric Jaye, Jim Rivaldo, Carole Migden, Richard Schlackman, Rose Pak, Rick Romagosa, Gunilde Walsh, Tim Farley, William Issel, Don Solem, Belva Davis, Spencer Michels, and Barbara Taylor.

On the East Coast, special thanks to Ellen Malcolm, Anita Dunn, Bill Gardner, Chuck Manatt, Mario Cuomo, Paul Kirk, April Boyd, Cory Alexander, Thomas Hollowak, Michael Sesay, Susan Graham, Stuart Chapman, Peter Angelos, the residents of Baltimore's Little Italy, and Tommy D'Alesandro III (who bristled when I tried to pay for our lunch at Della Notte Ristorante a block from his childhood home. "Not in my precinct," he said, grabbing the check. "Not in my precinct").

The book would not have been completed without the help of Bruce Cain, director of the University of California's Washington Center (UCDC), who provided the professional atmosphere, in addition to a much needed office, when my employment with the *San Francisco Chronicle* ended in the middle of this project. Research assistant Cody Gray enthusiastically turned out facts and statistics that were of great importance to the text.

At Rodale, editor Leigh Haber was the first to commit to the project and appreciate Pelosi's lasting importance. The careful editing of Nancy Elgin greatly improved the copy.

The idea for the book came from Amy Rennert, my agent, who recognized immediately the importance of telling Pelosi's story and encouraged someone accustomed to writing 1,000 words at a time that they were capable of writing several hundred pages.

Robin Mansfield offered great insights into the manuscript. Vernard Atkins, Chip Johnson, and Kevin Rayhill made every trip to the Bay Area an enjoyable one. And Malcolm Chesney helped me keep my sanity.

I could never express enough gratitude to my mother and father, Ina and

Terrance Sandalow, whose insights and fine editing skills are exceeded only by their love and encouragement. My brother, David, sister, Judith, and sister-in-law, Holly Hammonds, provided smart suggestions and unwavering support.

Few kids know more about Nancy Pelosi than my sons, Malcolm and Casey. They are the joy of my life and will grow up never thinking twice about a woman as Speaker or president.

No one deserves more gratitude than my wife, Marcie. In addition to serving as an editor and sounding board, Marcie provided boundless emotional and logistical backing. The book would not have been written without her.

Finally, special acknowledgment is due Nancy Pelosi. Though she did not cooperate for this project, she has for many years been gracious, generous, and dutiful with her time. My awe for her energy and commitment to public service grew with this book. However one views Pelosi's politics or the decisions she makes on policy or strategy, her devotion to improving the lives of others is something to revere. Many Americans cynically assume that most politicians are in it for money or glory. Pelosi needs neither. To assume otherwise is not to understand Nancy Pelosi.

INDEX

Abercrombie, Neil, 244
Abortion issue, 162–63
Abzug, Bella, 182
Agnos, Art, 52–53, 60, 71–72, 94,
  101–2, 122
AIDS issue, 91, 97, 100, 125–31
AIDS Memorial Quilt, 128
Alcatraz takeover, 61
Alioto, Joseph, 45, 54, 56, 59, 91, 184
Alioto, Michaela, 184
Anderson, John, 60
Angelos, Peter, 36, 66, 299
Appropriations Committee, 23,
  159–60, 178
Armed Services Committee, 117–18
Armey, Dick, 204, 219
Asner, Ed, 120

Babbit, Bruce, 135–36
Baker, James, 147
Baltimore, 11–16, 32
Baltimore Colts, 31–32
Baltimore Orioles, 31–32, 36, 66
Bankhead, William, 20
Barrett, Michael, 278
Bartholomew, Carolyn, 196
Bashford, Wilkes, 56–57
Bauer, Gary, 139, 153
Bean, Melissa, 277
Becerra, Xavier, 175
Beinert, Peter, 234
Bell, Chris, 212
Bennett, Tony, 287
Berkeley riots, 61–62
Bingham, Mark, 197
Bin Laden, Osama, 210
Blue Dogs, 183–84, 192, 252–53, 291,
  295
Blunt, Roy, 277
Boehner, John, 286–87
Bonior, David, 173–74, 177, 179, 181,
  186, 188, 190, 195, 200, 205,
  208, 224
Boxer, Barbara, 71, 118, 121, 134–35,
  152, 172, 198
Bradley, Bill, 186
Brewster, Daniel, 37–38, 178
Britt, Harry, 92–95, 97, 99–100,
  103–6, 109–10, 150, 160

Brooks, David, 224
Brooks, Jack, 140
Brown, Amos, 197–98
Brown, Edmund, 56
Brown, Jerry, 55–57, 59–60, 79, 206,
  287
Brown, Michael, 269–70
Brown, Willie, 1, 5, 50, 56–57,
  73–74, 77, 94–95
Brown v. Board of Education, 32
Buell, Mark, 284
Burton, Dan, 130
Burton, John, 1, 50, 53, 70–71,
  86–87, 89–92, 94, 109–10,
  176, 198–99, 206, 225, 251,
  271, 287
Burton, Philip (Phil), 49–50, 52–54,
  56, 70–72, 84, 92, 95,
  100–101, 105, 134–35, 140,
  169, 182, 192, 195, 255
Burton, Sala, 71–72, 84–90, 92, 110,
  116, 140
Bush, George H. W., 92, 122,
  141–42, 150
Bush, George W., 2–5, 49, 186–90,
  204, 207, 209–10, 221–23,
  234–35, 237–40, 252, 257,
  269–70, 275, 277, 285, 289,
  292–95, 300
Byrd, Robert, 81

Caen, Herb, 57, 85
California Democratic Party, 6,
  65–81, 88, 181–82
Campbell, Ben Nighthorse, 158
Cannon, Joe, 298
Capote, Truman, 66
Capps, Lois, 176
Cardin, Ben, 186
Carter, Jimmy, 55, 60, 66
Centers for Disease Control, 126
Central American Free Trade
  Agreement, 255
Chavez, Cesar, 95
Cheney, Dick, 204, 275, 294
China policy, 139–55, 179
Chisholm, Shirley, 2
Christopher, Warren, 149
Civil liberties issue, 197

Civil Rights Act (1964), 183
Clinton, Bill, 28, 37, 131, 138, 147,
  150–54, 158, 161–62, 168,
  173, 176, 179, 189, 254,
  280–81
Clinton, Hillary, 152, 209, 234, 274
Clyburn, James, 227
COBRA-Continuation Tax
  Disabilities Amendments
  (1989), 127
Coffee boycott, 120–21
Condit, Gary, 175, 183, 192
Congressional Black Caucus, 249,
  276
Congressional elections (2002),
  219–20
Congressional elections (2006), 1–7,
  267–68, 270–84
Congresswomen's Caucus, 118
Conyers, John, 200, 275
Council on Foreign Relations, 233
Courtney, Joe, 282
Cranston, Alan, 59
Crawford, George, 207–8
Crider, Jenn, 282
Crook, Howard E., 23
Cuban missile crisis (1962), 232
Cuomo, Mario, 59, 76–77, 83, 95
Curran, William, 20

D'Alesandro, Annunciata (Nancy)
  Lombardi, 12, 15–16,
  33–34, 116
D'Alesandro, Hector, 12, 26, 33
D'Alesandro, Joey (Jo-Jo), 12, 26, 33
D'Alesandro, Nancy Patricia. *See*
  Pelosi, Nancy Patricia
D'Alesandro, Nicky, 12, 26, 33, 36
D'Alesandro, Roosey, 12, 26, 30, 33
D'Alesandro, Thomas (Tommy) III,
  11, 13, 19, 24, 26, 33–35, 56,
  109, 284, 287–88, 299
D'Alesandro, Thomas (Tommy) Jr.,
  11–12, 16–25, 29–35, 116,
  285, 294
Daly, Brendan, 208, 238–39
Dannemeyer, William, 130
Daschle, Tom, 204, 209
Davis, Belva, 75

Davis, Gray, 198
Davis, Susan, 187
DCCC, 176, 190
Dean, Howard, 244–45, 274
Deegan, Joseph, 18
DeLauro, Rosa, 163, 175, 179, 221,
    255–56, 260
DeLay, Tom, 166–67, 181, 204–5,
    207–8, 239, 247–50, 259,
    272
Dellums, Ron, 118
Democratic Congressional
    Campaign Committee
    (DCCC), 176, 190
Democratic National Committee
    (DNC), 56, 76–81
Democratic National Convention
    (1960), 73–74
Democratic National Convention
    (1984), 72–74, 76
Democratic Party, 2–3, 6, 29, 56–57,
    60, 65–81, 88, 152, 158,
    161–62, 180–82, 187–90,
    201, 207, 216–17, 260–63,
    266–67, 270–76, 298
Democratic Platform Committee
    (1992), 161
"Democratic Vision," 274
Desegregation, 32, 45
Diaz, John, 164
Dingell, John, 200, 203, 205, 255
DNC, 56, 76–81
Dodd, Catherine, 105, 196
Dodd, Chris, 66
Downey, Tom, 121–22
Duckworth, Tammy, 273
Duncan, John, 136
Dunn, Tim, 273

Economic stimulus plan, 253
Edwards, Chet, 175
Edwards, Don, 88
Edwards, John, 209, 233
Eisenhower, Dwight D., 49
Ellsworth, Brad, 276
Emanuel, Rahm, 229, 245, 253,
    271–73, 280–81, 284
Epstein, Ed, 289
Eshoo, Anna, 200, 256, 287
Ethics Committee, 160, 165–68

Farber, Mrs. Seymour, 54
Farnen, Stacey, 199
Fazio, Vic, 172–74, 177, 221
Federal Emergency Management
    Agency (FEMA), 269
Feinstein, Dianne, 45, 51, 65, 73–74,
    93, 137, 153–54, 198
FEMA, 269
Ferraro, Geraldine, 2, 66, 74, 76,
    117–18
Fogarty, John, 49, 70
Foley, Mark, 225, 279
Foley, Tom, 160, 208

Folgers Coffee Company, 120–21
Foran, John, 52
Ford, Gerald, 62
Ford, Harold Jr., 223, 243
Frank, Barney, 99, 277
Franks, Tommy, 212
Freeh, Louis, 280
Friedman, Thomas, 234
From, Al, 226
Frost, Martin, 175, 179, 220–23

Ganz, Marshall, 95
Gardner, Bill, 72–73
Garrett, Duane, 78
Gay community and issues, 65, 75–76,
    99–103. See also AIDS issue
General Services Administration,
    138
Gephardt, Richard (Dick), 173–74,
    176–77, 179, 186, 188,
    190–91, 194, 197–98, 204,
    206, 210, 214, 220, 222–24,
    233, 254, 257
Gere, Richard, 287
Gingrich, Newt, 157–59, 165–68,
    184, 214
Goldwater, Barry, 49
Gore, Al, 186–89, 219
Goss, Porter, 197
Graves, Denyce, 206
Gulf War (1991), 236

Haas, Karen, 286
Haight-Ashbury scene (1960s and
    1970s), 61
Hambrecht, Bill and Sally, 176
Hammond, Darrell, 266
Hansen, James, 133, 138
Harman, Jane, 187
Harris, Kathleen, 189
Hart, Gary, 59, 96
Hart, Mickey, 205
Hastert, Dennis, 7, 197, 204, 242,
    247–50, 270, 279–80, 283,
    287, 293
Hearst, Patty, 62
Hébert, Edward, 118
Helms, Jesse, 130
Hitler, Adolf, 20
HIV, 126. See also AIDS issue
Holm, Paul, 197–98
Holmes, Eleanor, 191
Honda, Mike, 187, 212
Hostettler, John, 276–77
Hoyer, Steny, 38, 175, 177–79, 181,
    186–87, 191, 193, 198–201,
    227, 244–45, 288–90
Hsieh, Tom, 69
Hughes, Mary, 213
Human immunodeficiency virus
    (HIV), 126. See also AIDS
    issue
Hussein, Saddam, 209, 210–11,
    230–31, 234, 236–37

Immigration Act (1965), 49
Impeachment inquiry of Clinton,
    157, 168, 173, 179
Impeachment movement against
    George W. Bush, 275–76
Imus, Don, 223
Institute of Notre Dame, 27, 34–35
Integration, 32, 45
Intelligence Committee (House),
    146, 160, 210–11, 231
Iran-Contra affair, 81, 91, 97
Iraq troop surge, 294–95
Iraq war, 3, 229–45, 293–97
Iraq war funds and vote, 236–37,
    295–96
Iraq war resolution and vote, 209–11,
    216, 233–34
Iraq withdrawal measure, 295
Irving, Carl, 78
Israel, Steve, 258

Jackson, Jesse, 76
Jaicks, Agar, 57–58, 61, 67, 69, 72,
    83, 85–89
Jaye, Eric, 96, 110
Jefferson, William, 253–54, 276
Jiang Zemin, 153–54
Johnson, Lyndon B., 34, 255
Johnson, Nancy, 164
Jones, Ben, 145–46
Jones, Cleve, 128
Jones, Jim, 62–63
Jonestown deaths, 62–63

Kanjorski, Paul, 216–17
Kaptur, Marcy, 227
Katrina disaster, 5, 269–70
Kennedy, John F., 28, 35–36, 73,
    188, 204, 232, 251
Kennedy, Patrick, 194
Kennedy, Susan, 88
Kennedy, Ted, 59–60, 77–79, 96,
    225–26
Kennelly, Barbara, 121, 174
Kent State University shootings, 62
Kerry, John, 209, 233, 236, 240, 267
Kilduff, Marshall, 62
King, Carole, 287
King, Martin Luther Jr., 32, 38, 93
King, Rose, 67–68, 79, 88
Kirk, Paul, 77–78, 80, 181
Kirkpatrick, Jeanne, 76, 254, 279

LaFaille, Tom, 200
Lake, Tony, 152
Lakoff, George, 252
Lance, Bert, 76
Lee, Martin, 144–45
Lemons, Judy, 84–85, 140
Leno, Jay, 266
Levy, Chandra, 192
Lewinsky, Monica, 168, 179
Lewis, John, 175, 181, 187

Lewis, Michael, 184
Liebert, Larry, 69, 143
Lochhead, Carolyn, 164
Longworth, Nicolas, 121
Lugar, Richard, 297
Lyon, Phyllis, 91

Maher, Bill, 102, 104
Manatt, Charles (Chuck), 72, 76–77, 80
Martin, Del, 91
Martin, Lynn, 2, 117, 119
Martinez, Matt, 187
Mary Our Queen Cathedral, 38
Matsui, Bob, 148, 253–54
Matsui, Doris, 254
Matthews, Chris, 265–66
McAteer, Eugene, 52
McCain, John, 186
McCarthy, Leo, 51–56, 77, 83, 94–95, 102, 110, 188, 200, 206, 213
McClellan, Scott, 239
McCourt, Frank and Jamie, 251
McGovern, George, 80
McKenzie, Scott, 49
Medicare reform bill (2003), 257–60
Meehan, Marty, 243
Menendez, Robert, 175, 227
Michael, Paul, 286
Michels, Spencer, 97–98
Microtargeting, 108–9
Mikulski, Barbara, 28, 108, 287
Milk, Harvey, 51, 53, 63–65, 93–94, 100, 103
Miller, George, 70, 256, 286
Miller, John, 145–46
Miller, Lorraine, 208
Miller, Steve, 205
Mineta, Norman, 287
Mink, Patsy, 206, 212
Mitchell, George, 81, 95–96, 143, 147, 151
Mondale, Walter, 74, 76, 118
Moore, Sara Jane, 62
Moran, James, 175
Morin, Steve, 127
Moscone, George, 50, 52–53, 63–65, 73, 92, 109
Murphy, Austin, 119
Murphy, Chris, 282
Murphy, Patrick, 273
Murtha, John (Jack), 11, 119–20, 135, 160, 181, 183, 190–91, 200, 233, 241–45, 288–90

National Abortion and Reproductive Rights Action League, 163
National Park Service, 135–36
National Public Radio (NPR), 195–96
"Netroots," 3
New Deal and New Deal liberalism, 19–20, 22, 29, 32

Nickels, Don, 204
Niland, Mary Kevin, 260
9/11 terrorist attacks, 196–98, 209
Nixon, Richard, 32, 49, 188
Nolan, Mae, 2
North American Free Trade Agreement, 123, 298
Norton, Mary T., 115, 251
Novak, Robert, 163
NPR, 195–96

Oakar, Mary Rose, 161
Obey, David, 160
O'Neill, Tip, 4, 57, 71, 165, 237, 251
Oppedahl, John, 164
Oreck, Bruce, 211
Ortega, Daniel, 97
Out of Iraq Caucus, 297

Pak, Rose, 150
Palmisano, Vincent, 15, 19
Panetta, Leon, 150
Pelosi, Alexandra, 2, 44, 51, 59, 84, 86, 188, 196, 200, 252, 282
Pelosi, Christine, 44, 200, 236
Pelosi, David, 55
Pelosi, Jacqueline, 44, 212
Pelosi, Nancy Corinne, 44, 86
Pelosi, Nancy Patricia
    abortion issue and, 162–63
    AIDS issue and, 91, 100, 125–31
    ambitions of, questions about, 69–70, 169–70, 172, 177
    Appropriations Committee and, 159–60, 178
    Baltimore neighborhood of, 13–15
    birth of, 11–13, 20, 22
    brother-in-law of, 47–48, 54, 64, 92
    brothers of, 11–13, 19, 24, 26, 30, 34–36, 56, 109, 284, 287–88, 299
    Brown campaign and, 55–57, 60
    Bush criticisms by, 4, 237–40, 268–69, 300
    California Democratic Party and, 6, 65–81, 181–82
    childhood of, 25–27
    children of, 2, 39, 44, 51, 59, 84, 86, 188, 196, 200, 212, 236, 252, 282
    China policy and, 139–55, 179
    China trip (1991) and, 144–45
    civic duties of, early, 51
    civil liberties issue and, 197
    Clinton (Bill) criticisms by, 147, 151–52, 154
    coalition-building of, 122–23
    college years of, 35–37
    congressional campaign of, 88–111
    Congressional elections (2006) and, 1–7, 267–68, 270–84

Democratic minority in House and, 157–70, 219–27, 247–63
Democratic National Committee and, 77–81
Democratic Party and, 56–57, 60, 65–81, 152, 158, 216–17, 260–63, 266–67, 276, 298
Democratic Platform Committee (1992) and, 161
"Democratic Vision" and, 274
earthquake relief aid to Italy and, 66
economic stimulus plan and, 253
Ethics Committee and, 160, 165–68
father of, 11–12, 16–25, 29–35, 116
fear and, lack of, 6
as freshman congresswoman, 115–23, 127–28
fund-raising ability of, 175–77, 217, 223
fund-raising parties of, 51, 54–55
gay issues and, 75–76
Gingrich criticisms by, 165, 167–69
grandchildren of, 215, 282, 288
history-making by, 2, 4, 180, 182, 185, 195, 204, 206, 227, 286–87
husband of, 5, 37, 44, 57, 60, 121, 123, 146, 165, 178, 212, 216, 268–69, 281, 286
impeachment inquiry of Clinton (Bill) and, 157, 168, 173, 179
impeachment movement against Bush (George W.) and, 275–76
Intelligence Committee and, 160, 210–11
Iraq troop surge and, 295
Iraq war and, 3, 229–30, 234–45, 293–97
Iraq war funds and vote, 236–37, 295–96
Iraq war resolution and vote, 210–11, 222, 229–34, 230–34
Iraq withdrawal measure and, 295
jobs of, early, 37–38
leadership style and tactics of, 6, 205, 254–57, 260, 291
listening skills of, 108, 215
Medicare reform bill and, 257–60
Minnesota trip of, 278–79
as minority leader of House, 219–27, 247–63
mother of, 12, 15–16, 33–34, 116
multitasking ability of, 46–47, 57–59
office spaces of, 121, 251–52
political background of, 5–6, 15, 25
postelection to Speaker of House, 7, 299–300
Presidential election (2000) and, 187–90

Pelosi, Nancy Patricia (*cont.*)
    Presidio Army Base closing and
        bill, 133–38
    Presidio Terrace Association and, 54
    public awareness of, 224–25,
        277–78
    Reagan criticisms by, 68, 107
    in Republican-controlled
        Congress, 157–69
    Republican Party and, 4–5, 68–69,
        162–63, 208, 221–22, 243,
        260, 268–69, 298
    San Francisco neighborhood of,
        43–45, 48–49
    Saturday Night Live skit and,
        265–67
    Social Security privatization plan
        and, 260–62, 291–92, 295
    as Speaker of the House, 285–300
    State of the Union Address (2003)
        and, 236–37
    State of the Union Address (2007)
        and, 293–94
    steering committee meeting and,
        first, 248–49
    stereotype of, 5, 169, 214, 222,
        225–26, 276
    swearing in as whip, 203–7
    teenage years of, 27–29, 31–33
    terrorist attacks of Sept. 21, 2001
        and, 196–98, 207, 209
    Ways and Means Committee and,
        248–49
    wedding of, 38–39
    whip campaign of, 171–201
    as whip of House, 207–17, 220–21
Pelosi, Paul, 5, 37, 44, 57, 60, 121,
    123, 146, 165, 178, 212, 216,
    268–69, 281, 286
Pelosi, Paul Jr., 44
Pelosi, Ronald (Ron), 47–48, 54,
    64–65, 92
Pepper, Claude, 128
Perkins, Frances, 291
Perkins, John, 79–80
Perle, Richard, 235
Perot, Ross, 162
Peterson, Collin, 278
Poehler, Amy, 266
Powell, Colin, 233
Presidential election (2000), 186–90
Presidio Army Base closing and bill,
    133–38
Presidio Terrace, 45, 54, 103
Press, Bill, 56
Pryce, David, 244

Quigley, Carroll, 37

Racicot, Marc, 239
Ramer, Cyril, 63
Rangel, Charlie, 194
Rankin, Jeannette, 2
Rayburn, Sam, 4, 28, 90, 255

Reagan, Ronald, 49, 51, 60, 68, 73,
    81, 91, 107, 126
Reid, Harry, 81, 204, 267–68, 274, 294
Reilly, Clint, 95–96, 109
Republican Party, 4–5, 68–69, 158,
    162–63, 165–68, 180, 201,
    208, 214, 221–22, 243, 260,
    268–75, 298
Reynolds, Tom, 239
Richards, Ann, 208
Richards, Cecile, 208
Rivaldo, Jim, 94
Rivers, Lynn, 205, 255
Ronstadt, Linda, 56–57
Roosevelt, Franklin D., 12, 19–20,
    22, 93, 261, 291
Rose, Charlie, 182
Ross, Fred Jr., 95, 120–21
Rove, Karl, 280
Rumsfeld, Donald, 3, 274
Russert, Tim, 275–76
Ryan, Leo, 62–63
Ryan White Act, 130–31

St. Joseph's Church, 37
St. Leo's Church and School, 14–15,
    27, 235
Sandlin, Max, 249
Sanford, Terry, 78
San Francisco, 43–46, 48–49,
    61–62, 65
San Francisco Chronicle, ix, 46, 48,
    54, 57, 60, 69, 70, 85, 88,
    143, 164, 237, 267, 289
Saturday Night Live skit, 265–67
Schakowsky, Jan, 208–9
Schiff, Adam, 187
Schmidt, Jeanne, 242
Schmidt, Steve, 201
Schroeder, Pat, 115, 117–18, 182–83
Shays-Meehan campaign finance
    bill, 208
Sheehan, Cindy, 276
Shelby, Richard, 158
Shorenstein, Walter, 73
Shuler, Heath, 273
Silver, Carol Ruth, 98
"Six for 06," 275, 294
Skelton, Ike, 244
Slaughter, Louise, 175
Smith, Chris, 148, 153
Smith, Nick, 259
Social Security privatization plan,
    260–62, 291–92, 295
Solis, Hilda, 187
Sondheim, Walter Jr., 32
Spinoza, Tom, 97
Spratt, John, 252
Stark, Pete, 121, 164, 256, 258–59
Stenholm, Charlie, 175
Stevenson, Adlai, 29
Stivers, Jon, 224
Streisand, Barbra, 81
Studds, Gerry, 94, 99
Sullivan, Louis, 164

Tagliabue, Paul, 66
Tanner, John, 175
Tauscher, Ellen, 180, 193,
    244
Taylor, Barbara, 63–65
Terrorist attacks (Sept. 11, 2001),
    196–98, 207, 209
Thatcher, Margaret, 254
Thomas, Bill, 249
Thomas, Craig, 135
Thompson, Mike, 183–84, 200
Tiananmen Square massacre (1989),
    139–40, 154–55
Towns, Edolphus, 255
Tracey, Phil, 62
Trinity College, 34–37, 44
Trout, Jack, 252
Truman, Harry, 23, 31
Tubbs, Stephanie, 249
Turner, Jim, 253

Udall, Mark, 213
Underwood, Robert, 199–200
U.S. Supreme Court, 45, 189

Venetoulis, Ted, 56
Vietnam War opponents and
    demonstrations, 50,
    62

Walker, Doak, 93
Walker, Nancy, 87, 94
Wallace, George, 38
Warner, John, 297
Waters, Maxine, 164, 175
Watt, Mel, 276
Watts, J. C., 164
Wax, Mel, 64
Waxman, Henry, 129
Ways and Means Committee,
    248–49
Wei Jingsheng, 154
Weir, Bob, 205
Weiss, Ted, 129
Westwood, Jean, 80
White, Dan, 64–65
Wilson, Pete, 137
Wittman, Andrew, 213
Wolf, Frank, 148, 153
Wolff, Brian, 280–81
Women's suffrage and role in
    politics, 6
Wright, Jim, 50, 116, 165, 167,
    198–99, 208, 255
Wyman, Roz, 74, 188
Wynn, Albert, 255

Yaki, Michael, 123

Zodiac killer, 46
Zuur, Ted, 97–98